Praise for *The Fighting Bunch*

"Doggedly researched and briskly narrated, this rousing chronicle testifies to the importance of free and fair elections."

—*Publishers Weekly*

"An astounding and rarely told story of an (eventually) successful response to police violence and voter suppression. It's a story of a community acting with unity against an intensely oppressive and corrupt institution." —*Southern Review of Books*

"This is an especially timely tale in a year of social and political turmoil. The pulse-pounding narrative of *The Fighting Bunch* takes us to a place in America where the struggle against evil did not end when the war did and once more people of good will had to take a courageous stand." —Tom Clavin,

New York Times bestselling author of *Tombstone*

"In a remarkable feat of dogged, fresh reporting, historical research, and narrative aplomb, DeRose breathes new life into the little-remembered saga of the 1946 Battle of Athens, Tennessee, when a force of angry men, led by recent World War II veterans with the 'stamp of combat in their eyes,' mounted a successful armed rebellion against entrenched municipal corruption and police brutality." —Joe Sharkey, author of *Above Suspicion*

"History's best lessons are sometimes forgotten, and it's up to authors like Chris DeRose to resurrect them. He does so elegantly in *The Fighting Bunch*, the astonishing story of how, in August 1946, a band of World War II veterans summoned all

their courage and fighting skills to stand up to and destroy a corrupt political machine in McMinn County, Tennessee. It's likely you never knew about it before—but once you've read this book, their act will resonate in your mind forever."

—Jeff Guinn, *New York Times* bestselling author of
Manson and *The Road to Jonestown*

"Men who went overseas to defend the freedom for the world returned home to discover they had lost it here. How they fought to reclaim it is a riveting story that should remind every American of how precious and fragile are the freedoms we too often take for granted." —John Bicknell, author of *Lincoln's Pathfinder:*
John C. Fremont and the Violent Election of 1856 and *America 1844*

"In *The Fighting Bunch,* Chris DeRose unearths a fascinating and incredibly timely piece of American history. This lively and well-researched account of American GIs and their people-powered revolution, which restored democracy to McMinn County, Tennessee, soon after the war, is a lesson for us all—and a warning for those tempted by power or complacency not to forget the role that justice and fairness play in this country. Or to put it as one of the heroes might have (outside of polite company): Don't screw with democracy, the ballot box, or angry GIs. It's another reminder that the men and women who endured World War II were, in fact, members of the Greatest Generation."

—Jim DeFelice, *New York Times* bestselling coauthor of
American Sniper and *Every Man a Hero*

ALSO BY CHRIS DEROSE

*Founding Rivals: Madison vs. Monroe, the Bill of
Rights, and the Election That Saved a Nation*

*Congressman Lincoln: The Making of America's
Greatest President*

*The Presidents' War: Six American Presidents and
the Civil War That Divided Them*

*Star Spangled Scandal: Sex, Murder, and
the Trial That Changed America*

THE FIGHTING BUNCH

The Battle of Athens and How World War II Veterans Won
the Only Successful Armed Rebellion Since the Revolution

CHRIS DeROSE

ST. MARTIN'S GRIFFIN
NEW YORK

*For Ben, my son, who came to life along with this book. You were
eagerly awaited, joyously welcomed, and are completely loved, always.*

Published in the United States by St. Martin's Griffin, an imprint of St. Martin's
Publishing Group

THE FIGHTING BUNCH. Copyright © 2020 by Chris DeRose. All rights reserved. Printed in the United States of America. For information, address
St. Martin's Publishing Group, 120 Broadway, New York, NY 10271.

www.stmartins.com

Designed by Omar Chapa

The Library of Congress has cataloged the hardcover edition as follows:

Names: DeRose, Chris (Christopher), author.
Title: The fighting bunch : the Battle of Athens and how World War II
    veterans won the only successful armed rebellion since the Revolution /
    Chris DeRose.
Other titles: Battle of Athens and how World War II veterans won the
    only successful armed rebellion since the Revolution
Description: First edition. | New York : St. Martin's Press, 2020.
Identifiers: LCCN 2020024226 | ISBN 9781250266194 (hardcover) |
    ISBN 9781250266200 (ebook)
Subjects: LCSH: Riots—Tennessee—Athens—History—20th century. |
    McMinn County (Tenn.)—Politics and government—20th century. |
    Elections—Corrupt practices—Tennessee—McMinn County—
    History—20th century. | Veterans—Political activity—Tennessee—
    Athens—History—20th century. | Veterans—Political activity—
    Tennessee—McMinn County—History—20th century. | World War,
    1939–1945—Veterans—Tennessee—Athens. | World War, 1939–1945—
    Veterans—Tennessee—McMinn County. | White, Bill, 1924–2006.
Classification: LCC F444.A75 D47 2020 | DDC 976.8/865—dc23
LC record available at https://lccn.loc.gov/2020024226

ISBN 978-1-250-80852-3 (trade paperback)

Our books may be purchased in bulk for promotional, educational, or business
use. Please contact your local bookseller or the Macmillan Corporate and
Premium Sales Department at 1-800-221-7945, extension 5442, or by email at
MacmillanSpecialMarkets@macmillan.com.

First St. Martin's Griffin Edition: 2022

10 9 8 7 6 5 4 3 2 1

CONTENTS

A NOTE ON NAMES

The Americans who settled the lands beyond the Eastern Seaboard, predominantly from the border region of Scotland and England, joined siblings, cousins, aunts, uncles, and other members of their extended families. Generations later, people with the same last name, even an uncommon name, and even in a small county, are not necessarily closely related and may not even know one another.

PLAYERS

THE FIGHTING BUNCH

Bill White, Marine Corps

Bill Grubb, Army

Gene Gunter, Marines

David Hutsell, Army

Cecil Kennedy, Navy

Buck Landers, Army

Jimmy Lockmiller, Marines

Ken Mashburn, National
  Guard

Edgar Miller, Army

Thomas Shamblin, Army

Sam Simms, Navy

Edsel Underwood, Army

Millard Vincent, Army

Paul Weeks, Army

THE MACHINE

Paul Cantrell, sheriff of McMinn County and later state
  senator, chairman of the McMinn County Court, and
  chairman of the McMinn Democratic Party

Pat Mansfield, chief deputy sheriff and later sheriff

George Woods, state representative and later speaker of
  the Tennessee house

Minus Wilburn (pronounced Min-iss), deputy sheriff of
    McMinn County
Burch Biggs, boss of neighboring Polk County
Carl Neil, game warden

THE GI TICKET

Ralph Duggan, Lt. Commander, U.S. Navy, lawyer, lead
    strategist for the GI ticket
Otto Kennedy, chairman of the McMinn Republican Party
    and owner of Essankay Tire
Jim Buttram, campaign manager, GI ticket
Knox Henry, GI candidate for sheriff
Frank Carmichael, GI candidate for trustee
George Painter, GI candidate for county court clerk
Bill Hamby, GI candidate for clerk of the circuit court
Charlie Pickel, GI candidate for register of deeds

PROLOGUE

IN SEARCH OF HISTORY

"Yes, we broke the law. And so did George Washington."

—*Felix Herrod*

AUGUST 2, 1946

"I can only tell you half the story . . ."

Bill Downs delivered the first live broadcast from Normandy Beach and traveled with liberating armies through France and Germany. The CBS correspondent, one of Edward R. Murrow's "Boys," had covered the surrender of Japan and walked the streets of Hiroshima with the occupation force. Now he was broadcasting the news of an unlikely battle amid another occupying force. Downs stood in a "wrecked jail" interviewing the veterans, "fresh from combat all over the world," who controlled Athens, Tennessee, after a "bloody battle." The young men had the "stamp of combat in their eyes," said Downs, a fatigue familiar from the "hard days of the Normandy breakthrough and the Battle of the Bulge."

"They realize they have taken a serious step," said Downs, but "do not interpret their action as taking the law into their own hands. Rather they say they just put the law back in the hands of the people."

"It was a dictatorship down here," said one GI. "Elections were a farce" while they were away at war. They were warned not to run for office and to stay away from the polls when they came home. "No matter what happened," the machine promised, "they would win." Another put it simply: "We just got plain tired of being pushed around by a bunch of thugs."

They were interrupted by a white-haired woman shouting through a shattered window: "Billy, you come home right now and get your lunch." Billy may have overthrown the government the night before, said Downs, "but when his mother called, he went."

Downs had been an hour away at Oak Ridge National Laboratory, birthplace of the Bomb, for a ceremony marking the transition of atomic power from military to civilian use: "to serve man, rather than destroy him." He raced to Athens to cover another force, built for war and converted to civilian use, that returned to its previous purpose for one last fight.[1]

Bill Downs and the reporters who arrived in Athens could only tell "half the story." There were legal consequences to think about: Who knew how many laws the GIs had broken with all the shooting, bombing, kidnapping, and robbery? And winning last night's battle wouldn't save them from a bullet through their window or a knife at a bar. For years—and, in some cases, for the rest of their lives—the men who fought the Battle of Athens kept their mouths shut.

Their successful armed rebellion is without precedent since the American Revolution. I wanted to know the other half of the story.

Many had tried to get it without success. Reporters descended on this county seat between Knoxville and Chattanooga in the days after the battle, and it was front-page news in every corner of the country and from Buenos Aires to Berlin to Tokyo.

One of these reporters was Theodore White, wartime China correspondent for *Time*. Months earlier he'd been brought home by publisher Henry Luce for his refusal to write a cover story glorifying Chiang Kai-shek, a man he considered a tyrant.

White rented a "sunless apartment on East Twenty-Ninth Street" to write a book about what he saw in China: "a billion people who are tired of the world as it is . . . in such terrible bondage that they have nothing to lose but their chains. Less than a thousand years ago Europe lived this way. Then Europe revolted against the old system in a series of bloody wars that lifted it generation by generation to what we regard as civilization. The people of Asia are now going through the same process." The pages "rolled off" the typewriter.

Thunder Out of China was selected for the Book-of-the-Month Club. If it never sold another copy, he'd earn ten times the annual salary of the average American. Upon hearing the news White left his New York apartment and bought his first automobile. He drove south to Washington, where he aimed his car at the heart of the country and headed west. There must be stories out there, he thought.

White's car climbed out of the Shenandoah Valley and crossed into the hills of Tennessee, where he heard reports of the battle. He headed for Athens.

"You want to know how this started, eh?" said Jim Buttram, campaign manager for the GI ticket, a high school football star who had been wounded in France. "Well, all of us did a lot of thinking over there about the disgraceful way this gang was abusing our people here. When we got back, a group of us got together last December and decided we couldn't stand for this to go on."

"[Sheriff] Pat Mansfield said he was going to give us a fair and square election," said Otto Kennedy, bail bondsman, tire store owner, and chairman of the local Republican Party. "And then we have those sons of bitches, walking around with their guns and badges telling us to kiss their ass." (This became "kiss our neck" somewhere between the interview and publication.)

Ralph Duggan, a genteel Athens lawyer and strategist for the GIs, spent long nights in Pacific waters worried more about his home than the Axis military machine. "If democracy was good enough to put on the Germans and Japanese," he said, "it was good enough for McMinn County."

But nobody would talk about what everyone really wanted to know: "From dusk to dawn," wrote White, "the story of the siege of Athens dissolves into anonymity. No man knows or tells who played precisely what role on the night of Thursday, August 1, 1946."[2]

White submitted his story, "The Votes and Hearts of McMinn County," to *Harper's*. It ran under a new title, one that would forever give this event its name: "The Battle of Athens, Tennessee." He went on to national fame for his books on presidential elections but in his memoir, *In Search of History*, he still remembered Athens, "the last whiplash curl of violence from World War II," as his first lesson in American politics.

There was little reason to think that I could do better than Theodore White or any number of others who had tried to tell the story of this unlikely revolution. The challenge was to re-create events that were purposely concealed by people who are no longer alive. If I fell short I would find myself in good company. But if I succeeded, I would have preserved one of the great American stories.

I started with a tool my predecessors didn't have: the internet. Sure enough, there's a website about the Battle of Athens, run by Travis Davis, grandson of Bill White, a name long associated with the event. Speaking with Travis, I realized he was trying to correct the record, at least as it existed around town.

The vow of silence taken after the battle created an information void, filled by people making all kinds of claims. Travis knew his grandfather was telling the truth, and in exchange for his help Travis asked me for nothing but to dig as far as I could into the story and report what I found. He said it would vindicate his grandfather. He was right.

Bill White recorded his stories from World War II and the Battle of Athens on old cassette tapes, hours of firsthand recollections that had never been heard outside the White family. Bill identified the men who had fought alongside him, giving names to the shadowy, faceless veterans firing in the darkness. I searched for each of them. Time and again the first hit was for their obituary. Maybe their families knew something?

Ken Mashburn's daughter Patty remembered her father telling her as a little girl: "Do the right thing, even when it's not the easy thing." When he was young, he explained, he had risked getting killed or locked up in a firefight with a corrupt sheriff. "Really?" his young daughter asked.

David Hutsell's daughter worried that she didn't have any useful recollections. "Okay," I said. "Please call me if you think of anything." We talked almost every day for the next week as her memory refocused on old events. And it turned out that her father had told Gabe, his grandson, everything. I was able to interview him at his home in Athens.

Joe Grubb was living in San Francisco and retired as an agency head for the city. I got his number from his father's widow, whom I had called after reading his obituary. "Oh, yes," he said, "my father had a file labeled 'Battle of Athens.'" I thought he was messing with me. Letters in the aging manila folder told of the war, the GIs' shocking homecoming to McMinn, and the building of the veterans' club in a hotel basement that sprang the GI political movement.

Jim Buttram died the year I was born. His widow died a year before I started this project. But her passing required their children to clean out a safe they had never seen their parents open. His son Jim invited me to his home in Lenoir City to see for myself. Inside were his confidential papers detailing efforts to organize and elect the GI ticket.

The Ralph Duggan who greeted me at his home in Georgia was instantly recognizable as the man his namesake father might have aged into, had he not died so young. His father's private papers were meticulously organized, and he gladly opened them up for me.

Others never said a word until pressed, later in life. Knoxville police captain Randy Lockmiller was working security at the convention center when a stranger recognized his name: "Are you kin to Jimmy Lockmiller?" he asked.

"That's my dad," he said.

"Your father was involved in the Battle of Ballots and Bullets," he said, a local name used by some older residents.

Randy called his father that night: "What's this about the Battle of Ballots and Bullets?"

Jimmy paused. "Who have you been talking to?"

Ann Davis was a senior in high school when her father came to speak to her class. For the first time she learned of his extraordinary role on Election Day, 1946. As far as she knew, he never discussed it again. Years later, as the mayor of Athens, she took one call after another from media outlets around the world, asking about the fiftieth anniversary of the battle. No, there would not be a parade. No ceremony. No anything else.

Tom Edwards arrived in Athens to cover the anniversary for *The Wall Street Journal.* "Memory is tenacious in these parts," he wrote. Despite a half century's intervention, people wanted nothing to do with it. Edwards recorded one longtime friend saying to another: "You know, your father tried to kill my grandfather." How could these two live with each other unless they put it far out of their minds? One official after another told Edwards, "I'd lose my job if they knew I was talking to you." Edwards's article was titled "Gun Shy: Legacy of 1946 Battle Makes Town Uneasy."

But Athens would be remembered in spite of itself.

I found a master's thesis from 1948 at Emory University. The author, George Brasington, who went on to a long career as a professor at his alma mater, had traveled to Athens and interviewed people who never spoke to anyone else. I found it on the shelves, dusty, typewritten, where it had sat for more than seventy years.

I first traveled to Athens in December 2018. The McMinn County Living Heritage Museum, which had opened an exhibit on the battle only two months earlier, has a "Battle of Athens" box filled with scrapbooks and newspaper clippings. Reporters from Chattanooga and Knoxville had been on the scene, furiously scribbling in notepads while bullets bounced in every direction.

Also in the box was a letter from *Tennessee History Quarterly* rejecting an article by Thomas Baker, a professor at Tennessee Wesleyan College. I called *Tennessee History Quarterly* and was almost embarrassed to ask: Did they have a submission from 1969? Their files from that era are housed at the Tennessee State Archives—I would have to contact them. I sent an email, expecting nothing. I had the article the next day—forty-one pages of original research and interviews with key participants.

Congressman John Jennings had waged a fight for fair elections. He told newspapers that he had "submitted to the Department of Justice sworn evidence of wholesale fraud, force, and theft in McMinn County." Deep in the shelves of the National Archives are big boxes filled with dusty manila folders, and inside are hundreds of pages of letters and affidavits from the people of McMinn describing terrors more fitting of our World War II adversaries than the United States. I was the first person ever to request these files. The attorney general of the United States described them as the worst allegations of voter fraud ever brought to the Department of Justice.

Then there were court records: in the McMinn County Circuit Court; the federal Eastern District of Tennessee; and the state supreme court, with pleadings, depositions, and other testimony—preserving details that otherwise would have been long forgotten.

There were two live broadcasts of the battle: one from Chuck Redfern at the local station and another from Allen Stout and Bill Larkin of Knoxville. Redfern's broadcast has been lost to time. Johnny Pirkle, who became a legendary broadcaster from the area, was a young boy glued to the radio the night of the battle. As a WROL intern in the 1960s he found the original acetate recordings of Stout's broadcast. Some of these were still in condition to share the night we met for barbecue on Congress Parkway. There was the voice of Allen Stout, telling the story in real time, with bombs and bullets exploding in the background.

Otto Kennedy, who as chairman of the Republican Party led the wartime opposition to the machine, had died in 1988. But I found his granddaughter, Donna Cagle, a retired teacher in Athens. She had brought her grandpa to speak to her class in 1983 about the events surrounding the battle. And she taped every word.

For every breakthrough there was at least one setback. There are two documentaries on the battle: one by Ross Bagwell, who'd gotten his start as a producer on *Howdy Doody,* and another by the McMinn County Living Heritage Museum. Bagwell had financed the project at a loss, he told me, to keep the story alive. He promised all the raw footage he could find—which, tragically, turned out to be none. Nearly every person in the credits has heard from me, to no avail. The museum, however, had its uncut footage, yielding hours of eyewitness interviews.

Larry Eaton runs the most popular Facebook group in McMinn County and let me use it for whatever I needed. There is only one picture of the battle itself—nobody's face is visible. But in the immediate aftermath is a famous photo, snapped at the second a hated deputy had his throat cut while being guarded by a GI. I posted it in Larry's group, asking if anyone recognized the other man. I immediately heard from his grandson, who put me in touch with his son.

The newspapers published a list of everyone admitted to the hospital on August 1 and 2, a popular item in the days before privacy laws. I tracked down every name, confident that if you were shot, stabbed, or assaulted in Athens on these dates it was connected to the battle.

The wartime experience of these young men is a critical part of the story. In addition to his cassette tapes, Bill White sat for an oral history with the University of Tennessee. On another occasion, he was among the McMinn County veterans interviewed for the fiftieth anniversary of World War II. His interviewer was none other than Paul Willson, grandson of Paul Cantrell, the politician who had been overthrown in the Battle of Athens.

I met with Paul Willson my first day in Athens. He and Bill White were longtime friends, and in fact many of the men involved in the battle were among the most important friendships of his life. I began to sense that the story of the aftermath—how the community came back together—was as compelling as the battle.

I am confident I followed every lead as far as I could. For instance, in Jim Buttram's private safe was a letter from a Paul Pfretzschner of Buffalo, New York, a veteran and graduate student who asked some very interesting questions: whether the media "omitted any significant detail"; how the GI ticket came together; "how the Cantrell Machine operated." If Buttram responded, I wanted to read it. Unlike many of the people I sought out for this book, Paul Pfretzschner wasn't hard to find. But like most of the people I wanted to talk with, he was gone. His obituary gave me the name of his wife, who had since passed, and three daughters, one of whom I found on Facebook. I shared the letter with her and asked if she had the reply. Neither she nor her sisters had the letter, if Buttram ever sent it. But sharing with them a letter from a father they lost in 1986 was a heck of a consolation prize. I had many such opportunities in the course of this research.

Bill White's presence looms large in the home that he shared with his wife, Jean, though he's been gone thirteen years. Pictures and plaques on the wall reflect his time in the Marine Corps.

Bill and Jean had owned a hunting and fishing lodge in the mountains. The lodge and its proprietor had drawn the interest of journalists over the years. Jean shared some old articles with me. "Bill White is the kind of man John Wayne would've looked up to," wrote the Memphis *Commercial Appeal*. The reporter marveled at Bill's gun collection. "You name the war, he'll show you the gun which helped win that war," from Revolutionary flintlocks to Civil War rifles, "and give you as thorough a history on it as you have time for."

A magazine headline wondered: "What Kind of Man Would Hunt Wild Hogs with a Spear?" An article titled "Tennessee's Tough Guy" concluded, "There's a lot of Indian left in Bill White, perhaps the most unusual hog hunter of modern times. You might call him a bit crazy . . . but you'd better not say that to his face."

I read the interview. "Tennessee Russian boars are the most vicious game animals in the United States," Bill said. "A hunter would rather pit his dogs against five bears than one pig. The hunter has only one chance. Then it's the pig's turn." There was a picture of Bill with a four-hundred-pound hog. The curved, razor-sharp tusks and four-inch teeth could "rip open" someone "from bowel to brisket" with one shake of its head, Bill said. The magazine noted that people would pay top dollar to hunt with Bill and asked if he was available. Bill preferred to hunt alone, but promised to find a guide for anyone who asked.[3]

Jean told me that she'd first seen Bill White while working as a ticket taker at the Strand Theater. "Who is that?" she asked the boy she was working with.

"That's Bill White," said her co-worker.

"I'm going to marry him," Jean said.

Her co-worker laughed, aware of Bill's rough reputation. "He'll never get married."

Jean told me she had a strong intuition about certain things in her life and that when it spoke to her it was never wrong. Sure enough, years later, they met and he asked her out. Jean told her father. "Is that the Bill White who was in the Battle of Athens?" he asked, concerned.

They wound up eloping over the border to Georgia. Despite her father's misgivings, the marriage produced four children and lasted fifty-seven years, to the end of Bill's life.

I asked her: "What would Bill White want me to write about the Battle of Athens?"

"The truth," his widow said without hesitation. "The exact truth."

1

HOME, SWEET HOME

CAMP LEJEUNE, NORTH CAROLINA
September 24, 1945

Bill White had survived Guadalcanal and Tarawa. Now all that remained was a separation interview with Lieutenant F. L. Dixon, who rattled off a series of questions as he banged away on a typewriter.

The form called for basic information (RACE: W; SEX: M), the date he had joined (12JAN42), the fake birthdate he had used (4MAY23), and his time overseas (YEARS: 2; MONTHS: 4; DAYS: 11). The marines wanted to know where they were sending him (401 S. HILL ST., ATHENS, TENN.) and, finally, why: it was home, Bill said.

It was a long bus ride before familiar tall trees and rolling green fields came into view. The sign made it official: "Welcome to Athens—The Friendly City." The clock tower appeared, followed by the rest of the grand old courthouse.

Every train car and coach in America was crowded with men coming home from war. They were returning from jungles, fields, the desert, and ships surrounded by water, but they all shared the dream of going home. Someday, when the war was over, they would resume their interrupted lives.

The courthouse square was filled with life when the weather permitted: people gathered to sell, shop, gossip, play music, or hear itinerant preaching. But Bill could see it was mostly empty, except for some leafless maple trees.

Four sheriff's deputies wearing gold badges and guns were there to meet the bus at the dilapidated depot. They arrested a group of Bill's fellow passengers, still wearing their uniforms, for public drunkenness. They'd had a few beers to celebrate being alive, but far from enough to intoxicate a navy sailor.

"What's going on?" Bill asked a bystander.

"Those deputies meet every bus and every train, and if you're drinking a beer or anything they're arresting you and making you pay a fine."

Bill couldn't believe it. These boys had risked their lives. And now they were headed to jail and about to lose their mustering-out pay to a bunch of thugs. "Hellfire," Bill said.[1]

2

ON THE LITTLE TENNESSEE RIVER

1924-35

"I was born on the Little Tennessee River," remembered Bill White, with a sweetness and reverence he reserved for little else, "which flowed down out of the Cherokee Mountains."

His parents, Edd and Elizabeth White, had three boys followed by three girls. Bill found it easy to get lost among his siblings, especially Edd Jr., his faster and stronger older brother. Bill bristled under any kind of authority, and was known to hide all night in the woods rather than face discipline. But he had a special connection with Grandpa Wiggins, with whom he spent as much time as he could. "Those years were real good years," said Bill, "because my grandpa taught me a whole lot about hunting, and trapping, and fishing, and I admired and respected him."

Grandpa Wiggins led Bill on summertime treasure hunts for arrowheads, spear points, bone needles, and effigy pottery. These were left over from the Cherokee, he explained, who had lived in these mountains and along the river for many years, and Bill was descended from them through his great-grandmother.

Bill learned the legends of his ancestors, like Atagahi, "The Lake of the Wounded," hidden somewhere in those mountains, where injured animals could be restored to health by drinking the water. It was said that some Cherokee hunters found the lake by following a wounded animal, but once they left could never find it again, though some looked for the rest of their lives.[1]

Bill also learned about his family on his father's side. His relative James White had fought in the American Revolution and founded the city of Knoxville. White had served as a senator in the rogue government of Franklin, a failed attempt to form a new state from the western counties of North Carolina. The Cherokee considered James White a man of honor, and he had twice prevented outbreaks of violence along the frontier.[2]

Grandpa Wiggins and Bill sat on the banks of the Little Tennessee River and waited for catfish, buffalo fish, and trout. Supposedly the Dakwa lived in those waters, a fish large enough to swallow a man. It especially liked to eat boys who walked too close to the water's edge—at least that's what Grandpa Wiggins said.

Grandpa would take Bill "plum over across" the mountain to Bass Dockery's house when he wanted some whiskey. Bass had lost an arm in a shootout, and Bill helped him fire up the still and fed it with firewood. Bass let little Bill take a sip, sending him running to the spring behind the house to calm his mouth.[3]

Bill and his grandpa built traps for rabbits and wild hogs. They rode twelve miles to the mill to grind corn and flour and the same distance home to make corn bread and biscuits. Sunday mornings were for the First Baptist Church in the mountain town of Toccoa, where Bill's parents had met.

People called it a Great Depression, said Bill, but "we didn't have much to begin with. We lived about the same as our families had for the last one hundred and fifty years—just off the land. We were happy. We didn't know we were poor until somebody out of the city came out here and told us we were poor people."[4]

Bill once came across a tombstone in the woods: "Bushwhacked on Steer Creek Road While Cradling Oats." He asked Grandma Wiggins about it. The bushwhackers were a gang of rough men who'd been hired to defend a nearby plantation. After the Civil War they ran roughshod over the mountains, raiding farms, stealing cattle, and "killing anyone in their way." His grandma told Bill that they'd murdered her brother, a Union veteran who had fought at Lookout Mountain, shortly after his return from the war.

Then one day his time in the mountains with Grandpa Wiggins came to an end. Bill's mother told him that his father had gotten a job with the Tennessee Valley Authority, working at the new substation in Athens. He'd have to move with the rest of the family.

Bill cried. Couldn't he stay? He wanted to stay. He knew Grandpa Wiggins wanted him to stay.

Bill's mom explained to him. Grandpa and Grandma would love for you to stay. But they don't have enough food for the three of you. Bill had never thought about it. Then he remembered how Grandma always ate the crumbs of the corn bread after he was done. He moved to Athens with his family.[5]

3

WARRIOR ROOTS

McMinn County, Tennessee, sits along the Great Warrior Path of the Cherokee and U.S. Route 11. A tribal elder remembered "a lovely land of hill and dale, free from the extremes of heat in the summer, or the bitter cold in the winter; a land of health, of pure air and pure water, whose clear running streams in every valley were filled with the finest fish; a land of singing birds, of flowers and honey, of wild grapes and nuts in great variety, and over all extended one almost unbroken, open, grass grown forest where roamed countless numbers of deer, and other game, in thriving abundance. . . . Our days were passed like a happy dream, in the hunt, in idly fishing from our canoes, in feasting with our friends, and in the joyous assemblage around the campfire at night."[1]

Chief Atta-Kulla-Kulla was on a hunt when he discovered a badly wounded soldier fighting in the American Revolution. Nocatula, the chief's daughter, was charged with bringing him back to health. The soldier joined the tribe and was given the name "Conestoga," meaning "oak." Nocatula and Conestoga fell in love, fishing in her canoe and hiding away at her favorite bluff. Shortly before their wedding, Conestoga was ambushed by a rival suitor, Mocking Crow. Nocatula came across him as he lay dying, pulled the knife from his neck, and plunged it straight into her heart. "Slowly he opened his eyes and seeming to realize the dear face now pressed against his, he smiled, and with a last effort slowly raised his now stiffened right arm, and placed it across her shoulders."

The chief directed a hackberry seed to be placed in her hand and an acorn in his. They were buried together. When Bill White arrived in Athens, the oak and the hackberry tree had grown tall, their branches intertwined as though holding hands. They could be found on the campus of Tennessee Wesleyan College, founded on the eve of the Civil War, whose red brick buildings with white columns and porticos kept a respectful distance from the resting place of Nocatula and Conestoga.

The Hiwassee Purchase of 1819 opened East Tennessee to settlement. The Cherokee were curious about their new neighbors. The rest of America, it turns out, had been wondering the same thing since they first appeared on overcrowded docks.

The Quakers and Puritans had come to build Utopia; the Cavaliers, runners-up in the English Civil War, had come because they'd lost a political battle; the newest wave of immigrants were here because they'd lost every political battle.

They were dubbed Scotch-Irish, from the region spanning Scotland and England, descended from warrior Celts, the Romans who conquered them in A.D. 80, and the Saxons, Vikings, and Normans who invaded one after the other.[2]

They were Borderers—living near where one country ended and another began—and this was the central fact of their existence.

From 1040 and for the next seven centuries, every king of England invaded the Scots or was invaded. Or both.

Stone beacons dotted the high hills of the borderlands. A farmer could look up at any moment and see one lit, and know that any one of a number of bad things was about to happen.

It didn't matter which king was on top: the Borderers always lost. Marauding armies did just as much damage headed north as they did going south. Bandits preyed on this lawless region in the years between invasions. The Borderers relied on themselves and their families for survival, and hated the distant authorities that continually upended and endangered their lives. The chance to leave this world behind and start over in another one was the sweetest thing they could have imagined.[3]

There was one final indignity for them in their escape: a sea voyage with too many passengers, not enough food, and a mortality rate approaching that of slave ships.[4]

Borderers made awful servants. They became famous for not taking orders, beating up overbearing overseers, and, in at least one case, taking off with his master's wife and daughters. It was observed of one, and could have been said of many: "His looks spoke out that he would not fear the devil, should he meet him face to face."[5]

The Borderers loved their new home. People asked: "Where are you from?" The typical answers: Virginia, North Carolina, or maybe Pennsylvania. If pressed to name the city of their ancestors, many wouldn't know, or care. There was no nostalgia for the Old World or their place in it.[6]

McMinn County was carved from the Hiwasee Purchase and named for Tennessee's governor. The village of Pumpkintown was selected as the county seat and renamed Athens, after the cradle of Western civilization and birthplace of democracy, a signal toward their grand aspirations for the new community.[7]

Some expected trouble from two warrior cultures in new proximity. But they intermarried, lived as neighbors, and were buried together in the old cemeteries. The Cherokee "were living a settled, civilized existence that paralleled in every way that of their white counterparts," and possibly had greater formal education than the new arrivals.[8]

The trouble started over the border in Georgia in 1828. Gold had been discovered in the mountains on Cherokee land. Thousands of "gamblers, swindlers, debauchers, and profane blackguards with morals as bad as it is to conceive" rushed to stake their claims. President Andrew Jackson decided to settle the matter by relocating the entire Cherokee people to the west, a journey of hundreds of miles for some and more than a thousand for others.

General Winfield Scott arrived in McMinn County with seven thousand men in 1838. The people protested and resisted and did everything they could to save their neighbors, friends, and family. One resident recorded: "The Cherokees are nearly all prisoners . . . dragged from their houses and encamped in military places all over the area," with "no time to take with them anything except the clothes they have on. Well-furnished houses are left prey to plunderers who, like hungry wolves, follow in the train of the captors."

The people of McMinn had failed to save the Cherokee. But they never lost their hostility to oppressors. They petitioned the Tennessee Constitutional Convention to phase out slavery and overwhelmingly opposed Secession.

During the Civil War they found themselves in a position familiar to their ancestors, on the fault lines between two warring

parties. On any given day control could change from Union to
Confederate hands and back again. Close attention was paid to
the color of uniforms worn in the street. Men returned from
Union and Confederate armies at war's end and moved ahead
with life.[9]

4

HARD TIMES

Bill White and his family settled on Depot Hill, the high point of Athens, a neighborhood known as Happy Top, home to the workers in manufacturing, mills, and lumberyards.

Bill hated North City Elementary. He was new, short, and scrawny, and an inviting target for bullies. He had to "fight his way to school" and "fight his way home." There was no cafeteria: at noon he ran three miles home, wolfed down his lunch, and ran all the way back.

Bill couldn't understand why the school had so many rules. Why they had to line up in silence—rain or shine—at the beginning of the day. He told his teachers when he thought something wasn't right. "And there was a whole lot of things that wasn't right," Bill said. Outside of school, Bill was expected to help tend the family garden, fatten hogs, trap rabbits, and milk the cow. Edd, an electrical engineer for the Tennessee Valley Authority, was doing better than many, but these extra measures were necessary to get by. But however long and hard the day,

Bill was "glued" to the radio at night and the adventures of *The Lone Ranger*.[1]

McMinn County was in high spirits despite the Depression. "Athens is a true courthouse town," wrote one observer, "and the shady square is filled to overflowing with country people on Saturdays. They come on horseback, in mule drawn wagons, and in cars spattered with red clay."

The businesses around the courthouse had colorful awnings and distinctive trademarks, like the painting of a headdressed chief above Cherokee Hardware. Wooded hills and the distant peaks of the Unaka Mountains were visible along the horizon.

"When their trading is done the men lounge around the courthouse square, swapping gossip and political views while their women-folk attended the movies. . . . Soap box evangelists" and musicians give the scene a "holiday air."[2]

One of these traveling preachers was the Goat Man, who traveled the roads of the American South in a wagon pulled by an army of goats. People could smell his arrival, an awful offending odor from him, his goats, and the rubber tires he'd burn to stay warm at night.

There were softball games, musical performances, plays, and pie suppers. Young people danced in the ballroom of the Robert E. Lee Hotel. There were picnics with prizes: "a large cake for the prettiest girl, a jar of pickles for the ugliest boy, and a rolling pin for the most henpecked husband."[3]

Bill White and the other children had plenty of fun that money couldn't buy. They visited the farm of Judge Clem Jones, which became the unlikely home of many exotic animals when a Nashville zoo went bankrupt. They searched Starr Mountain for the cave of Mason Evans. Evans, the "Wild Man of Chilhowee," had abandoned society after being rejected by his true love, spending the remaining decades of his life in solitude, instantly recognizable by his tattered clothes and battered hat, with a featherless rooster as his only companion. The bravest among them explored Henderson's Hollow, where the tall trees grew so thick, it was dark in the middle of the day. A Big Black Thing, neither man nor beast, was said to inhabit the hollow and had chased one curious boy for his life.

McMinn County sits above the largest underground lake in North America. Ed "Coo" King, who spent most of his time in the caves searching for rocks, was glad to gift a ten- or twenty-pounder for someone to decorate their yard. Recipients nodded politely when King said the rocks would someday turn to gold.

In the midst of a hailstorm, Bullet Boyer chipped a huge block of ice from the chest and dropped it from a window of the Robert E. Lee Hotel. A crowd swelled around the largest hailstone anyone had ever seen. It was taken to the Redpath Café, where it was preserved in a freezer, brought out to satisfy curiosity seekers, and photographed for the cover of the next day's *Post-Athenian*. The great hailstone of McMinn County hit the wire service and made national news. When the initial buzz wore off, the café chopped it up and served it as ice for beverages, which people eagerly bought.

In addition to keeping their senses of humor, McMinn residents survived the Depression by supporting one another. The *Post-Athenian* reported: "There are deeds of kindness and more generosity shown at this time than has been recorded for years if ever before and the public does not know it."

A. G. Buttram's grocery store had crackers and a giant wheel of cheese at the end of the register. Anyone who wanted could come in and help themselves until they were full. People were re-luctant to accept charity, so Buttram agreed to keep a tab, which he promptly tore up. This game satisfied both hunger and pride. Every sewing club in the county set aside one day a week to make clothes for people who needed them. Banks worked tirelessly to keep people in their homes. In turn, there were no "runs" on the banks, as elsewhere, where panicked customers withdrew their savings, wiping out the bank and depositors behind them in line. A family with three references could receive flour from the Red Cross. Sheriff Boling Shoemaker took a 25 percent cut in his three-thousand-dollar salary. Doctors and brothers Carey and Ed Foree opened a hospital charging five dollars per day. But "nobody who came to the hospital needing help was turned away, not even if he didn't have a nickel."[4]

Etowah had boomed to be the second-biggest city in McMinn County. It was hit hard when the Louisville & Nash-ville Railroad cut its payroll from twenty-one hundred to eighty. Governor Franklin Roosevelt of New York campaigned in Etowah near the close of the 1932 election, his train arriving at the station near 11:00 P.M.: "My friends, it is mighty good of you to stay up at this hour of the night to see me." He promised the economy would bounce back and refused to "concede a single state—even Vermont." Democrats estimated the crowd at seven thousand, Republicans at fifteen hundred.[5]

Bill White had one favorite escape from school, bullies, and his crowded home. He'd go out into the woods and spend all day picking, usually blackberries, sometimes apples and grapes. Bill had two gallon buckets. Once they were full to overflowing, dragging his little shoulders down with them, he could walk to town and sell them for ten cents. That dime would get him one of 250 seats at the air-conditioned Strand Theater.

Tom Mix was his favorite actor. Bill didn't have any use for Gene Autry or Roy Rogers, the singing, guitar-playing cowboys ("They were stupid," he said). Bill liked "Westerns and shoot-'em-up movies—that's all I'd go to see." Mix was a tough guy who took on corrupt sheriffs and evil land barons and saved the day against long odds. *The Miracle Rider* came out in 1935. Mix had made the transition from silent films to talkies. Now he was fighting fedora-wearing gangsters, an anachronism in his cowboy clothes and hat.

The movie opened with dramatic music and Tom galloping on Tony the horse. Zaroff, an evil businessman, was terrorizing the Ravenhead Indians to drive them from their land, where he planned to mine a powerful explosive.

Mix looked like a goner as the movie neared its end, captured by Zaroff and his goons. "If it wasn't for your meddling," Zaroff said, "I'd be the most powerful man in the world."

"Thanks for the compliment," said Mix.

"Any last requests you'd like to make?"

"A condemned man usually smokes a cigarette before he dies." Mix used the diversion to kick one of the goons, grabbing his gun and escaping out the window.

Mix and a group of Texas Rangers opened fire on Zaroff's house from behind their car. Mix rolled an oil barrel toward the house, using it for cover, and, when he was close enough, threw tear gas bombs through the window until Zaroff's gang surrendered. "Throw those guns out the winda," Mix said. "Now come out with your hands in the air." He had saved the day again.

In the summer of 1936 McMinn was focused on local problems, of which they had more than enough. A long-awaited rain ended a near catastrophic drought. Hundreds of houses joined the electric grid. Athens opened up a typhoid clinic to beat back recent outbreaks.

But the pages of the *Post-Athenian* brought troubling news from the rest of the world: Japanese troops entered Beijing; Fascist Italy invaded Ethiopia; Stefan Lux, a Jewish journalist, walked onto the floor of the League of Nations and committed suicide by shooting. He had tried for years to call attention to the dangers posed by Adolf Hitler and the Nazi regime. Now he died in a final, desperate attempt to snap the world out of its fog.[6]

5

THE RISE OF PAUL CANTRELL

With the election of President Roosevelt a flurry of acronyms appeared to fight the Depression: AAA, NYA, NRA, WPA, CCC. The Civilian Conservation Corps opened a camp in Athens, putting hundreds to work planting trees and soil. The camp quickly had trouble with the sheriff's office.

Deputies earned money for every arrest they made. An arrest motivated by money, rather than public safety, was known as "fee grabbing." The men of the CCC with their government paychecks made for easy targets. The camp leader threatened to take his jobs elsewhere and did, ten weeks later when nothing changed. Sheriff Davy Crockett Duggan, named for his famous relative, couldn't or wouldn't put an end to fee grabbing, even to keep a valuable employer.[1]

Paul Cantrell decided to run for sheriff in 1936. He was the youngest son of the late Thomas Washington Cantrell. "Wash" Cantrell may have been the richest man in the county, generous to a fault with everyone he knew, but lived like a pauper. Wash could finance the biggest house in Athens and loan the county money to build a road. But he lived in a log cabin, and walked through three miles of mud every day on his way to the office. He founded Etowah Power and Light, the local utility, which became a reliable place for people to cash their paychecks. Wash realized that he was only one step away—the most profitable one—from being a bank. So instead of cashing checks to be deposited elsewhere, Cantrell Bank was born.[2]

Paul Cantrell had worked as a conductor on the L&N Railroad before becoming manager of his father's utility. He was a spellbinding speaker, a Democrat inspired by President Roosevelt, and believed he could break up a calcified Republican regime, much as his political hero had.[3]

The Republicans nominated Charles Scott Sr., the former chief deputy. He promised "as few deputy sheriffs as possible . . . men with good, clean records," and to fire any deputy making an arrest for improper reasons.

Paul Cantrell took out a full-page newspaper ad, pledging: "No fee grabbing deputies." He promised to end class discrimination in the office. "You can depend on me making a good and efficient sheriff," he wrote. His ad featured a picture of him in a black fedora, wearing a bow tie and glasses, his trademark look.[4]

The *Post-Athenian* loved to host its Election Night party: "Everybody invited—Republicans—Democrats—Socialists—and whatnot." Results would be tallied on a giant chalkboard outside the newspaper office. By 5:30 P.M. the street was completely full. People who showed up later watched from windows and rooftops across the street.[5]

The drizzle started around 8:00 P.M. Some ducked into doorways, but for most it "made little impression." Scott led by 171 votes at 10:00 P.M. The next update improved his margin to 270. His lead grew to 500, where it stayed for two hours.

But Cantrell had reason for optimism. The outstanding precincts were in his hometown of Etowah, where his brother Frank served as mayor. They reported around 1:00 A.M. 9,662 people had voted that day. By a margin of 128, Paul Cantrell was the new sheriff. "Cheers arose from the large crowd still lingering in the street, and whistles were blown and horns honked." The crowd stayed and discussed the result for another half hour.[6]

Cantrell hired Patrick Manuel Mansfield as his chief deputy. Cantrell knew Mansfield, a husky former fireman and engineer on the L&N, from his railroad days. Mansfield had been laid off and was working as night police chief in Etowah, earning $150 a month. The chief deputy position was a dramatic step up in pay and prestige, and he jumped at the chance.[7]

The McMinn County Court, the legislative body, remained firmly in Republican hands. They had long considered putting law enforcement on salary. The election of a Democrat gave them whatever remaining motivation they needed. The court capped Sheriff Cantrell's pay at five thousand dollars, with all excess fees returned to the county. Cantrell responded with a lawsuit that allowed him to keep collecting fees.[8]

It was six months after Paul Cantrell's upset victory. Bill White noticed his friend Jim Voiles was upset at school. Jim said that the night before, three sheriff's deputies had burst into his brother's room and shot him dead, claiming he had pointed a .22 rifle at them. Why were they in the house in the first place? The deputies said they were following through on a call about Carl's possible involvement in a fight. He was twenty-three years old and left a wife behind. The Voiles family pushed for charges against Deputy Oliver Nichols. Judge Sue Hicks dismissed the case. It was awful, Bill thought. But what could they do about it? They were just kids.[9]

Judge Hicks had gained fame as a young lawyer on the prosecution team in the Scopes Monkey Trial, testing Tennessee's prohibition on teaching the theory of evolution. He was named for his mother, Sue, who had died after childbirth, pursuant to her last request. Years later, he spoke at a judicial conference where author Shel Silverstein was in attendance. Silverstein thought about the challenges for a man with a woman's name ("I tell ya, life ain't easy for a boy named 'Sue'"). He wrote a song inspired by the judge and later recorded by Johnny Cash, who sent Hicks an autographed picture: "To Sue, how do you do?"[10]

The Johnson family lived down the road from Bill and were among the best friends he'd made in Athens. Hub Johnson had been widowed young, remarried, and finally became a father in his late forties. His daughter, Mabel, was a little older than Bill. Charles was Bill's age and George a few years younger. Hub found himself responsible for three young children when his wife died suddenly. They had a little farm and delivered newspapers as a family to make enough to live. They walked three miles to town, collected the papers, and delivered them, once in the morning and then in the afternoon. Sundays included.

Hub Johnson, now in his sixties, had weak kidneys. One day he had to relieve himself in the middle of his route and decided to go behind a billboard sign. Deputy Oliver Nichols saw Hub, and struck him repeatedly with a blackjack in front of his children, killing him. Bill couldn't believe the news. Deputy Nichols, the same one who had killed Carl Voiles not a year earlier. Why was he still on the force and in a position to hurt Mr. Johnson?

A private citizen could initiate criminal charges, and Mabel attempted to get justice for her father. Deputy Nichols testified that sixty-three-year-old Hub Johnson had struck him first and resisted arrest. Besides, Nichols testified, his fatal strike was "not a hard blow." The children told the judge that their father had done nothing to Nichols. Once again, Judge Hicks dismissed the case without ever letting it go to the jury. The Johnsons, already struggling to get by, suffered greatly with the loss of their father. "They really had a hard time of it," Bill said. "That was my first encounter with McMinn County politics."[11]

6

THE BEST FIGHTS OF THE SEASON

Sheriff Paul Cantrell stood for reelection in 1938 on a platform of having cut costs by half. That was "a deliberate falsehood," said Boling Shoemaker, his opponent, himself a former sheriff. Shoemaker said he'd drawn $9,755.38 in his first year, compared to $16,621 for Cantrell. Shoemaker's deputies earned $1,978 in that same time, compared to $4,567.13 for Cantrell's. The challenger urged voters: "If you want the laws enforced fairly and impartially without fear or favor; if you want gambling dives and bawdy houses eliminated; if you want clean honest government by McMinn County vote for me."[1]

From sunrise on Election Day, the streets were "congested to an almost unbelievable degree" as "farmers, railroaders, merchants, industrial workers, politicians, men, women, and children began swarming" to vote in "one of the most hotly contested elections."[2]

The election commission oversaw the voting process. A three-member board, it was made up of two members of the most numerous party in Tennessee, in this case the Democrats, and one member of the minority party, the Republicans. For every polling place, the commission appointed an officer of election, the person in charge; a three-member panel of election judges to referee disputes, which, like the commission, was made up of two Democrats and one Republican; and lastly, one clerk from each party. At closing time the officer of election would look at each ballot and announce the result while the clerks kept a running tally. The total for the two clerks had to match. Election judges would inspect the ballots to ensure the officer of election was calling them accurately. This system was designed for an immediate, public tabulation of the votes with input and observation from all sides. But things would work a little differently in practice.

The first trouble of the day came when Athens attorney Tom Taylor, candidate for circuit judge against Sue Hicks, got in a polling place fistfight with John Rogers, a top Cantrell ally, over a discrepancy in the list of eligible voters. Rogers's list was destroyed. "Guns were swinging wildly and the election booth was partially destroyed when the fighters were knocked through it."

There was more Election Day violence, not all related to politics. The festive atmosphere drew everyone to town, and therefore offered an opportunity to settle scores. Alton Richardson tried to break up a fight and had his throat slashed by accident, fatally wounding him. Two women fought at the Niota polling place over a "jealousy," while Lawrence Garrison and Ed Pickle, both barbers, fought for "nearly half an hour" outside the courthouse over professional differences, in what the *Post-Athenian* called one of the "best fights of the season." Vick Logan, a "well-known Athenian," walked into the Williamsburg polling place and "attempted to wreck the voting booths" with a hatchet. Nobody was sure why. "The jail was filled to capacity with drunks and disorderly characters."

The Claxton precinct ran out of ballots at 2:00 P.M. Officials decided to call it a day, over objections by Shoemaker supporters. The ballot box was removed from the polling place and brought to C. E. Cobb, the deputy trustee, a Democrat whose boss was running for reelection on a ticket with Paul Cantrell. The election commission decided that none of the ballots from Claxton would be counted. Cantrell had lost the precinct by 26 points two years earlier.

The *Post-Athenian* hosted an Election Night party. A crowd of three thousand showed up to watch the returns of the "biggest," "bitterest," and "hardest fought" election in county history. They "howled with delight" when a new precinct was reported. The Etowah precincts reported last, and as before, decided the race. Paul Cantrell was declared the winner over Shoemaker, 5,677 to 5,255. Only 422 votes separated them.

The next day's headline read: "Cantrell-Owen Sweep County: McMinn Election Bloody One—Man is Killed."[3]

7

CIVICS AT McMINN HIGH

Fred Puett was heading home. For years he had worked in the capitol at Nashville, drafting laws by day and learning the law at night. And now that he was finished there was no work for lawyers. He was lucky to get the job he had, at his old high school, teaching civics. Civics had not been a high priority at McMinn—he was replacing a teacher who was also the football coach and had often ditched his own classes.

Mr. Puett tried to get his students interested in politics. "The sheriff runs the jail as his private business," he said. "He hires a jailer and a cook out of his fees. He buys the food. It is a good business if the jail is kept full.

"The justices of the peace, who form the governing board of the county [county court], are also paid in fees. The result is that the justices co-operate in keeping the jail full. The standard fine for minor offenses: drunkenness, traffic violations, and simple assault—after the violator has been jailed by the arresting officer—is sixteen dollars and five cents. This breaks down as follows: six dollars to the arresting officer; four dollars and fifty-five cents to the justice of the peace; one dollar turnkey charge for letting the man in the jail and one dollar for letting him out; a dollar fifty for two days' meals at seventy-five cents a day, and two dollars for the county.

"Especially profitable are drunks arrested after supper and let out before breakfast. As every lawyer would agree, that means the prisoner spends two legal days in the jail and the sheriff is entitled to a dollar fifty for feeding him."

Why does the officer get six dollars?

"Two dollars for serving a warrant, two dollars for hauling the prisoner to jail if the distance is more than six miles, two dollars for subpoenaing four witnesses at fifty cents a witness. Of course the arresting officer does none of these things. He does not serve a warrant and he summons no witnesses and there often is no haulage. He may make the arrest a block from the jail. But it ha[s] become established that the officer g[ets] six dollars for every arrest. Ten arrests on a Saturday night—sixty dollars—[is] good business for a deputy sheriff."

Star football player Big Jim Buttram shifted his giant frame uncomfortably at his desk, thinking seriously about what he was hearing. He and some of the other students discussed Mr. Puett's class over milkshakes. Maybe someday they could make their community a better place to live.[1]

8

"POLITICOS IN McMINN SPLIT OVER VOTE ROBOTS"

Weeks of Campaigning . . . Court Litigation,
Will Come to an End Thursday
—*Daily Post-Athenian*

Both Parties in McMinn Plan to Swear Officers
—*Knoxville Journal*

The main attraction in downtown Athens in July 1940 was a model voting machine, purchased by the county court and on display so that people could gain familiarity before Election Day. A representative from American Voting Machines of Jamestown, New York, was on hand to answer questions.

A voter would walk up to the machine and pull a lever that closed a curtain around them. Next to every candidate's name was a little lever. The voter would switch the lever next to the name of their preferred candidates. When they had voted for every office, they pulled a lever on the side of the machine, which recorded their votes, reset the levers, and opened the curtain.

The running tally was recorded on a counter behind a locked panel. At the end of the day, the panel would be opened, and the results displayed for everyone to see. The voting machines weighed around eight hundred pounds and were not easily stuffed or swapped.[1]

The county court had the legal discretion on whether to use voting machines. Nevertheless, John Cate and Reuel Webb, the Democratic members of the election commission, made public statements that the machines would not be used. The Republican candidates filed suit on July 11. The hearing before Chancery Judge T. L. Stewart included extensive testimony about "voting robots" and how they worked. Stewart ordered the election commission to use the machines.[2]

Absentee voting was another matter of dispute. State law permitted voters who would be gone from the county on Election Day to mail their ballot. Strict rules governed the process: the election commission was required to write down the name of everyone requesting a ballot, in ink, on a publicly posted list; all absentee ballots had to be received by registered mail; the envelope containing the ballot had to be preserved; the date it arrived had to be recorded next to the name of the requester; and a certificate for each vote had to be delivered to the official in charge of that voter's precinct. The election commission ignored every one of these laws.

Without these safeguards, commissioners could create as many absentee ballots as they wanted and place them in ballot boxes, in the names of real people, dead people, and fictitious people. Ralph Duggan, the Republican member of the election commission, sued his colleagues to force them to follow the law.

Duggan, thirty-one, was the son of the previous sheriff, Davy

Crockett Duggan. He had gone to law school at the University of Georgia, where he had roomed with Herman Talmadge, son of the state's governor and himself a future governor and senator. Unlike Talmadge, a fiery segregationist, Duggan was gentle, polite, and believed the laws should apply equally to everyone. Duggan returned home in 1936 and opened his own practice. The tall, lanky lawyer had a reputation for honesty and integrity even among his political adversaries.

The trial court sided with Duggan, holding that the Democratic election commissioners had to comply with absentee ballot rules. Duggan was surprised shortly thereafter to find Chief Deputy Pat Mansfield at his house. Mansfield, the physically imposing former railroad man, had an order from the Tennessee Supreme Court, overturning the decision of the trial court. He wanted to deliver it personally. The supreme court gave no explanation.

State Representative Joe Taylor, Duggan's cousin and close friend, was the Republican nominee for sheriff. He promised to run the office with half as many men, all of whom would be competent and of good character; to accept only the five-thousand-dollar annual salary; to allow arrestees to contact their relatives, regardless of their party affiliation; and to ensure that neither he nor his deputies would serve as bail bondsmen. In a newspaper ad, he asked everyone to see "that the man who gets the most votes is elected."[3]

Election Day dawned with the arrival of twenty state highway patrolmen, who said they were there to "keep the peace."

Tom Taylor, Joe's son, campaigned for his father outside an Etowah polling place. He was arrested by Officer A. B. Blair on the charge of carrying a weapon. Blair, on foot patrol, ordered Taylor into his own car and directed him to drive to the jail at

Athens, with Blair sitting in the front passenger seat and Constable John McTeer in the back. Blair and McTeer discussed whether to kill Taylor when they got to the jail. Were they messing with him? Taylor didn't want to find out.

On the bridge over Chestua Creek, Taylor jerked the wheel and drove off the side into the water. Taylor swam to shore and started running with whatever energy he had left. The officers, reeling from the unexpected swim, chased after him. Taylor's mother and sister had heard of the arrest and were driving toward the jail. Taylor jumped in their car as they drove by. The officers hailed a taxi and forced it on a high-speed chase. Officer Blair told Taylor as he rearrested him that he was adding "attempted murder" to the charges. *The Knoxville News-Sentinel* said the only way this could be phonier is if Taylor had been accused of "attempted murder with a voting machine."[4]

Officials at the Mount Harmony precinct refused to have an election. They claimed to be waiting for instructions from election commissioner John Cate. Voters found a justice of the peace to swear in election officials who were willing to do their jobs. Fred Puett, civics teacher at McMinn High, agreed to be the officer of election. They conducted a smooth contest for the rest of the day. But the election commission would have the final word. They refused to count a single vote from Mount Harmony.

Democratic election officials disabled the voting machine at the Macedonia Precinct. No election was held. At Riceville the lever to vote for Joe Taylor was out of order for forty-five minutes.[5]

In the remaining twenty-one precincts, a custodian working for the county court operated the voting machine while appointees of the election commission used a ballot box, in defiance of the judge's order. Armed men showed up in Precinct 13, forcing custodian Elmer Duggan to remove the voting machine from the premises. The gunmen used a ballot box instead. Cantrell won the precinct, 200–3.

John Rogers, officer of election at Precinct 12, seized the key to the voting machine. He directed all voters to use the ballot box. Rogers, armed with a pistol, cursed and threatened anyone who asked to use the machine. He allowed a number of people from outside the county to vote. Rogers took the ballot box home with him for lunch. He returned with a ballot box and a shotgun, in case anyone had any questions. Why he bothered to do this is anyone's guess, since he and other armed men cleared the polling place at closing time, counting the ballots however they wanted. Why steal or stuff the ballot box if you control the count? This only made sense if the point was to demoralize voters, to break the rules in the most open and obvious ways and get away with it, to show them that they could never win. John Rogers declared Cantrell the winner at his precinct, 437–16, a total exceeding the number of eligible voters.

John's son, Clyde, an Etowah policeman, was officer of election at Precinct 19. A voter walked in with two premarked ballots for Cantrell. The Republican judge objected. Clyde accepted the premarked ballots and ordered the Republican judge arrested and brought to jail.

Ralph Duggan appeared at Precinct 19 at closing time to watch the count. He was told the ballot box had been moved to the Cantrell Bank Building. Duggan found the building guarded by Cantrell's deputies and members of the state highway patrol. Duggan approached a patrolman and asked what was going on.

He responded that he "could not permit anyone to enter the
building . . . he was taking his orders from inside," and if he
"acted contrary to their wishes he would lose his job."

Duggan insisted on his legal right to watch. Two of Cantrell's
deputies arrested Duggan and took him to the jail. Paul Cantrell
was declared the winner of Precinct 19, 799–15. The ballot box
for Precinct 20 had also been moved to the Cantrell Bank Building for counting. Cantrell was declared the winner of that precinct, too, 556–6.

Some ballot boxes were brought to the jail for "further tabulation." Precinct 7, which had been called 230–9 for Cantrell
at the close of the polls, was revised to 847–37. John Cate, chairman of the election commission, told the *Knoxville Journal* that
the count would likely "take all night," but that the Democrats
would win by a big majority.[6]

The election commission claimed to have fifteen hundred
absentee ballots. Knox County, with over eighty thousand
voters—more than six times that of McMinn—had never received more than six hundred absentee ballots.

Etowah reported turnout of twenty-eight hundred, from a
population of thirty-three hundred, well above the number of
eligible voters. Only two thousand Etowahans had voted in the
previous election.[7]

The election commission certified the results surrounded
by armed guards in a crowded courtroom. Joe Taylor crushed
Cantrell on the voting machines, winning 5,924 to 3,634.
Cantrell reportedly carried the paper balloting: 2,963 to 77. The
election commission decided to combine the two and declare
Paul Cantrell the winner, 6,597, to 6,001, a majority of 596.

Ralph Duggan demanded a list of the voters who had used paper ballots and to inspect the ballots for fraud. He was refused. Joe Taylor and two Republican candidates filed a lawsuit.[8]

Judge Pat Quinn ruled that there was no way to differentiate between absentee ballots legally cast and Election Day paper ballots, and he was therefore including all of them. Quinn was wrong: once the county court adopted machine voting, absentee ballots were to be added to the totals on the machine, rather than marked on paper. Further, Quinn said the burden was on the plaintiffs to prove how many of the ballots were illegal. Quinn did not explain how this could ever be done, with ballot boxes counted in secret and the list of voters withheld from the challengers. Quinn also held that plaintiffs had to prove who the illegal votes were for, another impossibility.

Quinn said that even if the election commission had broken the law, it wasn't fair to disenfranchise voters who had cast paper ballots, or to penalize Paul Cantrell. Quinn dismissed the case and ordered the plaintiffs to pay the attorneys' fees of the winners.[9]

Taylor filed a lengthy appeal with the Tennessee Supreme Court. In a one-page ruling, the court upheld Judge Quinn and imposed additional attorneys' fees on the plaintiffs.

How could this happen? Ballot boxes used instead of voting machines, despite the law and a judge's order; the son of a candidate arrested by an officer working for the sheriff's brother; a ballot box taken home for lunch; two ballot boxes counted in secret in a building owned by the sheriff's family; ballot boxes recounted in the jail; officials who disenfranchised an entire precinct by deciding not to have an election; and voters told by armed men that they could not observe the count. Why were twenty state troopers on hand, and why didn't they do anything? Why did a judge dismiss these serious allegations? Why did the state supreme court—twice—side with Paul Cantrell? The answer lay to the west, on the banks of the Mississippi River.

9

THE KING OF TENNESSEE

Athens, Tennessee, is closer to Dayton, Ohio, than it is to Memphis. Memphis, for its part, is closer to St. Louis than Athens—with a hundred miles to spare.

Edward Hull Crump lived in Memphis. He had grown up poor, the son of a Confederate cavalry captain who had died young. He sold peaches at train stations, did backbreaking work on farms, and clawed his way to a low-level bookkeeping job in a small town. This led to a similar job with a Memphis saddlery company. Six years later he bought the saddlery and married into a prominent family. Crump won an upset race for city council, pledging to take on graft and corruption. He was elected to the Board of Fire and Police Commissioners and demanded a midnight closing time for saloons. In a wildly popular stunt, he deputized twenty officers and took them on three raids, to prove to the police and public that the law was enforceable. Crump ran for mayor on the same good government platform and won by seventy-nine votes.

It seemed as though Crump would be good to his word.

The police force was professionalized. Two officers were fired for getting drunk and "attempt[ing] to shoot each other and fight bears at the zoo."

In truth, Crump had discreetly legalized gambling for establishments that kicked back 40 percent of their revenue. A newspaper observed that Sunday closing laws for bars weren't enforced, and saloonkeepers had taken a sudden interest in politics, registering voters and getting them to the polls. Crump earned supporters in a number of ways: fixing a traffic ticket, getting someone a city job, filling a pothole, or upgrading a school. Every city employee was expected to work on campaigns. The business community went along or faced negative consequences, such as No Parking signs in front of their stores or visits from city code inspectors. Crump once placed a police phalanx in front of a man's business, searching every potential customer. Cowed by the corruption of Memphis, the owner moved to Chicago.

Tennessee permitted "ouster lawsuits" against public officials for dereliction of duty. If a judge agreed, the public official would be removed from office. The district attorney general went after Crump for his nonenforcement of alcohol laws. It was impossible for him to defend himself—everyone in Memphis knew it was true. Crump was saved by timing: the Tennessee Supreme Court ruled that he was ousted as mayor from his previous term, which was about to expire. His new term would begin in a matter of days. And he could not be ousted from the term he had yet to begin. Crump's opponents announced there would be a new lawsuit immediately after his inauguration. Crump took the oath of office in secret, resigned his position, and convinced the city commission to replace him with his handpicked successor. Crump learned that it didn't matter what title the boss held, or if he held any at all.

With Memphis under his thumb, Crump set his sights on Shelby County, electing a full slate of officers, including a write-in candidate for sheriff who won despite widespread illiteracy among voters. From this power base Crump set his sights on the rest of Tennessee. Shelby County had the most voters, and by delivering them nearly as a bloc Crump could pick the winner of the Democratic primary statewide. A Democratic nominee was as good as elected.

Crump supported Hill McAlister for governor in 1932. McAlister, who had lost twice before, carried Shelby County by more than three to one, handing him the nomination. One defeated candidate sent volunteers to inspect Shelby's election books. They were arrested.

Crump identified friendly legislative candidates and made sure they had the money to win. One thousand dollars could tip an election in "a rural anti-Crump county," while a "bigger county might cost $2,500." If Crump had plenty of any one thing, it was money, and the craps tables and roadhouses of Memphis paid for election victories all across the state. Judges in Tennessee were elected, and Crump, with the ouster lawsuit fresh in his mind, recognized the importance of winning as many of these races as possible.

Crump's power snowballed. Increased influence at the state level gave him access to patronage jobs across Tennessee and lucrative contracts that multiplied the number of people who relied on him.

Sheriff Burch Biggs was Crump's closest ally in East Tennessee, "a bluff, hearty, loud mouthed, rough and tumble countryman," distinguished by his "ten-gallon hat and a free-swinging revolver," who had deputized his six-year-old grandson. Since

1930 he had run Polk County, McMinn's neighbor to the south, as his own personal "gunman-terrorized domain." Allied county bosses like Biggs and later Paul Cantrell delivered lopsided votes for Crump's statewide candidates, legislators, and judges.

Paul Cantrell's mother had been Biggs's schoolteacher. As Cantrell joked at a Democratic barbecue, his mother "taught Sheriff Biggs his ABCs," and "Sheriff Biggs started teaching me the ABCs in politics. . . . I am progressing fairly well."

Senator Kenneth McKellar extended Crump's reach to Washington and gave him federal patronage throughout Tennessee. In 1936, eager to show off his independence, he endorsed a candidate for governor without consulting Crump. This gave Crump no choice but to back the other candidate, Gordon Browning. Browning was not Crump's ideal man: he was independent and popular enough that he might be trouble once elected. But putting McKellar in his place was the first priority. Browning won 59,874 votes in Shelby County, to 825 for his opponent, on his way to being elected governor. McKellar learned his lesson. He might have been a four-term senator, but Crump was the boss.

Browning had no interest in doing Crump's bidding. Things came to a head when U.S. Senator Nathan Bachman died and Browning appointed his replacement without talking to Crump. Crump recruited Prentice Cooper, a young, second-term state senator, to challenge Browning in the 1938 primary.

Browning knew how Crump operated. He ordered the National Guard to Shelby County to monitor the election. Crump filed a lawsuit and a federal judge—Crump's cousin—ordered the U.S. marshal to "use force if necessary" to keep the Guard out. Governor Browning rented a sound truck and took it to the Memphis Fairgrounds: "The idea that a federal judge can interfere with my right to give orders to the National Guard is silly and absurd. I know my rights, and am determined that the czar of Memphis shall not steal this election."[1]

Helpless to stop voter fraud in Shelby County, Browning sent officials around the state to monitor the election. Ora Daugherty was assigned to McMinn. Daugherty had barely arrived when Cantrell deputy Jim Carmichael arrested him and threw him in jail.[2]

Cooper defeated Browning in Shelby County 56,213 to 8,992 on his way to winning the primary. Browning had won Shelby 59,874 to 825 just two years earlier. He had gone on to win the general election by the "greatest majority ever given a gubernatorial candidate in Tennessee." Now he was out of a job.[3]

For good measure, Crump's candidate defeated the U.S. senator that Browning had appointed. Such was the power of one man. And that man was standing behind the McMinn County machine.[4]

10

"FOR THE DURATION OF THE NATIONAL EMERGENCY"

Bill White dropped out of McMinn High in 1940. He felt like he wasn't getting anywhere, and with the family so hard up, it seemed selfish to stay in school when he could be working. He found a job as a steel rigger with Alcoa earning fifty dollars a week: setting up braces, hoisting equipment, splicing rope, building platforms, setting wires, and painting. On weekends he tried to get out hunting with his 12-gauge shotgun. But it was hard not to be bored. The year 1941 was dragging by. He wondered if this was all there was to life.

Takeo Yoshikawa was on a mission on the other side of the world. He sat in cafés and teahouses, went to dances in the Japanese community, and kept a close eye on everyone he saw. He planned to kill them all.

Yoshikawa was an experienced spy. He was sent under a pseudonym as a diplomat to the Japanese consulate in Honolulu. There were 180,000 islanders of Japanese descent, many immigrants and their children, who could help him study the islands and learn their defenses. He expected an easy infiltration. Instead, Yoshikawa was shocked by their "deep sense of belonging to the United States," even the recent arrivals. They were eager to tell him: "I am an American." He watched the ships coming and going from Pearl Harbor and fumed. What kind of place inspired this kind of loyalty? What kind of country was America?[1]

"Tokyo Prefers More Talk," read the *Post-Athenian* headline of December 5. There were stories on Etowah basketball, McMinn baseball, the parent-teacher association, and a house fire. But the international and local news, racing down parallel tracks through the Depression years, were on a collision course.[2]

Cora Duckworth walked up the steps to the red house with a green roof. It was the home of the White family, who had moved off Depot Hill and into town. Cora sold copies of *Encyclopedia Americana* door to door on weekends. Edd and Elizabeth White welcomed her in. She performed her well-rehearsed pitch, laying sample volumes on the floor and opening them to the most colorful pages, as she explained the installment payment plan. She suddenly stopped, stood up, walked over to the radio, and turned up the volume. She had caught the shift from soft music to news bulletin that the others hadn't.

This morning at 7:55 A.M., while Americans were peacefully sleeping, Imperial Japan launched a dastardly attack on the American fleet anchored at Pearl Harbor. Torpedoes struck our battleships, and bombs began to drop in the harbor. Confusion was almost complete. Destruction at this point can only be guessed at. The damage has dealt this nation a staggering blow.

They listened together in silence. The pitch was over. The *Encyclopedia Americana* was out of date.

People crowded the streets the next day to pick up a copy of the *Post-Athenian*: "WAR IS DECLARED."

Felix Harrod, an Athenian three years older than Bill White, was in class at the University of Chattanooga. Someone walked into the room with the news. The student behind Felix stood, walked to the window, and threw up. It pretty much summarized things. This generation had plans and dreams, professional and personal ambitions, and now they would have to put them on hold—indefinitely, maybe forever. Somehow nothing would be the same.

The question for most young men wasn't whether but how they would serve. It was the most important decision they had ever made, a matter of life and death, but despite this there was very little rhyme or reason behind how they signed up for war.

Charles Scott Jr., son of Paul Cantrell's 1936 opponent, had a gregarious, outgoing personality, earning him the nickname "Shy." Shy Scott wanted to serve in the infantry, but had lost the tip of his trigger finger to a saw in the family lumber mill. He was assigned to the Army Air Corps.[3]

Some were attracted to the Air Corps because it gave them a short reprieve. America had fewer than two thousand combat aircraft, less than 1 percent of what it would have by the war's end. There was an urgent need for pilots but not nearly enough planes and instructors. Felix was a junior in college and wanted to graduate "if possible." He joined the Air Corps reserves, with a guarantee not to be called up until his final semester.

Jim Buttram and his friends took advantage of a similar program, signing a deferred-entry agreement. This six-month extension of youth was used to the fullest. They graduated high school, the first class of World War II, piled into a car in their letterman jackets, and headed for Florida. At the end of six months they reported as scheduled for their Army Air Corps training.

But by now the needs of the army had changed: "You fellas are in the infantry."[4]

In the aftermath of Pearl Harbor the *Post-Athenian* published a letter from Marine Sergeant Dan Searcy: "I know that the men of this great country of ours do not have to be made to defend the traditions that are so sacred to us." Searcy wrote that he would be at the Athens Post Office from 5:00 A.M. to 7:00 P.M. "Volunteer today with the Leathernecks."

The Marine Corps stood at 66,000 men, and would have to grow quickly, eventually reaching 485,000. But the Japanese had been their best recruiters: 1,978 signed up in November; 10,224 in December; and 22,686 in January.[5]

The post office was within walking distance from Bill White's house. He had no unfinished business or loose ends to tie up. He went to find Sergeant Searcy: "I want to join up and fight with the Marine Corps."

"Come on in." There was a short interview and a cursory health test. "I believe you're going to make a good one," Bill was told. "How old are you?"

"Eighteen," he said, adding a year.

"You're going to have to get your parents to sign before I can take you."

Bill spent the next week working on Edd and Elizabeth. Before the war was over, all three of their sons would be serving, with Edd Jr. and J. B. in the army. Elizabeth, knowing Bill would eventually find a way in, grudgingly gave her permission.

On December 21, three military planes were spotted flying low over Athens. Some feared they were the next target of the Japanese. Suddenly there was a loud crash. It was a plane it-self, rather than a bomb, that had hit the ground. The pilot was brought to the Robert E. Lee Hotel, where he remained silent under questioning. He turned out to be an American army pilot on a training mission, who got lost and ran out of fuel.[6]

McMinn, priding itself as the Volunteer County of the Volunteer State, supplied more than thirty-five hundred servicemen from a total population of just over thirty thousand.[7]

Elbert and Essie Sims sent four sons to war. Elbert came home after taking his youngest to the recruiter. "Those boys over there tried to get me to enlist in the navy," he told his wife.

"You might as well go on," said Essie. "You won't be any good to me moping around here." Elbert went back to the recruiter: "If you're going to take all my boys, you might as well take me, too."

Walking the streets of Athens, now quiet with the departure of the young men, you could see the missing family members represented as candles in windows, breaking the darkness imposed by rationing. Houses with three or four were commonplace. Two McMinn mothers had six.[8]

Barbara Lockmiller hadn't seen her brother for two years. Jimmy was constantly bumping heads with his father and stepmother, so they'd sent him to St. Andrew's School, up in the mountains. One night he appeared in Barbara's second-story bedroom.

"Do you have any money?"

No, she didn't have any money. She was nine.

"Well, I'm getting ready," he said. "I've come to get my things and I'm leaving." Jimmy hoboed his way west, catching rides on trains. He broke horses on an Arizona cattle ranch and worked the rodeo before heading to Los Angeles. Jimmy made five dollars as an extra in *Gentleman Jim,* the Errol Flynn boxing biopic. He tried to enlist after Pearl Harbor but couldn't without his parents' permission, so he reluctantly made his way back to Athens.

"I figured you'd come," his father said. "If that's what you want, fine."

Ralph Duggan had every reason to stay. He was thirty-two, married, with an active law practice. His letters of recommendation were filled with praise from the most prominent citizens, attesting to his "ability," "integrity," "character," and "exceptionally good reputation." He submitted his application, agreeing to mobilize on twenty-four hours' notice.

Duggan was medically ineligible. He suffered from Bright's disease, a chronic condition of the kidneys, causing swelling in the feet and abdomen, dizziness, and convulsions. Duggan asked Dr. Foree to clear him for service. Foree was known for his blunt assessments, and was "as much psychologist as physician" for his community. Duggan wanted to be part of the fight against Japan. He pushed and pleaded and the tough doctor finally gave in.[9]

The *Post-Athenian* reported on the first marines to enlist from McMinn. Bill White and seven others ranged in age from seventeen to twenty-two. Several were asked about their motivations: "the defense of my country," "to do my part," "to serve the government." If interviewed, Bill may have said any of these, adding: "I was mad because they attacked Pearl Harbor."[10]

Bill was inducted at Nashville on January 12. Like other recruits, he signed up "for the duration of the national emergency" and solemnly swore to "bear true faith and allegiance to the United States of America" and to "serve them honestly and faithfully against their enemies whatsoever."

Bill was given a physical: blue eyes, blond hair, ruddy complexion; 20/20 eyesight; five feet, eight inches tall; 154 pounds.

(Men "didn't have to go on any diets like now," Bill said. "They was on a diet all the time because they didn't have enough to eat.") Bill was photographed, tested for blood type, and fingerprinted.[11]

Bill spent the next four days on a train to San Diego. He had never been farther than Chattanooga.

Bill saw the Pacific Ocean for the first time from boot camp. "A big pile of water," he decided, like an oversized pond back home. But he couldn't stop looking: the waves rushing in and out, water as far as he could see. "It was something else," he conceded privately. Bill strained to see the ocean without anyone catching on. He didn't want to look like a "dummy" for being too excited.

"Man!" Bill couldn't believe his new wardrobe. "Two pairs of dress shoes, three pairs of field shoes." Back home he had a pair of "run-over brogan shoes" that had to last until his toes were sticking out. Now he had five pairs of shoes and new pants and shirts, "a dozen socks," a "dozen pair of underwear, undershirts."

Bill felt "on top of the world." All the recruits did. They came from all over the United States but had being poor in common. Back home it was "thin gravy with a fork!" Now they sat at long tables and ate the best meals of their lives. "They passed the beans and chicken and everything right down the line; you got all you wanted to eat. Man, this is something else!" Bill realized that he had never been full before. He had to sign up for war before he'd ever sat down and had enough to eat. Another revelation was soon to follow. When the marines appeared to be doing something for your physical comfort, expect the worst.[12]

"The training was hard," Bill said. They "lived in the boondocks" and ran five or six miles every morning at sunup. They staged raids and war games. Bill and the recruits went on forest hikes—fifty or sixty miles over three or four days. "You'd think your feet was wore off plum up to your knees," he said. "It never seemed to quit." They never walked anywhere. It was always a run. They ran up hills with drill instructors shooting live ammunition at their feet.

There was a new vocabulary to learn. Underwear was "skivvies"; the bathroom was "the head"; "782 gear" was named for the form you had to sign. There were rough incentives to get things right. Drill instructors wouldn't think twice about hitting you with a stick. Rarer but not unheard of was a punch in the nose. If you dropped your rifle, they'd make you sleep on eight of them. Bill, who as a little boy had bucked the rules at North City School, regularly got into it with his instructors. He spent a lot of time restricted to bread and water and cleaned plenty of dirty plates on "kitchen patrol." It helped straighten him out "a little bit," he admitted. Bill resolved to be just good enough to avoid getting kicked out of the marines.[13]

The attack by the Empire of Japan had shocked Bill White, as it had the people of McMinn and communities across the United States. But some military leaders had expected a clash since before the Great War.

Marine Corps Major Pete Ellis thought Japan would initiate. The United States would have to capture their South Pacific territories and use them offensively to strike at the home islands. They would be heavily defended. Landing men on a fortified island under fire was possibly the most difficult feat in warfare. The military had no capacity for amphibious landings and knew nothing about these islands. Ellis decided to take a trip. He moved through the Marshalls and Palaus posing as a tourist. On the island of Koror he "took up residence with a native woman, drank heavily, and prowled around Japan's installations," followed by suspicious police. On May 12, 1923, the Japanese government reported that he "fell ill and died."

Congress, meanwhile, scoured the defense budget for savings. What was the point of the marines, some asked? In World War I they had fought on land, just like the army. Commandant John Lejeune proposed a distinct mission for the marines as an amphibious landing force.[14]

Japan invaded China in 1937. America embargoed scrap iron and steel outside the western hemisphere, with the exception of the United Kingdom. When Japan invaded Indochina, Roosevelt froze Japanese credits in the United States and embargoed sales of fuel. This put Japan in a bind: their war machine consumed four hundred tons of oil every hour of the day.

The Japanese demanded the United States stop arming the Chinese and building bases in the Pacific, and help the emperor find the natural resources he needed. In return they would leave China and agree not to invade the Philippines. America countered: Japan should withdraw troops from China and Indochina, abandon the Axis powers, and sign a nonaggression pact with its neighbors. The die was cast. American war planners wondered where the strike would come: "Thailand, Hong Kong, Borneo, the Kra Isthmus, Guam, Wake, or the Philippines?" Pearl Harbor was the only target they felt was safe. The attack came against them all.[15]

Admiral Ernest King was the chief of naval operations. His officers argued between blocking the Japanese advance or harassing them until America could build strength. King had another idea. They would drive them backward to Japan.[16]

11

EVERYTHING I NEEDED TO KNOW ABOUT GEOPOLITICS, I LEARNED FROM FRANK CAPRA

> Part of the process of preparing for war was to educate the military about the differences between our system of government and that of fascist dictatorships. As they began to learn more about the totalitarian methods of Japan and Germany, many of these young men began to pay more attention to the undemocratic methods of the Cantrell machine.
>
> —*Frank Carmichael, U.S. Army, McMinn County*

Frank Capra was one of the biggest names in Hollywood. He was the first director to sweep the top five Oscars for *It Happened One Night*. In *Mr. Smith Goes to Washington* he had portrayed a fearlessly honest man taking on government corruption. The Italian immigrant was fiercely patriotic and joined the army four days after Pearl Harbor. But he wasn't leaving the movie business. George Marshall, army chief of staff, thought it critical that his soldiers, 37 percent of whom had not completed high school, knew what they were fighting for and who they were up against. Major Capra went to Hollywood to make a film unlike anything he had done before. He had total authority over editing and was committed that everything in it be the absolute truth.[1]

Prelude to War, the first in a series, was finished in May 1942. America's warriors in training sat on uncomfortable chairs and watched in dark rooms on remote military bases. Not how they had planned on seeing the next Capra movie.

Walter Huston narrated: "Why are Americans on the march? Is it because of Pearl Harbor?" There were images of the bombing and wreckage. Then the Blitz over London, Nazis marching under the Arc de Triomphe, China bombed by Japanese planes, and Nazi fighters flying over the Acropolis of Athens.

"Just what was it made us change our way of living overnight?" A map of the world appeared with the words: "This is a fight between a free world and a slave world."

"How did it become free?" Huston asked. "Only through a long and unceasing struggle inspired by men of vision. 'We hold these truths to be self-evident, that all men are created equal.' It is the cornerstone on which our nation was built and the ideal of all our great liberators."

This was compared to a speech by a Japanese leader: "Stop thinking and follow your God emperor, and Japan will rule the world!"

Rights Americans take for granted were eliminated in the slave world, and the institutions that exist to protect those rights, elected legislative bodies and courts, had been co-opted or disbanded. The answer to all opposition, said Huston, was "the blackjack and the gun."

"Now what of our world, the democratic world? What did

we want? Peace and security." America had scrapped 60 percent of its naval tonnage after the last war and kept only 136,000 men under arms, sixty thousand fewer than Romania.

Huston continued:

"We let our hopes for peace become so strong that they grew into the determination not to fight unless directly attacked. We let ourselves be influenced by those who said that we could find security through isolation.

"We simply did not want to understand that our individual and national problems were, and always will be, dependent on the problems of the whole world."

While other countries had turned to strongmen in times of crisis, Americans "never had a thought of losing our free institutions. John Q. Public still ran the country . . . in Germany they had the choice of voting for Hitler, Hitler, or Hitler." John Q. Public voted for who he wanted, read what he wanted, and could worship anywhere he pleased. "Most of all, he got a kick out of seeing his kids grow up." There were images of carefree children playing on swings, drawing, painting, racing, and roller-skating.

A quote appeared on the screen, attributed to the Japanese army: "To die for the Emperor is to live forever."

"It was inevitable that these countries should gang up on us," Huston said. The Japanese had gone to war against their neighbors. When criticized by the international community, they smiled, stood up, and walked out of the League of Nations. "The green light had been given the aggressors. We and the rest of the world knew that these aggressors should be stopped and punished. But we were unwilling to make the necessary sacrifices to back up that opinion . . . we hadn't yet learned that peace for us depends on peace for all.

"For this is what we are fighting. Freedom's oldest enemy: the passion of the few to rule the many. This isn't just a war. This is a common man's life-and-death struggle against those who would put him back into slavery. We lose it, and we lose everything.

"That's what's at stake. It's us or them. The chips are down. Two worlds stand against each other. One must die. One must live."

It was a lot of responsibility to lay on these young people, many not old enough to vote, some not old enough to shave.

Meanwhile, Bill White and the ragtag boys he had signed up with began to look like something special. Uniformed, feet pointed forward, bodies turned to the left, hands steady, breathing controlled, the butt of the gun to their shoulder, firing at targets two hundred, then three hundred, then five hundred yards away.[2]

12

GEORGE THE RIPPER

The state representative seat from McMinn County was sacred, in a way. In 1920 it was held by twenty-four-year-old first-termer Harry T. Burn of Niota. The women's suffrage movement, begun at Seneca Falls, New York, in 1848, fought for the next seventy-one years to get a constitutional amendment through Congress. For a year it worked its way through state legislatures, with thirty-six needed for ratification. The movement hit a brick wall in March when Washington became state thirty-five. Some states rejected the measure while others refused consideration. Tennessee took up the amendment in August. Burn, two months from an election and facing a wave of opposition to women's suffrage, voted twice to delay consideration until the January session. The House was deadlocked, 48–48, on whether to postpone the vote. The Speaker of the House, an opponent of the amendment, decided to put the amendment to a vote. Burn privately supported the amendment, and had recently received a letter from his mother, urging him: "Hurrah and vote for suffrage." On the vote for final passage, Harry quickly said "Aye," in a voice so low that many couldn't hear him. But that barely audible affirmative vote in the House chamber at Nashville changed the Constitution, and guaranteed the right to vote for millions of women.

Twenty years later this seat was won by George Woods, a top ally of Paul Cantrell. Woods, "genial and plump," had variously worked as a bail bondsman, baker, and real estate developer. From Harry T. Burn's seat, Woods would destroy what was left of democracy in McMinn County.

Woods introduced a series of proposals, dubbed "The Ripper Bill" by the press: the lines of the McMinn County Court would be redrawn; twenty-two polling places would be reduced to twelve; the seventeen current elected court members would be replaced by eleven people named in the bill, including Cantrell stalwarts like Herman Moses, convicted in federal court of extorting campaign donations from government employees. The county court election of 1940, where voters picked fifteen Republicans and two Democrats, would be nullified, and Paul Cantrell handed a decisive majority.

The bill was a tough sell, even for the Crump-controlled legislature. Cantrell and Burch Biggs, boss of Polk County, came to Nashville to twist arms. They told one state senator that "he'd better change his position" or his father, a supreme court justice, "had just as well not run for re-election."[1]

The Ripper Bill appeared on the floor of the state senate on the final day of session. Governor Cooper's spokesman announced that it had been signed "immediately." There seemed to be one problem: the chief clerk of the senate told the Nashville *Tennessean,* "The bill did not pass the Senate and will not become law." State Senator Robert Lindsay, whose district included

McMinn, insisted: "It did not pass." When asked, Woods said: "It passed the House. I wasn't in the Senate."[2]

Ralph Duggan, before shipping off to the navy, filed a lawsuit on behalf of A. G. Buttram and A. W. Wade, two elected members of the county court. Chancellor Stewart ruled the Ripper Bill was constitutional. Duggan asked Stewart to delay his ruling pending appeal. Stewart declined.

The new county court created three positions—one of them, county purchasing agent, went to George Woods, at a salary of $150 a month. T. B. Ivins, a former sheriff and prohibition agent convicted of using WPA employees to build a road to his farm, became superintendent of public works at the same salary.[3]

Paul Cantrell drew $56,886 from the sheriff's office during his first four years, worth over a million dollars in today's purchasing power. With the county court under his thumb, he would earn $52,218 in the two years that followed. He was appointed superintendent of the county workhouse at a $2,200 annual salary. McMinn County did not have a workhouse, making its superintending easy. One newspaper estimated these "useless offices" cost the taxpayer $28,000. Chief Deputy Mansfield saw a $150 monthly pay raise, which was increased to $200 six months later.

The median Tennessee home in 1942 was worth $1,826; the starting salary for men enlisting to fight the war was $50 a month.[4]

Despite rationing, machine men had no trouble getting cars, tires, or fuel. The county court raised the property tax from 2.5 percent to 3.37 percent, the seventh-highest rate in Tennessee, and would later raise it again to 4.5 percent. The votes of the new county court were unanimous.

There was money that couldn't be accounted for. There were people listed as salaried employees who never did any work or received any money, and no telling where those funds went.

Then there was the money from illegal gambling, unlicensed bars, and houses of prostitution. There were dice games, cards, and slot machines, all paying protection money, as much as a thousand dollars a month. The leadership of McMinn County had a license to print money and no voter could do a thing about it.[5]

The last independent government in McMinn County was the city of Athens. On Election Day the voting booths were installed at city hall, as they had been for as long as anyone could remember. Voters arrived but found no election taking place.

The ballot boxes were in the courthouse suite of the Democratic trustee. One state patrolman was the officer of election; another was an election judge; the second election judge was Oliver Nichols, who had killed Carl Voiles and Hub Johnson, and was still one of Cantrell's deputies. Two of Burch Biggs's gunmen from Polk County were on hand. One of them, Bill Heddon, had killed his own father. Five months after the election, Heddon murdered his sister-in-law and a second woman "in an advanced stage of pregnancy," along with a fourteen-month-old boy. This was the kind of human being that the people who ran McMinn County relied on to enforce their will and placed in between their neighbors and the ballot box.

In case these men weren't enough, there were "numerous other gunmen unknown to the citizens of Athens," including one recently released from the penitentiary. Many voters who figured out the new location for the election decided to stay away.

The Republican election judge was Oscar Frazier, a disabled

veteran of the Great War. When Frazier tried to view the count he was dragged into the hallway and beaten, leaving him paralyzed "for some time."

Harry Anderson walked to the window outside the courthouse to try and listen to the votes as they were called. Deputy Joe Cardin walked up to him and hit him in the head with a gun. "Get away from here, you damned son of a bitch."

Oliver Nichols placed "several hundred ballots" into the box. Rather than sit and be a party to fraud, poll worker Mack Price tried to leave the building. One of the gunmen fired at him and missed. Dr. Ed Foree showed up at the courthouse to treat the wounded.

The ballot box was moved upstairs and the door to the room was guarded by armed men. The machine candidates were declared the winners.[6]

The McMinn High School band played in the courthouse square. Reverend T. L. Williams said a prayer that was followed by speeches. The goal for the audience was to find every last piece of metal and put it toward the war effort. They regrouped at 2:00 P.M. with forty-three tons of salvage. This effort was one of many. The Kiwanis found fifty thousand pounds of iron, steel, metal, and tin. The Boy Scouts collected seventy tons of paper, rubber, and rags. As the men of McMinn prepared to fight overseas, their community was strongly behind them.[7]

13

"WE WERE LIKE YOUNG TIGERS"

Alvaro de Mendaña sailed from Peru in 1567, in search of the Ophir, a biblical land that supplied the gold for King Solomon's temple. But for nearly two months Mendaña saw nothing but water. One night a stubborn wind kept him from his course. By daylight he saw that if he had gotten his way, his ships would have crashed on unseen shoals. "We all rendered thanks to God for having delivered us from this danger, recognizing that His hand had sent the contrary winds to save us from destruction."

Soon they saw islands, made landfall, and met the people who lived there. Their chief explained that they should trade names out of friendship. And so the chief became "Alvaro de Mendaña," and Mendaña became "Bile." Not every encounter went as well. On another island a native "invoked the devil," drawing a circle on the ground, shouting and trembling as though about to fall, and pointed a lance at Mendaña.

Mendaña named the Isla de Flores—Florida Island—and climbed to the top of Guadalcanal, looking out over thirty villages. Mendaña was certain he had found what he was looking for—Islas Salomon, the Solomon Islands.

Marine Corps General Alexander Vandegrift, grandson of Civil War veterans, had never heard of the Solomon Islands before he was ordered to seize them. He was given a month. It would be a total disaster, he predicted. This earned him an extra week.

Guadalcanal and Tulagi were the primary targets: the first to stop the Japanese from completing their airport, the second for its harbor. Striking at the Solomons would reverse a Japanese drive that threatened to cut Australia and New Zealand off from the United States.

Vandegrift put together nineteen thousand men, mostly new recruits, including Bill White. Lacking intelligence on the Solomons, Vandegrift resorted to reading a Jack London story, "The Red One," which was set there. London wrote: "If I were a king, the worst punishment I could inflict upon my enemies would be to banish them to the Solomons."

"We could not get there fast enough," said Bill White. "We were like young tigers." After months of waiting they finally had their orders: "You're on your way. You're going to be in the first convoy to fight."

I'm ready, Bill thought. I'm ready for it. He thought the others were as well.

The instructors tried to temper their enthusiasm: "They've got the land, air, and sea superiority." It didn't work. They were grateful to be in the first batch of fighters. Some worried they'd miss the war if they weren't. They had no idea what they were up against.

Hitler ruled from the "Arctic waters in the north to the Libyan Desert," and from the English Channel to within "a day's march of the Caspian Sea." The "Japanese empire dwarfed Hitler's," stretching "five thousand miles in every direction: Formosa, the Philippines, Indochina, Thailand, and Burma; Malaya, Sumatra, Borneo, Java, and the Celebes; the Kuril Islands, the Bonins, the Ryukyus, Marianas, Carolines, Palaus, Marshalls, and Gilberts; northern New Guinea; two Alaskan islands; most of inhabited China; and almost all of the Solomons." The Japanese controlled a "seventh of the globe," a dominion "three times as large as the United States and Europe combined."[1]

Bill White departed San Diego on July 1, 1942, nearly seven months after Pearl Harbor. Since then the Japanese had taken Wake Island and Guam from the marines, kicked the army out of the Philippines, and taken the Dutch East Indies.[2]

The marines traveled on three ships: the USS *Hayes, Jackson,* and *Adams,* known as the Unholy Three. Bill was on the *Jackson,* named for President Andrew, another Borderer from Tennessee. It was hot and sticky and humid, and the ships were badly overcrowded and poorly ventilated. Long days came and went surrounded by sea.

The marines stopped and stretched their legs on Tonga and were greeted by Queen Salote. A few days later they practiced a landing on Fiji. The Higgins boats, smaller transports for around forty men, dropped down the side of the massive ships. The marines scrambled down the nets to the Higgins boats. It was a mess, one that hardly improved with a second attempt. "A complete bust," said one officer.[3]

Tokyo Rose, a Japanese propaganda broadcast, repeated a message on August 6: "Where are the United States Marines hiding? The marines are supposed to be the finest soldiers in the world, but no one has seen them yet!"[4]

FRIDAY, AUGUST 7, 1942
3:00 A.M.—USS *Jackson*

Bill White finally got a hot shower. But there was always a catch. The soap and water were to clean his body of germs and minimize the risk of infection if he was shot or stabbed. A bean breakfast followed, "the last for some of the men and the last for many hours for all."

Bill was a member of Company B, First Battalion, Second Marine Division. Their mission was to take out heavy guns that could interfere with landings on nearby islands. They scrambled down nets toward the Higgins boats that would take them to Florida Island, each man bearing an average of eighty-four pounds, "the most heavily laden foot soldier in the history of warfare." Bill White and the men of his company ran through the foam, onto the beaches, the first Americans of the war to land in hostile territory.[5]

Their eyes darted across the jungle. The breeze blew the tall trees and grass. But there were no signs of the enemy. They passed through small villages. Abandoned. They charged the bluffs and found nothing at the top.

"We've been duped," someone said. Tricked, they were sure, by other marines who wanted all the fighting for themselves.

"What the hell is this, another training exercise?" a marine yelled.[6]

News crackled over the radio as marines cursed the empty island. The marines who had landed on Gavutu were being slaughtered. They ran back to the boats as fast as they could.

Bill had been told that the Japanese weren't very good fighters. On Gavutu it looked to him like they had put up a pretty good fight. "They'd just about killed all the paratroopers," Bill said. Some shot between the eyes.

The added firepower brought by Bill and Company B nearly cleared Gavutu of the Japanese. But snipers kept taking shots at them from the nearby island of Tanambogo. The commanders assumed there were around fifteen, who could be dealt with relatively easily. It was decided that Bill's company would make an amphibious landing on Tanambogo, eliminate the snipers, and reinforce the final push on Gavutu.

At 6:00 P.M., navy shells fired over the Higgins boats onto Tanambogo. One fell short, wounding an American coxswain and sending his boat in the wrong direction. Other ships unwittingly followed.

The three boats that made it to Tanambogo encountered a wall of fire stretching fifty feet out to sea. The Japanese had doused the beach and water with gasoline. Some of the boats caught on fire. The Japanese opened up with machine guns. Bill returned fire using the motor of the Higgins boat as cover. The machine gunner at the front of Bill's boat was shot and "bounced back dead." Another marine took his place and was killed within seconds. The front of Bill's boat burst into flames. Bill jumped out into the water and tried to get to the beach.

Marines who had jumped or fallen from the burning boats and made it to shore were chopped with Japanese sabers and thrown alive into the beach bonfire. The air was filled with the sounds of gunfire and screaming marines.

Bill hated the Japanese. He wanted to kill them all. But for now the marines retreated to the boats, to Gavutu, where they would pass an uneasy night under the threat of death from Japanese soldiers and the unbowed snipers of Tanambogo.

It was their first day of war.

14

"A MONSTROUS, SHOCKING, AND REVOLTING STATE OF AFFAIRS"

> At present the people of McMinn County have no more rights than the people of occupied France!
>
> —*Walter White, resident of Athens*

Paul Cantrell, term limited as sheriff, announced for the state senate, seeking the betterment of "schools, old-age pensions, and free textbooks." Pat Mansfield, his chief deputy, would run to replace him. A supportive newspaper ad called Mansfield a "splendid, fearless, and upright officer" for "dangerous and troublesome times."

The county court sold the barely used voting machines for $5,250. It had paid $32,000 for them just two years earlier. They would use paper ballots and boxes.[1]

Abe Trew, a "prominent miller," was the Republican nominee for sheriff. He promised "honesty in elections" and to make "fee grabbing" by deputies a "thing of the past."[2]

The Ripper Bill eliminated ten precincts, all of them in rural communities. Voters had to travel up to twelve miles to cast a ballot. The election commission never told the public where the new precincts were, and many never figured it out. John Anderson, who had replaced Ralph Duggan as the Republican election commissioner, didn't know—he hadn't been invited to meetings.

Fewer precincts increased the machine advantage. For starters, eliminating polling places made it harder to vote. It made every ballot box that was swapped, or taken to the jail or Cantrell Bank Building for counting, that much more valuable. And perhaps most important, the machine relied on election workers who were willing to turn away eligible voters while allowing illegal ballots, men who would order their neighbors away from the count, at gunpoint if necessary, and physically remove them from the polling place despite their legal right to observe. Then they had to look at a ballot that one of their neighbors had marked for Abe Trew and call it for Pat Mansfield. The machine had access to money, power, and items rationed by war. But most people have limits to what they would do. And it was easier to find the manpower for twelve polling places than twenty-two. But even with the new districts the machine was leaving nothing to chance. As before, the Democratic commissioners claimed receipt of a massive absentee vote, more than twelve hundred ballots.[3]

The machine had the muscle, the money, the badge, and the courts, but supporters of fair elections in McMinn could count on at least one powerful ally: Judge John J. Jennings Jr., known as "The Five J's of Jellicoe," the town where he lived. He was now a congressman but preferred his old judicial title.

A childhood friend described Jennings as a fighter, but added that as a freckle-faced redhead he'd had little choice. "He calls a spade a spade, a rooster a rooster and not a hen, and this applies to men."

Jennings was still a fighter at sixty-two, though his hair was now gray. He elbowed his way onto the attorney general's calendar, wrote letters to J. Edgar Hoover of the FBI, and publicly denounced the McMinn machine in the newspapers. Jennings wanted investigations, arrests, and prosecutions for previous misconduct, and observers to guarantee the integrity of future elections. His district was based in Knoxville and made up of solidly Republican counties, and he did not depend on Crump or his allies for support.[4]

Jennings flooded McMinn with flyers detailing election laws: specifically, no armed man was allowed within ten feet of the polling place. He encouraged voters to report any threats or acts of violence. "Go to the polls, vote, and stay and watch the count as you have a right to do. The law protects you in so doing, and I will see that it is enforced."

It was a paper promise. At least two armed men were there to greet every voter in the August 1942 election. Every mother, father, grandparent, and sister of the men fighting the war had to run this gauntlet to cast a ballot. One Democrat who had planned on bolting his party was held in jail for two hours to prevent him from voting. Valid poll tax receipts, proof of eligibility to vote, were deemed void, in some cases by the very official who had issued them. In the run-up to the election, T. B. Ivins had made it known among indigent senior citizens that old-age pensions would be held up unless they voted "the right way."

Two years before he became sheriff, Paul Cantrell, as chairman of the election commission, invalidated the results of the entire Mecca Precinct because a deputy was peeking at the voters' ballots. Was he against the practice on principle? Or because it was a Republican deputy and precinct? Either way, by 1942, it was his show, and the secret ballot in McMinn County was all but dead. Thin, transparent ballots were used. Election officials would hold them up to the light, see how a person voted, and mark them down as a friend or foe of the machine.[5]

Reverend H. L. Love of Mars Hill Church proposed a partnership of pastors to escort frightened voters to the polls. They liked the idea, they said, they really did. But they had machine men in their congregations, and couldn't really get involved. Even if he had to do it alone, said Love, "I intend to fight to the end for the restoration of honest elections."[6]

Sheriff's Deputy Joe Cardin approached the crowd in the courthouse square and offered cash in exchange for votes. He bragged that his own wife had already voted twice.

Roe Rucker, officer of election at the courthouse, refused to allow the Republican judge into the building. John Anderson appeared in person to demand his admission. Rucker told Anderson, a member of the election commission, that he "did not have a damned thing to do with the election," and that "we are running the damned election." Rucker and two gunmen forced him from the courthouse. Will Balew had to convince Rucker he was a Democrat before he was handed a ballot. Bryan Stephens, who lived outside the county, voted twice in a row. Roe Rucker stopped taking poll tax receipts in the afternoon, allowing anyone to vote whom he wanted. Bootlegger Charlie Riddle handed marked ballots to Pink Gossett, a drunk, who walked them into the courthouse and placed them in the ballot box. Riddle was handing out whiskey and money downtown in exchange for votes.

Rucker shut off the lights at 10:00 P.M., in the middle of counting ballots, and placed two flashlights on the table. "That's enough light," he said.

There were protests that the count couldn't be seen.

"It's nobody's damned business," Rucker said. He put two guns on the table and said, "I will unload my artillery." The Republican clerk, a young woman, felt she ought to go home. Rucker turned the lights on when she left.

Deputy John Morgan was the officer of election at Riceville. He kept calling votes for Mansfield that were marked for Abe Trew. The Republicans in the room objected. "Sit down or I will shoot you down," said Morgan, grabbing his gun handle. "If you don't like my count, take it to the supreme court."

Absentee ballots were announced for people who had voted in person that day. Another for a man who had been dead three years.

John Rogers was the officer of election at Etowah City Hall. Groups of people walked in throughout the day claiming to be blind. This allowed Rogers to mark a ballot on their behalf. There was never any discussion as to their preference. Rogers also failed to sign the ballot where he had assisted the voter, as required by law. At closing time the ballot box was moved to the Cantrell Bank Building for counting in secret.

Deputy Minus Wilburn was the officer of election at an Athens polling place. Wilburn was unremarkable in appearance, not handsome, not ugly, not big, a little shorter than the average man. But nobody would kill you faster or for less. Years later, when Wilburn met his own violent and sudden end, his own mother said, "Now he's in Hell."

In full view of everyone, Wilburn took one young girl after another into the voting booth and marked their ballot for them. Wilburn wore an outfit with hidden pockets, sewn by his wife, for bringing premarked ballots into the polling place. [7]

Paul Cantrell was unopposed in his primary for state senate.

He also ran for a seat on the county court as Etowah justice of the peace. The election commission named his brother, Jim Cantrell, as officer of election, which was held in the fire station. The ballot box was removed to the Cantrell Bank Building for counting. Neither the incumbent justice of the peace nor any member of the public was allowed to observe. Cantrell was declared the winner.[8]

Democrats swept all countywide offices for the first time anyone could remember. Sheriff-elect Pat Mansfield took out an ad to say "thanks" for "the overwhelming vote of confidence," and promised to "at all times be at your service." Mansfield was declared the winner, 5,158 to 2,251. Republicans did worse from there. They won a single justice of the peace spot in the town of Niota. They couldn't even find a candidate for county court clerk.[9]

"We had no democracy," wrote Zeb Aldridge to Congressman Jennings. Athens attorney Clay Matlock wrote letters to the editor of the *Knoxville Journal* and *Chattanooga Daily Times* calling the election a "shame and outrage and disgrace to a free people anywhere on earth."

Congressman Jennings conducted an investigation into absentee balloting. He drove to post offices and interviewed clerks. At the Knoxville Post Office he learned that batches of absentee ballots had been mailed to the Democratic commissioners of McMinn County in this election and in 1940. Jennings was told that Sam Moser, a state highway patrolman, had gone to the Knoxville Post Office and mailed 65 absentee ballots to the chairman of the McMinn County election commission.[10]

It was "a monstrous, shocking, and revolting state of affairs," wrote Jennings. But what could they do about it?[11]

15

"HIGH, DRY, AND BARE ASSED"

SATURDAY, AUGUST 8, 1942

Snipers killed marines on Gavutu throughout the night. Bombers pounded Tanambogo the next day in preparation for a second landing attempt. Japanese emerged from caves when it was finished, waving the rising sun flag.

Bill and a group of marines charged behind two tanks across a causeway connecting Tanambogo and Gavutu. The commander of the first tank lifted his head out of the hatch to try and work the machine gun and was killed. The second tank moved too far ahead of the infantry and was surrounded and set on fire. The crew had to scramble out to escape the extreme heat. All but one was shot dead before they hit the ground. The survivor was beaten and stabbed while still on fire.[1]

At the end of the causeway the Japanese leapt screaming from holes in the ground and charged the marines, swords first. The marines pushed them back with bayonets and point-blank rifle fire. "They killed a lot of us," Bill said, "but we still learned how to fight them."

When the Americans were the only ones left on Gavutu and
Tanambogo, they turned to burying their dead. Bill and others
dug a long trench. They found a bent Japanese bugle and someone who knew how to play taps. The fallen were lowered into
the ground, and a squad fired shots over their grave as the bugle played. The sun began to set over the ocean, casting strange
colors over the sea and sky: "Bright yellow, red, purple, green,
every other color you could think of," Bill said. "It was a beautiful sight. And a sad sight, too. The coconut palm trees were all
bent over and seemed as though they were weeping right along
with us."

Bill and Company B headed next to Tulagi.

The Japanese would not be taken prisoner. Those who survived the initial invasion had accepted their death as inevitable.
Their sole remaining motivation was to kill as many Americans
as they could. They were trained to "think of yourself as an
avenger come at last face to face with his father's murderer. Here
is the man whose death will lighten your heart of its burden of
brooding anger. If you fail to destroy him utterly you can never
rest in peace."[2]

The marines searched out every possible hiding place for sur-
vivors. Bill and his lieutenant stood at the mouth of a cave. "Bill,
go in there and see if there are any Japs." Bill threw a grenade
inside and waited for the explosion. "Let me tie this rope around
your leg here in case you get killed in there," said the lieutenant.
"I can drag you out and give you a Christian burial."

With this encouragement, Bill crawled in through the top
and saw a Japanese soldier who had survived the blast. He shot
him immediately. They repeated this in cave after cave. Bill
charged in behind an explosion. Sometimes he encountered an

enemy with a split second to kill or be killed. Sometimes he found himself alone with his heart beating out of his chest. Bill started using a long stick with dynamite tied to the end, wrapped in barbed wire to stop the Japanese from grabbing it and sending it back. A flaming mattress proved the most effective at clearing out a cave, but those were in short supply.

Late in the night the marines listened and watched as a battle raged at sea. There were "flashes and explosions and then new salvos." The rain poured and flooded the islands into a swampy, muddy mess.

Bill White was witnessing one of the worst naval defeats in American history. Three U.S. heavy cruisers and one from Australia sank, lit by the flames of the transport *George F. Elliott*. More than a thousand American and Australian sailors were crushed, burned, drowned, or eaten by sharks.[3]

The remaining fleet, with fourteen hundred marines and badly needed supplies, withdrew from the Solomons. The eighteen thousand marines on the islands had rations for three days and ammunition for four. Day three was just beginning.[4]

They were left "high and dry and bare assed," Bill said. The marines adopted the attitude of the Japanese: "Never surrender, never retreat, take no prisoners, and fight to the death."

"Do you think for a minute I'd give up, let them abuse me, and torture me, and then kill me?" Bill asked. "No! That's silly."

Death could come at any minute, from any direction. "Our bodies were so tense," Bill said, "it was like pulling back a bowstring." They were "alert all of the time." Needless to say, "you never slept much."

They adapted to their new surroundings. "When it rained we got wet," Bill said. "When the sun came out we dried off. We slept where we fell." They learned to rest in rock piles, swamps, and foxholes with water. Bill's feet were covered with blisters and sores, a shared condition the men called "jungle rot."

Bill was awed by the bravery of his fellow marines. "If you got shot, you died," Bill said. There was no way to get to a hospital. He watched boys his own age accept their fate without complaint. "Just laid down and died. Hundreds of them."

AUGUST 19

The navy was gone. The Japanese ruled the seas. They shelled the marines with impunity, who in turn "could only scrunch lower and lower in the shallow trenches and hope and, perhaps, pray."[5]

The daily ration of a marine at war was not generous to begin with. It was reduced by two-thirds. They resorted to eating roots and weeds. Bill learned every way to eat a coconut: raw, fried, bald. He ate weevil-infested barley, with "more weevils than barley."

Bill and the men he served with couldn't afford cigarettes in civilian life. The marines had gotten them started: "It'll calm your nerves." Now they dealt with severe nicotine withdrawals.

Dead bodies swelled in the heat and burst. Flies multiplied and grew fat. They could land on your food for a split second and give you dysentery. It seemed like everyone got it: fever, chills, nausea, vomiting, stomach pain, and near constant diarrhea. Men used the latrine as often as thirty times a day. Some needed to be carried. The men used old newspapers for toilet paper, until they ran out. Their favorite was an issue of *The New York Times,* headlined: "Navy Keeps Supplies Flowing In."[6]

The average marine lost twenty-five pounds. Men went blind at night for lack of vitamin A. Somehow they had to keep working, to fortify Tulagi against a counterattack. Malaria was no excuse—everyone had it. If your fever was below 103, you were working.

Bill's First Battalion was ordered to take their Higgins boats from Tulagi to Guadalcanal to defend a village of missionaries against the Japanese. Ten miles from the island Bill was blinded by a searchlight from an enemy destroyer. A shell hit the Higgins boat in front of him, filling the water with marines. A second shell hit Bill's boat, pitching it forward, and he was in the water.

The waves handled him like a rag doll. He was helpless as a giant swell tossed him far from the boats. Then he was pitched forward, near where his ship had been shelled. Bill felt a hard bump against his leg. Then another. Sharks! They had passed on Bill for the moment in favor of the bleeding. But they'd get to him before long.

Bill tried to keep calm and remember his training. He held his arms out like they had practiced. Someone on a rescue boat would hook their arms into his and pull him aboard. The first attempt failed and the boat passed him by. Well, good God, he thought. I don't believe they're going to get me. The next wave threw him near the edge of a boat. He held out his arms again. He felt another set of arms lock with his and yank him aboard.

They landed on Guadalcanal and made their way to the village, where they drove out the Japanese in a firefight over the next few hours. The marines secured the town, but the residents had already been killed, including priests and nuns. They blew up Japanese trucks and an ammunition dump until they were counterattacked. Bill and the rest fought their way back to the Higgins boats and returned to Tulagi.[7]

16

"U.S. INDICTS SIX FOR VOTE FRAUD"

The election laws were raped again in McMinn
County in last Tuesday's election. . . . Such
conduct is beyond endurance by free men in a
free country. We sorely need the relief that can
come through the Department of Justice.

—*S. C. Brown to Congressman John Jennings*

So many citizens of Athens, and of McMinn
County, had begun to feel that the situation was
hopeless, but are watching the coming trial in
federal court in Winchester, Tennessee, with
new hope. We have all seen things, in the past
two years, that we never dreamed could happen
in a free country.

—*Paul Walker to U.S. Attorney General Francis Biddle*

Congressman Jennings gave a speech in Athens denouncing
the August election as "the most corrupt thing I ever saw." If

November followed suit, he would not stop "until all the men who violate the laws are behind bars in the federal prison."[1]

America was striking out at the Axis powers in the East and readying their attack in the West. Jennings was ready to open two new fronts of his own. His first target was the McMinn County Election Commission, specifically the two Democratic commissioners. Jennings wanted an ouster lawsuit to remove them from office. Beecher Witt, the district attorney general, found himself in a tough spot. He was the local prosecutor for the region including McMinn and a Republican, like most voters in the district. But he saw no advantage in picking fights with Paul Cantrell or Burch Biggs. He left them alone, and so far they had left him alone. But the 1942 election featured new lows of lawlessness, well documented and publicized. And now he had a congressman from his own party demanding an ouster suit. It would have to be filed.

The suit charged that commissioners John Cate and Reuel Webb "knowingly and willfully misconducted themselves in office" and "neglected to perform the duties enjoined upon them": allowing armed deputies in polling places; disregarding absentee voting rules; and barring members of the public from observing the counts, all in violation of state law. Cate and Webb "persistently, arbitrarily, and illegally disregarded the rights of citizens and voters . . . substituted the law of pistol and blackjack for that of the ballot . . . made elections in McMinn County a hiss, a byword, and a reproach to free government." Their appointees were "schooled and . . . experienced and hardened in their repeated violations of the election laws . . . men known to be of desperate and dangerous character, who habitually go armed and who are expert in the use of deadly weapons."[2]

Reuel Webb responded with a letter to the editor: "Anyone

knows that the election last August was the calmest and most peaceful of any election in the state of Tennessee. There was no Republican organization and practically no opposition." Webb wrote, "Men of the highest type and character will hold our elections in November and Mr. Jennings and all his cohorts and investigators are heartily welcome to witness the proceedings, which will sound the death knell for John Jennings Jr."[3]

Jennings had another surprise for Cantrell and company. He had spent the last two years pushing the Department of Justice to prosecute. Finally, the U.S. attorney general agreed to present a limited number of charges to the Chattanooga grand jury. Grand juries determine whether probable cause exists to proceed to trial, "a reasonable ground for supposing that a charge is well-founded." The Department of Justice presented mountains of evidence. No honest grand jury would fail to indict in these circumstances. But Chattanooga didn't have one.

The DOJ had been reluctant to get involved. The Chattanooga grand jury had considered the charges multiple times and would not indict. They could say they tried and move on. But Jennings wouldn't let them. He pressed to make the case to the grand jury at Winchester, Tennessee, where it wouldn't be expected.

The news was splashed across the front page of the *Post-Athenian*: "U.S. Indicts Six for Vote Fraud." Two election commissioners were facing ouster, and six henchmen were facing prison. Both cases would undoubtedly yield more evidence, and more convictions. And they wouldn't dare try and steal the November election now. Would they?[4]

On the eve of the November election, State Senator Robert Lindsay made a shocking announcement: "I have been elected to the state senate from McMinn, Bradley, Roane, and Anderson counties for three terms, each time by fair and honest methods. I might be elected again, but if I did so it would be necessary for my friends in Bradley, Roane, and Anderson to resort to the same kind of methods my opposition has convinced me it will use in McMinn. I do not intend to use such methods and I do not intend to ask my friends to use them." The presses ran all night printing new ballots bearing the name of the only candidate for state senate: Paul Cantrell.[5]

Elizabeth White prayed for her son every morning. Mothers tend to fear the worst, and if she did she wasn't far from the mark. On September 27, 1942, she wrote the Marine Corps: Bill "was sent to San Diego California for training and never did get to come back home he was just eighteen years of age and has since been sent overseas and we haven't heard from him since the fifteenth of June and he always wrote every week and more and we are awful worried about him if you can tell us where he is sure would appreciate it."

The response was swift but antiseptic. "It is not deemed advisable to furnish information regarding the exact whereabouts of your son, inasmuch as the location of the organization with which he is serving is confidential. The delay in receiving mail from him is no doubt due to the present irregular mail deliveries, and it is hoped that you will hear from him in the near future." She was assured that "any news of importance regarding his welfare" would be brought to her attention.[6]

NOVEMBER 3, 1942

With the county races won in August, and legislative races unopposed, the leadership of McMinn County had one priority for the general election. John O'Connor, head of the Knox County Red

Cross, was the Democratic nominee against their sworn enemy, Congressman John J. Jennings Jr.

R. T. Bryan, sheriff's deputy and jailer, ran the election in Precinct 12. People handed him their folded ballots. He opened them, took note of who they voted for, and then refolded and placed them in the ballot box. After seeing a ballot he didn't like, he asked the voter: "Have you got your poll tax receipt?"

The voter, a senior citizen, explained that he was exempt due to age.

"You are under arrest," said Bryan, snatching the ballot out of his hand. "I will take you to jail." All voting ceased while Bryan was gone.

Deputy Minus Wilburn came and went, whispering to the election judges and escorting supportive voters to the polls. Precinct 12 was in a store, and when Bryan was ready to tally the vote he moved behind the counter. Claude Hutsell, the Republican poll watcher, and W. T. Wade, Republican election judge, sat down to watch the count. They witnessed Bryan call three ballots for O'Connor that were cast for Jennings.

Bryan didn't like being watched. "Get back and stay back thirty feet," he said. Bryan flew around the counter in a rage and grabbed Hutsell's chair out from under him. "You ain't watching nothing. I'll put you out. I am running this."

Deputy Wilburn stood at the door, ensuring no one got in—or out. Hutsell and Wade moved to the back of the store, near the stove, where at least they'd be warm. Hutsell and Wade scribbled down the votes as Bryan called them. When the count was finished, the clerks announced that O'Connor had 256 votes; Jennings, 144 votes, for a total of 400 votes exactly. Only 365 people had voted at Precinct 12 that day.

Bryan walked over to where Hutsell and Wade were seated. "What are you doing?" he said, ripping up their notes.

"We are keeping tally of votes as you called them out."

"You ain't keeping nothing," he said.[7]

Holland Vestal was the Republican poll watcher at Precinct 11. Vestal was one of the largest employers in the county, a sixty-two-year-old businessman running four hosiery mills, with a son serving in the Pacific.

Carl Neil was the regional game warden and officer of election. When the polls closed he took the ballot box and sat with his back to the wall. Vestal asked him to move so that he could see the ballots as he called them. Neil ordered him to stay back. Vestal protested three times.

"You have no right to be closer than ten feet," Neil said. Every ballot cast that day came down to whatever Neil said it was, with nobody in a position to disagree.[8]

M. A. Barnett, a sixty-five-year-old farmer, was a poll watcher for Jennings in Etowah. Deputy Erwin White, officer of the election, was calling the ballots too fast to keep a reliable count. Barnett objected to a ballot, clearly marked for Jennings, that had been called for O'Connor.

"What right have you got to watch this count?" asked White.

Barnett showed him his credential. White and Robert Biggs, a Democratic election judge, grabbed Barnett and physically dragged him outside. They then tore up his poll watcher credential in front of him. He recalled 359 votes cast. The scene repeated itself in Englewood as Burt Vaughn was thrown out by Tom Tallent.[9]

The worst was still to come.

William Rucker was a policeman in Etowah under Mayor

Frank Cantrell, Paul's brother. A year earlier Rucker had shot and killed Deputy Raymond Count King in front of the Etowah jail. Supposedly it was over a fee dispute from two arrests.

Raymond's father had told him in no uncertain terms—do not go to work as a deputy for Paul Cantrell. When he took the job anyway, his father forced him to move, refusing to accept a machine man living under his roof. Before long what Raymond saw and was asked to do were too much for his conscience to bear. King was planning to leave the department when he was killed, and his family believed it was for this reason, rather than a fee dispute, that he died. At best, he was killed by a fellow officer over a few dollars; at worst, he was assassinated to keep him quiet.

The grand jury refused to indict Rucker, for the second time that year. In the first, he and his brother Roe had been accused of killing Charlie McQueen, whose bullet-ridden skeleton had been identified by his clothes on Starr Mountain. McQueen had been suspected in the death of another Rucker brother, and wasn't smart enough to get as far out of town as he possibly could.[10]

Despite the last year—because of it, really—William Rucker was still a police officer and was selected as officer of election at an Etowah polling place. At the end of the day he moved the ballot box to a table in the corner of the room, where no one could see over his shoulder. He began to call the votes so quickly that they couldn't be counted. Zeb Aldridge, the Republican election judge, strained to see as best he could, even after a Democratic judge moved to block his view. Aldridge saw a Jennings ballot called for O'Connor and objected.

"Made a mistake," Rucker said. But the clerks never changed the count. It happened again and Aldridge objected. Rucker ignored him. Aldridge objected again. And again.

"Get the hell around there and sit down," Rucker told him.

"No, I will stand up where I can see them called."

Rucker kept calling ballots. Rucker folded a ballot without calling it and tossed it on the pile. Aldridge picked it up and looked at it. It was for Jennings. Aldridge insisted that Rucker call it.

Rucker stood up and punched him in the ear. "Get the hell out of here. And I don't mean maybe." Rucker unholstered his gun.

Aldridge walked to the door. "You mean for me to get out, and me a judge?"

"I do," said Rucker, "damn quick."

Jennings was reelected, carrying all but three counties: Knox, O'Connor's home, where he trailed by a handful of votes; Monroe, an allied county of Polk and McMinn, where he lost 1,459 to 1,183; and McMinn, where he was alleged to have lost 1,832 to 884.[11]

17

"COME TO THE RESCUE OF A HELPLESS PEOPLE"

NOVEMBER 8, 1942

Five days after the election

Les Dooley of Athens found himself in water up to his neck, wading ashore on the beaches of Morocco, among the first Americans to fight in the western theater. He was a twenty-one-year-old army lieutenant, commanding antitank guns, charged with laying down fire to protect the rest of the landing party. The first people he encountered were Moroccans trying to sell him cigarettes.

Two miles in, he received a desperate call for help from the front: one of his 37-millimeter guns was "vastly outnumbered" and under attack. Dooley took a truck and raced to back them up. The windshield shattered as the truck was sprayed with machine gun fire. He and his men jumped out seconds before it exploded. Every man at the front had been wounded. Dooley watched as tanks sped toward them, firing their guns. "There wasn't time" to be scared, he said. His only thought was to return fire. Dooley and the men who had come with him to the front destroyed a French tank. Then another.

The French killed one of his gunners. Dooley stood in the dead man's place. The gunner next to him was shot. A shell hit the gun Dooley was using, jamming it. He felt something strike his left wrist, sending him to the ground, praying like he never had before. He watched as others did the same. The French tanks sped toward them and he was sure they were about to get run over. He hugged the ground and braced himself. The tanks stopped abruptly, five feet from crushing him. An officer got out and started "jabbering in French." Dooley and his crew were captured by the Vichy, the French government allied with the Nazis, which controlled France's North African colonies. The first Americans to die in the western theater were killed by the people they were there to save.

Les Dooley and his men were prisoners. A French doctor operated on his forearm, but it had to be amputated. They ate two meals a day—lots of goat meat. "They must've forgotten to skin the goats," Dooley thought. Four days later he was taken to another town and handed over to U.S. troops. The next day he boarded a ship for home. He had been in Africa for one week.

"The good ol' USA never looked better," Dooley said. He was sent to Walter Reed Hospital and thrilled to see his friend Oliver Kirby of Athens. But Oliver wouldn't be much for talking—his jaw had been shot off.

Dooley was awarded the Distinguished Service Cross "for heroism and gallantry in action." He felt he left more than his arm in Africa. "Maybe it's my heart," he said. "I'd like to be carrying on with my buddies there."[1]

The *Post-Athenian* interviewed Representative George Woods about the upcoming legislative session. A measure to repeal the poll tax was gaining momentum as the war heated up.

With so many young men in harm's way fighting for freedom, was it right to keep charging people for the right to vote? Woods declined to join the effort. He said it would be divisive, adding: "This is no time for any fight on the home front." He also thought debating and voting on the poll tax would needlessly protract the session, and distract him from his "important tasks" in the war effort.[2]

But the public pressure was overwhelming. The state's largest newspaper, *The Tennessean,* told the legislature: "We are three million behind you. What are you afraid of? Get on your feet and fight." For the first time anyone could remember, a bill opposed by Ed Crump passed the legislature and was signed by the governor. Burch Biggs filed a lawsuit in Polk County. One of his elected judges ruled that the legislature of Tennessee *could not* repeal its own law. The decision was appealed to the state supreme court. They upheld the trial court, 3–2. The chief justice, in dissent, wrote that the idea that a legislature could not repeal one of its own acts was "unknown in the history of English and American jurisprudence." The deciding vote was a new justice from Shelby County, who had publicly referred to Boss Crump as "our leader."[3]

Meanwhile, Congressman Jennings met U.S. Attorney General Francis Biddle and his team, setting "out the great frauds and violations of law perpetrated in McMinn County," resulting "in the theft from me of at least one thousand votes."[4]

The Department of Justice claimed surprise at "repetitions of former violations." They shouldn't have been, considering the machine's methods were effective, profitable, and almost entirely without consequence.

Rhea Hammer, an Athens hardware store owner, wrote the

attorney general: "The good people of this county are sacrificing for the cause of America's freedom but have lost their freedom at home. Both parties have lost the freedom of the ballot box, a dictatorship has been set up, the county treasury is being raided at the expense of the taxpayers, and the good people of this county would like to sell their property and move away. Your department is our last line of defense. Please, for God's sake come to the rescue of a helpless people."[5]

Rev. H. L. Love, pastor of Mars Hill Church in Athens, who had tried to rally faith leaders to escort voters to the polls, wrote to Biddle of "a ruthless exploitation at the hands of unscrupulous men who sacrifice public liberties for the sake of private gain . . . nothing has been considered too low if it will enable them to perpetuate themselves in office.

"Decent citizens feared to bring their wives to the polls, and often felt it unwise to cast their own ballots." Love said it felt more like "Gestapo in Nazi Germany" than "free America." He asked for an FBI investigation. "It is not possible for a letter to contain information concerning all the subversive and unscrupulous activities that have taken place in this county."[6]

Holland Vestal wrote directly to Biddle as well: "The good citizens felt they would endanger their lives if they tried to correct the evil. We feel we will have to go out of the state of Tennessee to secure justice. The good citizens of McMinn County, Tennessee are begging for justice. Will you help us?"[7]

John Proffitt, an Athens department store owner, told Biddle: "We who call ourselves Americans have looked down on Hitler and his methods but here in McMinn County we have conditions which make Hitler look like an angel with a dirty face."[8]

Pastor Frank Porter of Tennessee Wesleyan College wrote

that the county was run by "a gang of outlaws," adding, "You will of course have no occasion to publish this letter."[9]

Three women of Athens traveled to Washington to press their case. Kathaleen Reed, Rosabel Boyd, and Loree Matthews met with the attorney general himself. Sylvester Meyers, section chief for the Civil Rights Division, sat down with them for an interview.

Meyers took notes on life in McMinn County, where "election frauds and irregularities were the rule and honest voting the exception."

"Cantrell has openly boasted that he has after 8 years graduated from the political school of Burch Biggs," wrote Meyers. Cantrell and Biggs planned to build a statewide machine that would overtake Boss Crump's.

Kathaleen Reed and her husband owned a pool hall where machine men liked to hang out. They enjoyed bragging to the ladies, who they felt were no threat. Pat Mansfield told Kathaleen that "at the very last minute of the last day" before the election, he took $7,000 worth of poll tax receipts and "fill[ed] in names of dead" and "fictitious persons." One constable stuffed 600 ballots in a box in exchange for a better job. James Evans bragged to her about forging 150 ballots "and would do it again." Evans told Kathaleen that he never paid a penny in income tax "and had no intention of doing so." Our "gang is running this part of the sticks," he said, "and the federal government doesn't even know it exists." The women were sure that a charge of income tax evasion could be made against other machine members—including Paul Cantrell.

The women described how the machine made money from illegal activity. Lee Fisher was the machine's point man on gambling, paying $5,200 for the privilege.

The women described a state of fear surrounding voting in McMinn County. People stayed home rather than risk being "pushed around by the armed guards," bent on "intimidating the honest citizen." Transparent ballots were used to ensure people had "voted right." In light of the consequences for "voting wrong," it's a wonder the opposition received any votes at all: "City officials have ruthlessly stopped people in Athens and about the county," wrote Meyers, "with the object of extorting fines. Many of the alleged victims have been the younger children of the prominent families opposed to the gang."[10]

The attorney general wrote Congressman Jennings: "the alleged violations in McMinn County were the worst ever brought to the attention of the Department of Justice."[11]

18

"SAY A PRAYER FOR YOUR PAL ON GUADALCANAL"

They called Guadalcanal "the island of death." It was covered by a thick canopy of hundred-foot treetops that looked solid enough to walk across. Beneath were 2,000 square miles of land crabs, fist-sized spiders, finger-sized wasps, and screaming birds. Americans had seized the airport—in the center and north of the island—in the initial invasion. The Japanese had them surrounded.

Bill White's Higgins boat landed on the beach next to the airport. He walked past a field hospital with far more wounded than tents or doctors. Bill saw marines with gunshot wounds to the arms and legs and stomach "lying all over the place." There was still no sign of the navy.

It was a battle of sudden, violent raids and attrition: get in, kill as many men as you can, steal or destroy weapons and supplies, try to get back in one piece. Bill came under machine gun fire on his second day. He dived into a hut of coconut limbs and leaves. Bill realized he wasn't alone, but lying on top of the bodies of four or five dead Japanese who had been there for days. Bill was covered in "goo." It was an awful, overpowering odor, the worst ever. The machine gun "clattered and clattered" outside. Bill thought about standing up and getting his head blown off so that he wouldn't have to smell it another second. But he stayed until it was safe to leave.

Bill couldn't find water to wash for two days. The sand and the "goo" stuck to his uniform and he never could quite get it off.

It was a great day when two small ships from Australia made it to port. Bill and others unloaded them with all the energy they had for the next two hours. The ships rushed back to sea when Japanese bombers appeared. Bill ate a gallon of apricots in one sitting. For the rest of his life he would never eat another. In addition to some longed-for food, they managed to unload Australian bush knives: over two feet long, with big black handles.

The blades came in handy in a battle across the Tenaru River. The Japanese were attempting to cross and the marines were trying to push them back. The fighting was at close quarters and hand to hand. When the day was over, Bill looked at the river and realized that he could cross over bodies without getting his feet wet. He had gripped his knife so tightly and stabbed so many times and so hard that his hand swelled up and went numb. He had to use one hand to pry the bush knife out of the other.

The next day a sniper killed the man standing next to Bill. He yelled for a medical corpsman. The corpsman who responded was shot. A second corpsman who attended both of them was shot. Bill looked desperately for the sniper and couldn't find him. He watched helplessly as a third corpsman was shot. Bill and others walked up behind where they figured the sniper to be, found him, and killed him.

They held their own and gained ground on Guadalcanal. But Japanese ships and planes could rain hell itself on the stranded marines. The worst was October 11: "No marine who lived through that night will ever forget it. No marine who did not can fully imagine it, or have it adequately described." Destroyers and battleships raked the Americans with fire. One bomber after another after another flew over and opened up on them.

Bill thought the shells sounded like freight trains. A single one could collapse your foxhole. He had to physically grab his legs to keep them from shaking. Bill popped his head up with the first light. He was surprised by how many had survived the night and were doing the same. He thought it looked like a field of groundhogs.[1]

Bill was on a scouting mission the day after a raid. It was unbearably hot—maybe 120 degrees. It began to drizzle and then rain. He found a Japanese camp and observed for as long as he could. The sun began to set and he felt it was too dangerous to try and return to camp. He lay down in tall elephant grass and went to sleep. He woke up fast when someone kicked the bottom of his foot. A Japanese soldier on patrol had walked right into him. Bill sat up, but a bayonet to the shoulder pinned him right back to the ground. Bill struggled, pulled out his .45, and shot the man in the chin. The bayonet slid out of his shoulder as the soldier fell backward, dead. Bill went farther into the jungle and tried to find a safer place to sleep. The next day Bill inspected the man's body. Bill's life was apparently not the only one he'd saved. The man was a scout and carried detailed maps of the marine positions. He had watched the marines planting mines and took detailed notes, "a layout of that minefield down to a tee."

Meanwhile, Bill was as miserable as he had been since he'd arrived in the islands. His shoulder ached. There was little in the way of medical supplies. Maggots infested the wound. "It's a good thing those maggots got in there," said the doctor, when Bill was finally seen at a field hospital. "It might have been gangrene." The doctor said a new drug might help and they needed volunteers—Bill agreed to try penicillin.

The U.S. Navy returned for a rematch on November 12. Both sides fired at such close range that they routinely struck their own. Two American antiaircraft cruisers and four destroyers were sunk. Three other ships were damaged. Two days later the navies reengaged, with continuous bombing by American B-17s from the Guadalcanal airfield. Seven Japanese transports were sunk. The Americans had taken the seas and skies of the Solomon Islands.[2]

The Japanese had been evicted from Florida Island, Gavutu, Tanambogo, Tulagi, and now Guadalcanal. Twelve hundred marines had died and twenty-eight hundred were wounded. Twenty-four thousand Japanese were killed.[3]

It was time for the marines who had won the islands to leave them. Some men were too thin and weak to board the ships under their own strength. They were carried. Their "skins were cracked and furrowed and wrinkled and their eyes held all the memories of the frightful nights and awful days they had somehow survived."

The Japanese had been using the Solomons as stepping-stones to New Zealand and beyond. Now the Allies were using them on the road to Tokyo. Bill White boarded the USS *Jackson* wearing the same clothes as when he'd left, 188 days before.[4]

19

UNITED STATES V. LATTIMORE ET AL.

The ouster lawsuit against election commissioners, which held out the promise of publicized hearings, revealing testimony, and further evidence against the machine, sputtered out. Cate and Webb resigned their offices, making the ouster lawsuit moot. "[T]hey served the racketeers of that county well," wrote Walter White, an Athens attorney. Representative George Woods and Sheriff Pat Mansfield were named the new commissioners. But there was still the criminal trial arising from the 1940 election.

Congressman Jennings wanted nothing left to chance. "My friends, at the peril of their lives, have aided in bringing these violations to light," he wrote Attorney General Biddle. For years he had promised the people of McMinn that if they would take the risk of coming forward, prosecutions would result. "Our people are anxious for speedy action. So am I."[1]

The U.S. attorney, J. B. Frazier, was appointed at the behest of the U.S. senators, both of whom were beholden to Crump.

In fact, Frazier was seen meeting with Burch Biggs and Judge Leslie Darr that November. Jennings insisted on a "vigorous prosecutor" sent from Washington instead of Frazier.[2]

An out-of-town prosecutor had been used in the trial of Tom Pendergast, the boss of Kansas City who launched the career of Harry Truman. Walter White wrote to Jennings: "Pendergast and his crowd were Sunday-School Teachers compared with the crowd you are fighting. . . . Unless it is carefully safeguarded, the jury in the McMinn case will be tampered with by certain powerful chiefs. . . . I am afraid of a whitewash."[3]

Assistant Attorney General Roy Frank arrived from Washington to try the case. It was rumored that defendant Spurgeon Simpson might flip on Paul Cantrell. Apparently, his brother and wife encouraged him to talk—to say that he had been specifically instructed to shut down a polling place and paid seventy-five dollars for that purpose.[4]

Roy Frank delivered his opening statement to the jury: "This is the beginning of the end. The depriving of the rights of American voters is striking at the very foundation of democracy, the basic structure of our national government. If we take that away, we have no democracy at all but descend to the same autocracy of Germany and Italy."[5]

The charges focused on the closure of the Claxton precinct at 10:00 A.M. during the August 1940 election. Paul Cantrell was called to the stand. He testified that he had helped the defendants assemble their legal team and prepared them for trial.

Roy Carver testified that he had brought three people with him to vote, including his seventy-seven-year-old father. Ralph Lattimore, a deputy of the then-sheriff Cantrell, ordered him to "get out." Carver insisted that he had a right to vote. Deputy

Lattimore hit him with a blackjack. Fewer than fifty ballots had been cast when the polling place was closed.

Thomas Davis testified that Lattimore and Deputy Frank Green refused to let him vote, physically removing him from the polling place. One woman testified that before walking in to vote she prayed: "Lord, don't let me get killed in there!" The prosecution called sixty-seven witnesses in total.[6]

Defense attorney Phil Whittaker dismissed the matter as "a little precinct squabble," but then claimed that the heavily armed deputies "were afraid for their lives. Wasn't it better to close the polls at that particular place to keep someone from getting killed?" He said the defendants were involved in important war duties and should be acquitted so that they could return.

Judge Darr began dismissing charges with the flimsiest pretense. Barnes Foster, another of Cantrell's deputies, had entered the polling place and removed the ballot box. Darr said he believed the taking of the ballot box did not demonstrate an intent to keep people from voting, since "another box could have been obtained by election officials." This was a question for the jury by any measure. But Darr set him free.

Darr also threw out the charges against Doore Jenkins, doorkeeper at the polling place. He ruled that to be guilty Jenkins had to deprive people of their right to vote in his official capacity. Since there was no statutory job of doorkeeper, he had no official capacity. By this logic, the machine could create illegal positions and fill them with people to commit illegal acts and never be convicted, because they were not acting under "color of office."

Witnesses testified that Mrs. Hester Burris, election clerk, had left before the ballot box was stolen. As a contested matter, Darr should've let the jury decide. But he acquitted her as well.[7]

Three defendants remained. Lattimore testified that he had blackjacked Carter because he tried to arrest him and that he resisted arrest. Sheriff Pat Mansfield testified as a character witness, along with Clyde Rogers, an Etowah policeman who as officer of election had accepted batches of premarked ballots and jailed a Republican judge who objected.

It took the jury a little over two hours to convict Lattimore, Spurgeon, and Green. Roy Frank spoke to the press: "The successful conclusion of this case represents an important victory for civil liberties, not only in Tennessee, but everywhere else in the country as well. At the same time it serves notice on our detractors among the Axis nations that Democracy is a dynamic faith, fully capable of putting up a fight for its preservation."[8]

"There is rejoicing among the good people of McMinn County," wrote S. C. Brown, an eighty-eight-year-old retired judge, in a letter to Jennings, "as the result of these convictions and deep gloom among those who have been abusing the people so long."[9]

Athens businessman Rhea Hammer wrote Jennings with his hope that people would once again "want to live here and invest their money here rather than as at present when men want to dispose of their real estate and move away from the place of their birth."[10]

The USS *Jackson* had seemed like a prison six months earlier. After Guadalcanal it felt like a "floating palace." For starters, no one was trying to kill them in their sleep. There was food, soap, and hot water. But all this was nothing compared to their next destination. The marines pulled into Auckland, New Zealand, on February 7, 1943.[11]

It may as well have been heaven. An island of grateful young women. The men of fighting age were in North Africa battling Nazis. More than six hundred marines would be engaged or married before they left New Zealand. Between ice-cream sodas and milkshakes the marines cleaned out the country's creameries. They drank "jump whiskey," so named because a sip would make you leap like a kangaroo.[12]

There were dances at the Hotel Cecil, the Grand, and the St. George. The Cecil had a map of the United States covering one wall, on which marines wrote their names and the towns they were from. Virtually every home in the country was open to these young men who had saved them from invasion.

Bill met a half-Melanesian woman, with blue eyes, olive skin, and blond hair, who insisted on bringing him back to her house. Bill realized that she lived with her family and wondered how this was going to work. The woman took his hand and led him to her bedroom, where she gave him a push toward the bed and closed the door. She insisted he stay for breakfast. Bill couldn't believe how pleasant her father was.

Bill stayed for days and found it hard to leave. He returned to camp past his appointed time and was punished with twenty days of solitary confinement, placed on a diet of bread and water, assigned to extra duties for three months, and fined $150.[13]

A federal jury had convicted Lattimore, Green, and Simpson. Now it fell to Judge Darr to issue a sentence.

Roy Frank argued for meaningful jail time: "I do not think a fine would have any effect in this case. A fine would be paid by a collection of certain people up in McMinn County, who were the ones to be benefitted by the acts of the defendants." The defendants weren't paying their own legal fees. Why would they pay the fine?[14]

"This court is strongly impressed with the idea that it is the duty of local communities to take care of their own elections," Darr said, "clean up their own houses and not bring their troubles to the federal government to clean up for them." Judge Darr fined them a penny.[15]

"The privilege of voting in a general election in Tennessee is now worth, on the appraisal of the federal courts, something less than one cent," wrote the *Knoxville Journal*.[16]

Congressman Jennings denounced Darr on the floor of the U.S. House. He "virtually turned them loose." Their associates "openly stated" that "they would not be punished—that the case was fixed." Now it seemed they were right. Darr "placed his blessing on the convicted offenders . . . said they were men of good character, and in effect, told the people of that county who had been robbed of their votes, blackjacked, and driven from the polls at the point of a pistol, to go to hell.

"If his verdict breeds no indignation," said Jennings, "then this talk of fighting a world war to preserve our own constitutional rights is all eyewash."

Jennings received a letter from Maggie Giles, the mother of six Athens men away at war: "I do think there will have to be a cleaning up at home before we can hope for a lasting peace. It is hard to see our boys making the sacrifice they are making for a freedom that we don't have in our own country."

Jennings thought it "a travesty and . . . mockery of law enforcement when a mother such as this, along with other citizens of Athens must walk through lines of armed thugs when they go to the ballot box."[17]

"We have just begun to fight," Jennings wrote, "and will ultimately win."[18]

Judge Darr had a history of doing the machine's bidding. Herman Moses, a top Cantrell lieutenant and one of his hand-picked county court members under the Ripper Bill, had been a supervisor for the Works Progress Administration. He was convicted of extorting campaign donations from his workers for Congressman Jennings's opponent. Darr had sentenced him to one hour in jail. T. B. Ivins, a former McMinn sheriff who served as superintendent of public works, forced WPA employees to build a road to his farm. The road cost a thousand dollars in public funds and increased the value of his land immeasurably. He was fined fifty dollars by Judge Darr.[19]

Paul Cantrell was sworn in as a new state senator at the capitol in Nashville. He had also been elected Etowah justice of the peace, giving him a seat on the county court, which selected him as chairman. At the same meeting they renewed the term of George Woods as county purchasing agent and budget clerk, salaried jobs he held in addition to his duties as a state representative.[20]

Two days later, Cantrell introduced his first proposal in the Tennessee senate. It was a "Ripper Bill" for Bradley County, cutting the districts for its county court from four to two, abolishing the current county court, which was Republican by a margin of eight to two, and replacing it with four members, all of them Democrats named in the bill. His cosponsor in the House was Broughton Biggs, son of Burch. The bill was introduced on January 7, 1943, and signed by Governor Cooper on January 15. A mass meeting of citizens from Bradley County condemned the measure. A group of more than fifty residents went to the houses of the new county court members to tell them they hadn't won their votes, didn't have their consent to govern, and asked them to resign. The new court members refused.

Cantrell's next bill, cosponsored with Woods, was to fund the position of McMinn County attorney for eighteen hundred dollars per year. Reuel Webb, the election commissioner who had resigned to avoid an ouster suit for gross misconduct, was named in the legislation as the first holder of the office.[21]

20

"NO ATHEISTS ON TARAWA"

OCTOBER 17, 1943

Bill White said good-bye to a land that he loved—his stay in the brig excepted—and boarded the USS *Harry Lee* at Wellington.

The marines played endless card games on deck, pausing only to move into shifting shade, and traded books to read until they were worn out. They didn't know where they were going. The news could come at any minute that they were heading back into battle. The transports offered no relief from the punishing Pacific heat. Even after dark, men lay in their beds in hot, cramped quarters and sweat through the night.[1]

The Gilbert Islands consisted of sixteen atolls, one of which, Tarawa, was made up of thirty-eight islets, and one of these, Betio, was home to an airfield fifteen hundred yards long. Whoever controlled it could project air power over thousands of miles of the Pacific.[2]

NOVEMBER 20, 1943

The battle would be commanded by admirals on both sides. The Japanese bragged that a "million men cannot take Tarawa in a hundred years."

Shortly after 5:00 A.M. the navy opened up on Tarawa, flying fireballs lighting the sky like noontime with a thundering crash on impact.

Bill felt like the shelling had lasted three hours and the sun still hadn't risen. He could see the flash on the island where the shells landed. B-24s bombed the island for seven minutes. The navy resumed shelling for the next two hours, covering every inch of the island with three thousand tons.

But the concrete bunkers, especially the ones underground, had been heavily reinforced to withstand just such a bombardment. If the marines wanted the island, they were going to have to go ashore and take it.[3]

8:24 A.M.

The navy badly misjudged the tide—affecting how close the boats could get and how far the marines would have to run under fire. The first landing boats ran aground on Betio's coral reef.

Bill White climbed out onto the coral reef in chest-deep water. If he survived the seventy-five yards to the beach he would face a well-fortified force protected by concrete blockhouses behind a four-foot seawall with a hundred machine guns aimed at the top. Marines were "falling, falling, falling . . . singly, in groups, and in rows."[4]

"I saw 'em being killed by the hundreds," Bill said. A bullet struck his helmet and broke his chin strap. Another hit his rifle and he nearly dropped it.

He floated in with the tide and dug his feet into the sand to keep from being washed out. He lay flat pretending to be dead. When the tide returned he'd ride it to get closer to the seawall. Then he'd dig in his feet again. He cracked an eye open to take in the scene.

You're in a hell of a shape, White, he thought. They ain't gonna get nobody in here. A machine gun firing above him ruptured his eardrum. "There was a time on Tarawa when the only hope we had was in God," Bill said. "Believe you me, there were no atheists on Tarawa."[5]

Bill noticed a body on the beach that didn't wash out with the others. He realized that he wasn't the only one who had faked his way to the shore. This changed his outlook: "With two marines you could do some fighting." Bill threw grenades over the seawall in the direction of the machine guns until he ran out. Two more marines joined them on the beach. Through grenades and gunfire they opened up a "dead zone" in the Japanese defense. The marines started flooding into the beach. Bill climbed over the seawall. When he landed on the other side, he was shocked he hadn't been killed or even shot. He looked straight ahead at a concrete blockhouse. It seemed like every defender inside was dead.

The man next to Bill had been shot in the jaw. Bill dragged him into the blockhouse. Bill left the blockhouse and saw a marine lying on the ground.

"Get up and let's go," Bill said.

"I can't," he responded.

"What's the matter?"

"Looky here." He pointed toward his stomach.

Bill lifted the man's shirt. His guts were spilling out from four machine gun holes in his belly. Bill carried him into the blockhouse. "I'll put some morphine into you. I know you're hurting." Bill knew that he was a goner and hoped for his sake he would die fast.

Bill left the blockhouse again and found another wounded marine. "They shot my kneecap off," he said. "I can't walk." Bill dragged him into the blockhouse.

Inside, a Japanese officer thought to be dead staggered up. Bill had left his rifle at the doorway while bringing in the last wounded man. Bill spun around and grabbed for it. The officer pointed a pistol at Bill. Bill fired first, the bullet going through the officer's hand and into his stomach. Bill bayoneted him in the throat and shot him twice more to make sure he was dead.

"He'd have killed every one of us in here," said the navy corpsman who was attending the wounded.

"Yeah, he might have," Bill said. He walked around the blockhouse with his bayonet to make sure that every enemy who appeared to be dead was dead.

Bill had learned that a dead man bleeds differently than a live one. He found another that was alive. The man jumped up and Bill bayoneted him in the back. He broke free and Bill shot and killed him.

Bill and other marines fought their way toward the airport, facing fire "from the left, on the right, to the front of us, and occasionally behind us." Some of the fighting was at a distance and some close up and hand to hand. "Just about any way you want to fight, you had it on that island."

Bill's rifle was shot "plumb out" of his hand when a bullet hit his bayonet. The man in front of him was shot in the neck.

At the airport, Bill bandaged his wound. Only then did Bill realize he'd been shot through the hip. All the bullets fired at him
since day one and someone had finally got him. But he "didn't
have nowhere to go. Might as well stay here and fight." The men
bedded down after dark in an airport hangar. There was gunfire
throughout the night.

At the end of the day the marines had made it two hundred
yards from the beach, with a tenuous hold on "one-tenth of a
square mile of stinking coral, blown to useless bits and stained
with great draughts of American blood."[6]

In the morning, marines who had landed the day before attacked to the south and west while trying to hold the bunkers
they had captured.[7]

Two of Bill's officers arrived in the morning. "Where had
they been hiding?" he wondered. His captain ordered: "White,
take a bunch of these men across there into that big ditch." It was
a gap dug to prevent American tanks from advancing. Bill and his
men began covering the ditch. In the distance he saw a Japanese
officer at the head of a large group of men. Bill "took aim" and
"shot him." He shot two more before they took cover in a thicket.

"What are you shooting at?" asked the lieutenant. "You quit
that shooting!" The lieutenant, standing in the ditch, couldn't see
what was happening.

"Lieutenant, I'm shooting at Japs, what do you think I'm
shooting at?"

"They might be marines!" he said.

Bill laughed at the new officer in his first battle. "Lieutenant,
if they're marines, there's three dead marines laying up there."

The lieutenant didn't find it funny. The captain looked at Bill
as if he could kill him. The lieutenant took a group of men to go

see for himself. Bill offered to cover them as they advanced. The lieutenant ordered him not to. A short while later, Bill saw the lieutenant on a stretcher carried by four men. He had been shot through the hand and stomach. He'd gotten four of his marines killed.

Bill was ordered to take men to clear out some remaining Japanese blockhouses. "We was losing some," Bill said; "they was losing a whole lot." Two of the blockhouses had been destroyed without much effort. The third put up a surprising resistance. Bill sent one of his men to find a can of gasoline. They splashed it on the blockhouse and set it on fire. The men defending it ran out, some of them in flames, and were shot.

Bill took a box of Japanese socks out of a blockhouse. He sat on his helmet and pulled off his boots. It was a treat to pull off his "sweaty, stinky" socks and put on a clean pair. He offered another pair to his machine gunner, seated on a box of ammo. "Swede, you want a pair of clean socks?"

Swede took off his boots and tried his new socks. There was a crack. Bill felt a bullet whiz past his ear. He saw Swede's helmet fill up with blood. Bill was so mad he thought he'd "blow a stack." He ran into the blockhouse, looking for the shooter. The windows provided little daylight and he couldn't see anyone inside. He saw where the shot came from—a little doorway in the middle of the blockhouse led to another room that he hadn't seen before. Bill took a grenade and threw it inside. It exploded. Bill walked in after it. The room was pitch-black. He bumped into a steel table. Hard. He couldn't see a thing. He heard "swish, swish." Someone was swinging a sword at him. Bill fell back and focused on a small sliver of light created by a crack in the door. Eventually the swordsman would cross into that light. When he did, Bill shot him with a split second of visibility. Bill charged and bayoneted him in the throat. The man swung his saber at Bill, scraping the side of his rifle barrel and slicing his thumb. Bill heard his death rattle as he went down.

Bill found a light and brought it back to the room. He was struck by the man's neat, fancy uniform and manicured fingers. He grabbed the sword, the fanciest he had ever seen.

"Oh my heck," Bill said, looking at the sharkskin scabbard and gold trim. "This dude's somebody." Bill took the sword for himself.

The battle for Tarawa ended seventy-six hours after it began. Bill White stretched to his full height and looked around. Everything was damaged or destroyed and scattered. All the trees had been shot down to stumps. There were gaping holes in the ground. "My God, this is the first time I really got a good look at this battlefield." It was 120 degrees. The dead were everywhere, over six thousand in a square mile. Bodies were swelling up and bursting.

"If you hadn't been used to it, you couldn't have stood it," Bill said. His lips were swollen, cracked, and bleeding, like every man on the island. Their ragged clothes were hanging off them. And their skin looked like worn-out leather. Their hair was matted to the point where it didn't look like hair. They were so dirty, you couldn't recognize your best friend. "That's war," Bill said. "I don't know if people like that or not, but I'm going to tell them the way it was. And what it was."

But "they felt proud because they survived that battle." Looking around at the complete destruction and the devastating human loss, they were struck by the fact that they had been spared.

Bill was back on a ship November 24, three days after he'd arrived. The "death smell of Tarawa" filled the USS *Doyen*. Marines died of their injuries every day at sea, and every day they were draped in flags and lowered into the ocean. It was a long two thousand miles and eleven days to Hawaii.

Then there was more bad news. They weren't making camp on the beach but up in the mountains. It seemed the marines had found the coldest place in the islands, with the least amount of sun. They were hoping it would help cure the men of malaria. And there was a second, less spoken fear, of mixing these marines with Hawaiians of Japanese descent.

Up in the mountains between two great volcanoes, the marines who survived Tarawa learned that they would be building the camp themselves. For three weeks they slept outside in freezing temperatures. By day they engaged in the backbreaking labor of building barracks, mess halls, and bathrooms.

With the Marines at Tarawa, a first-of-its-kind combat film, showed both sides in action. General Robert Denig hurried it out to the public. When it premiered, he waited breathlessly for the results. Enlistments in the Marine Corps dropped 35 percent.[8]

Bill's long-suffering mother received a gilded samurai sword in the mail with a short note from her son: "It was a tough fight but we won."[9]

Bill White had joined the marines as a response to Pearl Harbor. He had given much thought to his decision in the two years since. He realized that, yes, he was fighting for his fellow marines and, certainly, fighting for his country, but at heart he was fighting for Athens, McMinn County. Home.

21

UNITED STATES V. WILLIAM RUCKER

Zeb Aldridge sat at Whittaker's Café in Athens. Deputy Erwin White approached him: "When have you been in Chattanooga?"

"November 8," he answered. Aldridge was testifying before the grand jury against William Rucker, the Etowah police chief who had assaulted him and thrown him out of the polling place. White clearly knew and wanted him to know that he knew.

Aldridge was catching up with friends a few days later outside Gentry's Feed Store. White walked toward him and stood six feet away. He beckoned him over. "Why did you go to Chattanooga?"

Aldridge told him the truth. "I was summoned to Chattanooga as a witness before the federal grand jury."

"You don't have to go," said White. "You are going to have serious trouble over this."

"In what way will I have trouble?"

"You will find out," White said. "I will be seeing you."[1]

Rucker was easily indicted by the grand jury for depriving

the people of Pleasant Grove precinct of "the right . . . to have their votes counted as cast in the general election."[2]

Paul Cantrell personally posted his bail. Rucker's release could have been secured in any number of ways. But that would have defeated the purpose. This was a signal of approval for what Rucker had done. And a message for the others, that if by some small chance they found themselves in trouble with the law, Paul Cantrell would do everything he could to help you.[3]

Judge Darr had been pounded in the press and flayed on the floor of the U.S. House of Representatives for his role in the last case. There was even talk of impeachment. He recused himself from the Rucker prosecution. A judge from Cynthiana, Kentucky, traveled to Chattanooga to hear the case.

Rucker had certified 114 votes for O'Connor and 20 for Jennings as officer of election. The prosecution submitted forty-eight affidavits from residents swearing that they had voted for John Jennings. Assuming that everyone who voted for Jennings had been located and that each had willingly sworn out an affidavit against a violent police chief, he had still reduced Jennings's vote by 240 percent.[4]

The jury took an hour and five minutes to convict. The judge sentenced Rucker to sixty days in jail and a five-hundred-dollar fine. Rucker's lawyer asked for release on bond pending appeal. Denied.

Jennings claimed victory in Cantrell's backyard. Speaking in Etowah, he said the "election thief is the lowest kind of thief in the world." He demanded a fair election in August, promising prison time for offenders if it wasn't. And not just for the henchmen, but "the higher-ups."

"Those thieves, instead of their stooges, will be carried down to jail. That time is coming." No longer could the machine count on a "cheap, good-for-nothing judge by the name of Darr."[5]

Rucker reported to the Hamblen County jail on June 15. A month later a reporter was surprised to find Rucker seated comfortably outside—holding its keys in his hand. "I am serving as a trusty here," he said.

The reporter asked whether he had to stay in his cell.

"No. I have to stay pretty close, however."[6]

In fact, Rucker's wife had moved to Hamblen County and taken an apartment next to the jail. Rucker was staying there with her.

Jennings sent the attorney general an article about the "considerate and tender" treatment Rucker was receiving in jail. "This is but an amazing reward [for a] man who has been tried and convicted in federal courts for violating federal election laws." Rucker was moved to a new jail for the few remaining days of his sentence.[7]

FROM ATHENS TO NORMANDY

Captain Frank Carmichael, a heavy weapons company commander, had been activated in 1940 as a member of the Tennessee National Guard. After four years it was finally time to fight.

The words of General George Patton were ringing in his ears as he rode south across England in a convoy of tanks, artillery, weapons, and equipment that seemed to stretch out forever in every direction. Enough to sink the south of England, he thought.

At Southampton they boarded ships bound for France, landing on Omaha Beach on June 14, a week and a day after D-Day.

The soldiers made their way ashore. Depending on where they stepped the water was up to their knees, shoulders, or over their heads. Men struggled to hold on to their rifles and packs, and in some cases lost them. Frank thought of the men who had taken this beach under fire—he was having enough trouble without being shot at. Frank and his men marched to an apple orchard, where they made camp. They took refuge in a foxhole while the Germans shelled them. Their destination was the village of Carentan, where they would relieve the 101st Airborne.

Germans shelled them at crossroads and they'd jump into ditches. They ran across every bridge, where they were especially vulnerable.

They camped at the edge of a pasture, filled with horses and cattle, "some still living, and some dead, bloated, and turned over on their backs with their legs sticking straight up." It was bad news when the wind blew in their direction. Frank watched as exploding shells caused a horse to jump sideways. "If battle fatigue could do that to a horse, I wondered what it could do to my men."

The fighting started at 4:00 A.M. on the Fourth of July, against a river island filled with storm troopers. Artillery and machine gun fire was exchanged by both sides. Frank was standing next to Staff Sergeant Clement when an 88-millimeter shell landed in front of him, "killing him instantly."

The first men returned from the front around noon. They had fought in close quarters and were repulsed by German guns and grenades. The attack had failed.

A lieutenant came looking for Frank: "Where's Captain Carmichael?" Frank heard it as a threat. He snuck up on the lieutenant and grabbed his arm, which was holding a pistol. The lieutenant, who had planned on killing Frank for what he saw as today's failure, was strapped to a stretcher and removed from the battlefield. Frank knew he'd have his hands full with the Germans—he hadn't expected it from his own men.

Earlier that morning he had jumped over a hedgerow and his foot landed on a rock. It swelled and turned black until he couldn't move it in any direction. It was midnight when Frank could finally seek medical attention. The doctor wrapped his left leg almost to the knee. Then he slapped Frank on the butt and told him he would make it.

A truck came for the dead the next day. "They were stacked in like stovewood—four to five deep." The driver had been drinking. Frank didn't say anything. "I guess he had to drink to endure his job."

Frank heard the wounded crying for help at night as shells fell into their camp. Frank's hands were shaking as he put them together in prayer: please, let me be strong for my men. He felt "a complete peace" and was never again shaken as before.

Frank and his men were sent to find Germans who had broken into American lines. They marched behind two tanks along a road "littered with German and some American dead." He watched the tanks crush the dead bodies and felt sick—"the worst sight I had ever seen."

They encountered the Germans at the village of Sainteny. The tank next to Frank was hit by a German shell and burst into flames. The men abandoned the tank. "Some were on fire and one had his leg torn off by the shell." Another shell landed nearby and knocked Frank unconscious.

Frank's ears were bleeding when he came to. He couldn't hear a sound. His telephone orderly "was dead, with a piece of shrapnel in his head." Another soldier had his "muscle blown off" and "two large gashes in his face." Major Holt was alive. Frank put his hand under the artery in Holt's arm and lifted him, and somehow they walked to the aid station. Frank tried to get back to the front. "Every time I tried to go toward the door, I went in another direction." The doctor grabbed him. He wasn't going anywhere.

Frank was loaded into an ambulance. As an aide closed the back door, he was hit by a shell and killed. The blast knocked

Frank out. He awoke—full of shrapnel—on top of the ambulance driver and his assistant. Frank was taken to another aid station, where the shrapnel was removed and he was given a tetanus shot. He was placed on a ship to Southampton.

Frank wanted to get back to his company. A doctor explained that his hearing loss could endanger his men on the battlefield. And another blast would leave him permanently deaf. Only then did he give up. He was sent to London and put to work censoring mail. It was surprising what men would try to write to their girlfriends and relatives, he thought.

Frank used the opportunity to write Sergeant Clement's widow with the details of her husband's death. Without letters like these, family members would often be left wondering how their loved one died. Clement's widow thanked him for supplying these missing details. And still, she wrote, every night she went to the front door and looked down the sidewalk expecting to see her husband, refusing to accept that he was gone.[1]

One soldier from Athens celebrated his twenty-first birthday in Normandy with a predawn attack across the Vire River. Though he didn't know when or whether he would get to use it, he realized that he now had the right to vote. A week later a package from home found its way to him.

It contained surprisingly fresh cookies and a letter from his mother: "I don't mean to worry you, but we had a little trouble last week. You know that deputy . . . he stopped your brother last week for reckless driving—Jimmy said he was driving fine—and wanted to take him to jail. Jimmy said he wasn't going, and the deputy hit him across the side of the face with his blackjack. It knocked him out, and he started bleeding bad enough to scare the deputy. Instead of arresting him, he stopped a car and made these people from Sweetwater take him to Doc Ed. Jimmy's OK now."

For the rest of the war, that soldier saw the deputy's face on every Nazi. He had to survive the war. He had to get home and make it right.[2]

23

"I DON'T KNOW WHICH WAY IS UP"

Camp Tarawa may have been up in the Hawaiian mountains, as far from sunshine and water as you could get, but the marines were having fun. There were boxing matches, baseball games, and even rodeos. Some of the big-city boys gave bull riding a try, with "many failures but no major casualties."[1]

At Camp Tarawa, a navy corpsman told Bill that a captain's orderly had taken a gun from the Japanese officer he had killed. They had given the orderly a Silver Star for what Bill had done. The corpsman was indignant. He wanted to go to the captain.

"It won't do no good to go to the captain," Bill said. The captain "wanted to find a way to give him a Silver Star. If they want to go around and punch their big chests out with medals hung all over that they didn't earn that's all right with me." Bill received a Purple Heart for being shot in the fight to the Tarawa airport.

Bill was promoted to corporal and would lead a sixteen-man squad into the next battle. They were "well-trained, good fighters," Bill said. "I really loved them. I just loved to be a squad leader."

On May 21, 1944, they boarded ships at Pearl Harbor and prepared to return to the fight. There was a sudden explosion, followed by others. A blast threw Bill into the water. Ships were on fire. Bill floated past "pieces of hot metal, some almost as big as a house." Bill was rescued after an hour in the water, shaken but otherwise fine. Nearly two hundred men had died and four hundred were injured. Six landing ships sank in the next twenty-four hours. The West Loch disaster was censored from the press and the men involved were ordered never to speak of it. The men who could explain its cause definitively were the first to perish. The official inquiry revealed that a shell had been dropped or accidentally ignited.

Bill was reassigned to light duty at the Naval Ammunition Depot.

One day a medical team came looking for him. "Where's Bill White?" they asked. "We're sending you back to the States." Bill wouldn't hear of it. He was going to lead a squad against the Japanese.

"Listen," they said, "you had malaria fever—hospitalized with it a dozen times. You've been wounded twice. We're sending you out of here." Bill had no say in the matter. "You have battle fatigue and would want to fight all the time."

"Well, so what?" Bill asked.[2]

A sharp-eyed Knoxville reporter noticed Representative George Woods hanging around city hall. Woods said he was there to talk to the city manager about laying concrete on the highway. "I'm not here on politics," he said. He was.

Congressman Jennings was the last elected official opposing the machine. He had beaten back their attempt to defeat him in the 1942 general election, thanks in part to the big Republican majority in his district. But what if the machine could get their own Republican? They'd recruit the mayor of Knoxville, the largest city in the district, to run against Jennings in a primary. Mayor E. E. Patton was promised votes and financial support from Paul Cantrell.[3]

John Anderson, Republican member of the election commission, published a letter to his Democratic colleagues, George Woods and Pat Mansfield, challenging them to hold a fair election in 1944: appoint "men of unimpeachable integrity," uninvolved in previous election problems; protect voter privacy by eliminating see-through ballots; do not allow armed men within ten feet of a polling place entrance; and post the absentee voter list.

Woods responded that the list had been posted on July 26, on the south side of the courthouse, in the "presence of several witnesses." He thanked Anderson for his help in holding "honest elections in McMinn County. We must and we will have honest elections." Meanwhile, Woods made a bet that Jennings would lose the county by one thousand votes.

Claude Hutsell challenged Pat Mansfield for sheriff. The Republicans could only find four candidates for office. Most races went uncontested. It was hard enough to get people to vote, much less run.[4]

Two elections were held on August 3, 1944: one for county offices, conducted by the machine, and another, a Republican primary for congress, conducted by the party.

Walter Calhoun was the Republican poll watcher at the courthouse precinct. His objections were ignored throughout the day as fifteen- and sixteen-year-olds walked in and voted. At one point bootlegger Clyde Davis dumped a batch of ballots into the box. Sheriff Mansfield and the Athens police chief were there and saw it happen. Calhoun recorded everything he'd seen on a pad of paper, including this latest incident. The deputies seized Calhoun and began roughing him up. Mansfield joined in and grabbed him around the waist. Another deputy took his left arm and wheeled it backward until it was ready to snap. "If you move I'll break your damn arm," said the deputy. Calhoun felt hands cover his face and others feeling up and down his body. His knife was removed.

Mansfield ordered him to "go over in the corner" and not write another word. "If I catch you over on this side anymore, I'll put you in the damn jail, and there you will stay." Mansfield ripped up his notes in front of him.

Six people entered the polling place at closing time, asserting their right to witness the count. They were ordered out, as well as Calhoun. A deputy grabbed him by the arm and shoved him out the door. "You don't have any damned right to be in here," he said, threatening to shoot him. The ballots would be counted in private. The results would be what the officer of election said they were.

John Walker was the poll watcher at Precinct 8. He thought it looked more like "an armed camp," with four deputies carrying pistols and blackjacks. At closing time, Deputy R. T. Bryan took the ballot box and locked himself in the school office. After some time had passed he returned and announced that the count would be held in the auditorium.

"You're calling the ballots wrong," said Walker, watching Republican votes called for Democratic candidates.

"I am doing this, you sit down," said Bryan. He continued, calling Democratic ballots twice and not calling Republican ballots. He sometimes called ballots by the handful.

Walker protested.

"If you don't sit down you'll be sorry for it."

Walker grabbed a Republican ballot that had been called for a Democrat and showed it to the Democratic election judges. "What are you going to do about it?" Walker asked. They said it was Bryan's call. Bryan's call was to have Walker arrested.

Game Warden Carl Neil was running Precinct 11. Two unknown gunmen stood all day on the sidewalk outside. Periodically, one would go inside to talk to Chief Deputy Boe Dunn.

The machine had the county election under control. But the Republican Party conducted its own primary. The machine leaders overestimated their ability to win an honest election, such as it ever was.

Robert Biggs, a Democratic hired gun, appeared at a Republican polling place in the afternoon: "How is the election going?"

"I don't know," said an election judge.

Biggs demanded to be let inside. H. E. Williams, a sixty-nine-year-old poll worker, informed him that he had no right to enter a Republican polling place.

Biggs, thirty years younger and weighing 220 pounds, struck Williams in the head with his pistol. Horace Reynolds, age seventy-five, tried to intervene.

"Damn you, I will kill you," he said to Reynolds, slamming his gun against his head. Biggs then aimed at Williams and fired point-blank. Williams managed to tap the gun with his cane, deflecting a likely fatal shot.

The bullet broke a window and went into the polling place.

A. C. Sawyer, who typically avoided politics because it was "not organized" and "not worth the trouble," was struck with broken glass as the bullet whizzed over his head. A group of deputies appeared and gently escorted Biggs away before things got worse. Horace Reynolds never recovered from his injuries, mentally or physically.[5]

Bessie Ballew and Mrs. J. P. Thompson were poll watchers at the Old Etowah Post Office. Thompson complained about the steady stream of underage voters and kept notes. Deputy Erwin White approached her "in a threatening manner" and said: "Do you know you are violating the law? You cannot write anything of that nature and take it out from the election."

At closing time White took the ballot box and walked out of the polling place. The ladies weren't going to let him get away with it. Thompson flew out the door after him. Cars were speeding past them in the middle of the busy street. He'd advance a little; she'd advance a little. They'd move forward or back to avoid getting hit by cars. Bessie was a few paces behind. Another car sped by and barely missed White, and Bessie was sure he was clear of Thompson. Thompson ran right in front of the car. Bessie thought she was about to see her friend get killed. Somehow she made it past. White reached the sidewalk with Thompson right behind him.

"Open the door," he yelled. The door to the Cantrell Bank Building cracked just enough to admit White and the ballot box and slammed in Thompson's face. After a few minutes, White's wife, who had no role in the election, opened the door and stood guard in front of it.

"Wait a minute," she said to Thompson and Bessie, who had now joined her. "Wait a minute, we'll let you in." Thompson tried to reach around her.

The door opened and they were all admitted. A ballot box was on the floor. Was it the one from the polling place, untampered? White had gone to a lot of trouble if it was.

The ballot box was opened, with absentee ballots placed on top of the ballots in the box. It was plain to see, thought Bessie, that all the absentee ballots had been filled out by no more than three people. Then there were the ballots that supposedly had been cast throughout the day. Beneath them, at the bottom of the box, was another layer of absentee ballots. Everyone in the room knew what had happened: this was a stuffed ballot box that had been swapped for the real one.[6]

Mansfield was declared the winner, 3,498 to 1,281. In 1934 turnout had been 8,590. In 1936, when Paul Cantrell won his first term, there were 9,662 votes; 10,932 in 1938; 12,516 in 1940; 7,409 in 1942; and now 4,779. The people of McMinn County were convinced their votes didn't matter—that somehow the machine would win in the end. It wasn't worth risking assault or arrest or retaliation for voting the wrong way.[7]

Jennings won the Republican primary 19,421 to 3,907, carrying every county. The Republicans were not interested in replacing their congressman with one handpicked by Democratic bosses.[8]

Jennings won McMinn 2,442 to 43, in an election conducted by the Republican Party that drew no complaints. In the county elections, held the same day and run by the machine, Republican Claude Hutsell received 1,281 votes for sheriff, for a difference of 1,161. Why would so many voters show up to support Congressman Jennings in his crusade against the machine but fail to vote against the machine itself? There are three possibilities: they were afraid to vote against Mansfield, they knew the election would be stolen regardless, or they did vote and had their votes discarded. All were undoubtedly at play.

Congressman Jennings and his allies collected one thousand affidavits of voter fraud and presented them to the Department of Justice. It would have been much higher, said Jennings, but for "fear of reprisal." Fred Stephenson was kept busy as the lone notary willing to witness these statements.[9]

The local grand jury declined to file charges arising from the 1944 election: not even for the assaults on seventy-five-year-old Horace Reynolds and sixty-five-year-old H. E. Williams. "It's legal to shoot Republicans," became the saying.[10]

The *Knoxville Journal* looked ahead to the November election: "Every Tennessean Concerned Should Adopt Slogan . . . Beat Cantrell; Beat Woods. [T]he only reason there has not been a bloody civil war fought during the past few years" in McMinn is that its citizens have not "followed [the machine's] lead in making force, in the form of firearms, the arbiter of the citizens' rights. Fortunately, however, human nature is so constituted that it will tolerate injustice, even when backed by force of arms, only so long."

There were rumblings of a "Ripper Bill" for Knox County, similar to the one that had given Cantrell dominance in McMinn and the one he had sponsored for Bradley. *The Knoxville News-Sentinel* reported that Cantrell and Biggs were "rapidly establishing a 'Little Shelby'" in East Tennessee.[11]

Governor Prentice Cooper was term limited. There had been a meeting with Paul Cantrell, Burch Biggs, and other East Tennessee bosses, like Wiley Couch of Chattanooga, to encourage Crump to make a pick from their region.

Cantrell traveled to Memphis to see Ed Crump in person.

Crump told him that this governor talk was "out of school" and "the sooner the situation was cleared up the better for all concerned."

Cantrell didn't appreciate Crump's heavy-handedness. He showed up in Knoxville on the night of the Republican Lincoln Day Dinner, knowing he'd find a number of party leaders. He pitched the idea of a fusion ticket for governor: disaffected Democrats and the Republicans united against whatever stooge could be found by Crump. The idea fell apart after a Republican state senator declared for the nomination.

Cantrell denied the entire affair as reported by the *News-Sentinel*. The newspaper pointed to a meeting he'd had in Sevier County with key Democrats and Republicans. "It is improbable," wrote the newspaper, "that the public will believe a group of well-known political figures gathered in a mountain cabin, months before the summer season, just to talk about the weather."[12]

Crump's endorsement of Jim McCord, one-term congressman and auctioneer, did not sit well with everyone in his network. But McCord won the Democratic primary for governor, 132,466 to 11,659 to 4,510. He won 22,022 votes in Shelby County, compared to 436 for his opponents. Cantrell delivered McCord a margin of 2,161 to 137 in McMinn. There would be other opportunities in the future to be Crump's candidate or to be the nominee of his own political faction.

Crump bragged that McCord's election was his 101st win in forty-two years, which he said must be a record.[13]

Les Dooley started the war commanding antitank guns over Casablanca. His last posting was as manager of a hotel. The Grove Park resort in Asheville, North Carolina, was one of several that had been converted to military use. Men returning from war could stay there free of charge, with their wives if married. After months or years of hell, they would get a few days of luxury to transition to civilian life. The ten-day stay consisted of classes on the GI Bill of Rights, physical assessments, relaxation, and recovery. "I wonder if I'm dreaming," said the wife of a returning GI. "It's all like a fairy story." For Dooley, who had lost his left arm in Africa, it gave him a chance to continue to serve.[14]

Ralph Duggan had been commissioned in the navy in the summer of 1942. He'd received high marks for intelligence, judgment, and moral authority. "Extremely dependable . . . conscientious," wrote one reviewer. "Well qualified for administrative work," wrote another. Duggan wanted a combat role, but found himself assigned to the assistant discipline officer at the Bureau of Naval Personnel. He had been stationed at Hollywood, Florida; Savannah; and Boston. But from the start he had requested a destroyer in the Pacific. He failed at his first attempt to qualify for a combat specialty. "He has worked hard but his scholastic background severely handicapped him," wrote one instructor. Duggan excelled at the other courses but failed ordnance and navigation. He was on leave from Beach Battalion School in August when he visited with his wife, Claudia, in Chicago at the Drake Hotel. With her was his son, whom he met for the first time. The visit went far too fast, he thought. Duggan wrote her a letter that would be waiting when she got home:

"My Darling, being with you was wonderful, but it has made me so homesick I feel like taking the next train back. I don't know which way is up. And our boy is the finest youngster I ever saw. I don't deserve such a fine wife and boy and I feel very humble and proud. We have so very much to look forward to."

Unwritten, never far from his mind, was the political situation back home. He telegrammed Congressman Jennings his "best wishes for an overwhelming victory," which "because of your record in attempting to restore honesty and decency in government is well deserved." But first up were the Japanese. He was finally getting his chance to see combat, as a deck officer aboard the USS *Leonard Wood,* headed for the liberation of the Philippines.[15]

24

"KILLED IN THE SERVICE OF HIS COUNTRY IN ATHENS, TENNESSEE"

SEPTEMBER 25, 1944

Earl Ford, a navy Seabee, was happy to be home after sixteen months. It was his first night of leave and he wanted a drink and to hear some music. He and Luke Miller, another sailor, went to the Halfway Court, two miles out of Athens on the Sweetwater Road. Ford asked to use the telephone, which was in plain view. They told him they didn't have one. Ford got up to leave. His friend went with him.

Deputy Minus Wilburn thought they looked like easy marks. Servicemen always had money. He'd arrest them and pocket a nice fee. He deputized George Spurling and Clyde Davis, notorious criminals both, as officers of the law in order to assist him in making an arrest. They caught up with the sailors in the parking lot.

Spurling clubbed Ford repeatedly over the head. Ford, stumbling, backed up, his hands raised in surrender. "Don't move or I'll blow you in two," said Spurling. Ford didn't move. Spurling shot him in the chest from ten feet away. Ford staggered, struggling to stand, trying to comprehend what was happening to him. Earl Ford fell to the ground, where he was left for twenty minutes. Ford was pronounced dead at Foree Hospital.

Sheriff Mansfield defended the shooting to the newspaper: Wilburn "undertook to subdue a bunch of disorderly sailors and others, and deputized Spurling and others on the scene to help him." Mansfield claimed that they had pulled Ford off Spurling's back and that Ford had charged Spurling with a knife. Why hadn't anyone else seen the knife?

Wilburn claimed the knife was found under Ford's body. He did not explain how a knife, held out in front of a man, could wind up behind and under him when he was shot. W. O. Swindler, a cattleman from South Carolina, was traveling through town with his son and didn't know anyone involved. They were the first to come to Ford's aid. Neither saw any weapons anywhere near the body. A doctor who came outside the Halfway Court and attempted to save Ford's life saw no weapon. In fact, Ford was wearing a sailor's uniform with no pockets, and had nowhere to conceal a knife. Two witnesses told a reporter that Ford "never did offer threat or resistance to Spurling."[1]

Ford's funeral attracted "one of the largest crowds ever to assemble in Decatur." His epitaph reads: "Killed in the service of his country in Athens, Tennessee." Ford's family pushed for Spurling's prosecution. Trial was scheduled for October. Luke Miller, who had been blackjacked by Wilburn, was still in the hospital and couldn't testify. The sheriff's office told the newspaper that he'd be arrested for resisting arrest upon his release—an unsubtle threat to keep him off the witness stand.[2]

The machine controlled law enforcement. They controlled the courts. They controlled elections. If they could murder an active-duty sailor in the middle of World War II and get away with it, then they could kill anyone. And who was going to stop them?

Bill White arrived on the MS *Kota Agoeng* from Pearl Harbor to San Francisco on Columbus Day, October 8, 1944. An actor dressed as the explorer landed in an amphibious jeep and led a parade through Union Square to the Civic Center.

Bill had been gone for more than two years. He had dreamed of leading men on the drive to Tokyo. Now he was headed in the exact opposite direction, to teach jungle warfare on Parris Island. Bill laughed when he realized that he "wasn't much different" from the drill instructors he'd hated in boot camp.[3]

25

"THE AMERICAN WAY OF LIFE"

NOVEMBER 8, 1944

Congressman Jennings sent an urgent wire to the attorney general: George Woods, in his capacity as election commissioner, claimed to have fifteen hundred absentee ballots, and "profanely refused" when asked for the voter list. "Unless you put FBI men on this gigantic fraud at once it will be consummated and all evidence of the names and residences of these alleged voters will be destroyed. Please reply." He heard nothing back.

Woods won reelection by eleven hundred votes, less than the number of absentee ballots he controlled as election commissioner. Knox County, with nearly ten times the population of McMinn, had only three hundred absentee voters that year.

The stress of his duties in the House and the fight for fair elections were getting to Jennings. He collapsed in the dining room of the House of Representatives. "Overwork" was said to be the cause. He was expected to make a full recovery.[1]

George Woods became the new Speaker of the Tennessee House, with the backing of the governor-elect, McCord.

The *Knoxville Journal* called Woods "a politician who symbol-izes as vicious and un-American election practices as are to be found in the United States." Woods called the *Journal* a "scandal sheet."[2]

On January 9, Tennessee legislators gave speeches attacking the press for its critical coverage of McMinn County, Ed Crump, and George Woods.

Senator Paul Cantrell said he was "mighty proud" of his af-filiation with Ed Crump's Shelby organization. He referred to Congressman Jennings as "a red-necked man" and claimed that he had not told the truth about elections in McMinn.

Woods shouted his speech into the microphone, bragging of his wins in a Republican county: "I admit I am affiliated with the Biggs and Cantrell organization in East Tennessee and the Crump machine on the banks of the Mississippi," he said. "I am proud to be a member of the Biggs-Cantrell Machine."[3]

Senator Cantrell "voted straight down the groove with Memphis." But he also worked on some worthwhile issues. One of his bills required accreditation for fly-by-night business schools that charged high tuition while offering limited job prospects. Another addressed unfairness in workman's compensation—giving the worker a say in picking a physician to review their claim rather than one provided by the employer. These were the kinds of issues that had propelled Paul Cantrell into politics. If he regretted the means he used to gain power, or the time he spent holding on to power in favor of advancing these policies, those thoughts are unknown.[4]

Speaker Woods introduced a bill to repeal the rules for ab-sentee balloting, the ones he hadn't been following anyway.

Congressman Jennings said it would "sanction election thefts" and "rob the honest people of their right to honest elections." He said McMinn elections are "a stench in the nostrils of the decent people of Tennessee and have long since assumed the proportions of a national scandal," and should be exposed to the "pitiless light of publicity."[5]

Woods also redrew the congressional map of Tennessee for the sole purpose of removing McMinn from Jennings's district. But they were mistaken if they thought they were rid of him.[6]

"I wish you to always feel that I am your representative," Jennings wrote to Clay Matlock in Athens. "I shall never forget the loyal, unselfish, and fearless fight that you all have made, as you say, 'to restore in your county the American Way of life.'"[7]

Two weeks later, the American way of life secured victory in Europe with the surrender of Nazi Germany.

Bill White was at Parris Island, training marines for the invasion of Japan, when he learned that Grandpa Wiggins had died. Bill returned to Tennessee for the funeral—his first trip home in more than three years. His father sent him to the rationing board to get stamps for the drive into the mountains.

Gasoline was rationed not for its own sake, but to preserve the rubber in tires. Nearly fifty thousand Sherman tanks had been built for the war, each requiring half a ton of rubber. A battleship had twenty thousand rubber parts. America had a two-month supply when the war began, and 90 percent of the world's rubber was controlled by Japan.[8]

Bill walked to the Fisher Building, where Robert Fisher,

president of the local rationing board and owner of a hosiery mill, sat behind the desk that had been his duty station during the war.

Bill asked for five gallons of gas.

No, said Fisher. "Don't you know there's a war going on?"

Bill considered a number of responses, none of which would get him closer to his grandpa's funeral. He gave Fisher a look: "Well, I just want five gallons."

"You can't have it."

"Alright," Bill said. "That's alright."

Leaving the Fisher Building he saw a friend on the street. He told him that he needed gas, but "ration boy wouldn't let me have it."

"Well that's easy, Bill," said his friend. "There stands the chief of police," he said, pointing. "Give him five dollars and he'll give it to you."

Bill ordered ten gallons, twice as much as he needed, rather than risk this humiliation a second time. He watched as the police chief calmly counted out his stamps and put Bill's money directly in his pocket.

Bill told his father the story when he came home. His father, it turned out, had a story for him, one that had happened while Bill was away. Edd White was proud and quiet, a cavalryman of the First World War. He walked five miles a day to work at the power station on Railroad Avenue. He carried his lunch in a brown paper bag and a pint of milk from Mayfield's Dairy. While walking past the jail on his way home he saw four deputies stare at him, get in a car, and start the engine. As he walked past the courthouse, the car was in the middle of the street, following him. He lowered his head and kept walking. He walked past the bus station and they were right alongside him. Edd picked up the pace. They accelerated. He didn't know what they wanted with him or why. But he knew it wasn't good. He panicked and started running to his house. The car pulled in front of him and slammed on its brakes. Four deputies jumped out with clubs in their hands. He was arrested and taken to jail. Now it was time to figure out a reason. The deputies took his milk bottle out of the bag and passed it around, taking a sniff. "Smells funny," they agreed. The deputies who protected the roadhouses and honky-tonks and lined their pockets with kickbacks from bootleggers and pimps decided the remnant of Edd White's milk was alcohol. He was fined $16.05, several days' pay.

The situation back home had been "a big surprise" to Bill. His family had consciously left it out of letters. "I had plenty of worries over there," Bill said. Now he was home, and "everything, everything, *everything* you've been told you're supposed to be fighting for wasn't there."[9]

Bill said good-bye to Grandpa Wiggins at the country chapel in Hopewell. Time and mountain weather had wiped out the writing on most of the graves in the old churchyard. The cemetery's longest residents were marked simply by rocks. Grandpa Wiggins was buried next to Grandma, who had died five years earlier. "Asleep in Jesus," read their simple gravestone.[10]

As a young man Carl Anderson had broken the Hindenburg line, the supposedly impenetrable barrier of concrete, steel, and barbed wire defended by the best of the kaiser's army. Now he worked as a grocer and served as a major in the state guard. He was a Democrat, an Athens alderman unaffiliated with the machine, whose son, Carl Anderson Jr., was a German prisoner of war. Major Anderson formed a nonpartisan Citizens Ticket to oppose the machine majority on the Athens City Council. Anderson ran for mayor in 1945 on a pledge to have city council meetings (which hadn't happened for four months) and to open them to the public.

Anderson's newspaper ad dissected Mayor Paul Walker's record. Walker boasted of bringing in competent auditors. Yes, Anderson agreed, and they found "the city suffered greatly by comparison with former years."

Anderson's Citizens Ticket touted their independence from any "clique, organization, or individual" and freedom to "act for the best interests of the people of Athens."

Deputy Minus Wilburn served as officer of election with police officers patrolling the courthouse. Mayor Walker won by a margin of 861–154.[11]

Jimmy Lockmiller, seventeen, who had run away to California and returned to Athens to enlist in the marines, was on guard duty on Guadalcanal on the night of August 6, 1943. He had barely slept for months. Lockmiller had gotten malaria and was given a medication known to cause psychosis. He became "greatly agitated and disturbed." He was relieved from duty and put to bed. A medical corpsman went to check on him and determined he had "shell shock."

Lockmiller was taken to a mobile navy hospital. Lockmiller said he was "exhausted and had not been able to sleep on the ship coming over and had been overworked while at Guadalcanal." He was sent to hospitals in San Francisco and Fort Worth and was honorably discharged on January 1, 1944. The newspaper took note of his numerous medals, and wrote that "Jimmy was delighted to be home and his family are delighted to have him, but he speaks about his experience reluctantly." The truth was, Jimmy was sick about being back.[12]

Jimmy was hired at Oak Ridge National Laboratory, near Knoxville, as a security guard. He didn't know what they were working on, but it was clearly something important. Security was tight—everyone had to wear badges with different levels of access, and the entire place was under lock and key. Most of the employees lived on-site. He turned out to be protecting the headquarters for the Manhattan Project. The atomic bomb that emerged was unleashed on Hiroshima and Nagasaki in the first week of August 1945. This devastation triggered the surrender of Japan on August 15, and with it the end of the war. In his own way, Jimmy Lockmiller had seen through to completion the conflict he had been eager to join and unwilling to leave.[13]

Ralph Duggan came back to Athens, his wife, son, law practice, and political problems in November 1945. "I am delighted to know Ralph is back," Congressman Jennings wrote to Holland Vestal, "because he is able and determined to right the wrongs you have labored under, and is unafraid."[14]

Major Anderson, who had tried and failed to beat the machine at the Athens city elections, sought Duggan out. Anderson was a Democrat, Duggan a Republican. Why didn't they work together? The two men stayed in touch in the final days of 1945.[15]

Bill White roughly reentered civilian life six weeks after the surrender of Japan. "I'd slug you in a New York minute if you even said 'howdy' to me," Bill said. "You better not look at me wrong, because you would have to pick yourself off the floor." He didn't want to talk to anyone he'd served with. "I done already seen all I wanted to see of them." At night in his boyhood room in Athens he could hear the screams of the marines who were burned on the first day of war at Tanambogo beach.

Bill had longed for his bed, but after so many nights on the ground he couldn't get comfortable. He lay on the floor instead. Bill was hypersensitive to his surroundings. In the jungle this meant survival. At home it meant he couldn't sleep, with the dog moving around the house or someone walking in downtown Athens, two blocks away. And then there were the hogs, who tore up the corn patch he'd planted in the yard. Bill couldn't fire a gun in the city limits and it wasn't hog season. He made a wooden spear, like the Solomon Islanders had taught him, taking a stick and hardening the end over a fire. And he waited for the pigs to come back.

Bill's experiences were familiar to many of the 6.3 million who returned to civilian life by the end of 1945. And they were the lucky ones—the rest were still under arms and anxious to return. A rally of twenty thousand servicemen in Manila demanded to go home. A general addressed them by radio, promising their replacements would come as soon as possible. He was noisily booed. Dwight Eisenhower was "waylaid" en route to testify before Congress by a group of wives demanding he give back their husbands.[16]

A poet in *Stars and Stripes* wrote:

> *Please, Mr. Truman, won't you send us home?*
> *We have captured Napoli and liberated Rome.*

We have licked the master race.
Now there's lots of shipping space.
So, won't you send us home?
Let the boys at home see Rome.[17]

26

THE BEST YEAR OF THEIR LIVES

The New Year's Day edition of the *Daily Post-Athenian* reflected the optimism of the moment. In each corner of the front page a dove carried a banner in its mouth: "Peace 1946."

The prominent image was a husband and wife sitting on a couch with their backs to the reader. His arm is around her shoulders. They're looking at images of long-sought consumer goods, as the mighty American economy that had obliterated the Axis powers directed its focus toward a future of ease over hardship, abundance over scarcity, peace instead of war.

"The New Year is the one we've been waiting for," read the caption, "the year when reconversion will be completed and production brings realization of the war years' dream of a new washing machine, a new refrigerator, car, bicycle, camera, and whatnot—including NYLONS!"

Lowell Arterburn, publisher of the *Post-Athenian*, shared his thoughts in a front-page column, on the "significant" year that had passed, the war that "will be imbedded in our minds as long as we live," and the challenges ahead: "1946 begins as every year does, with a question mark. And it is well to remember that you and I and the rest of the common people–by God's grace—alone hold the answer."

The first McMinn baby of the year was born to the Moses family, a girl, arriving at 6:15 A.M. and weighing seven and a half pounds. Liza Reeps was the last to die, peacefully, on the afternoon of New Year's Eve, at the end of a good long life. She had been born in 1855, during the presidency of Franklin Pierce, six years before the Civil War.

Even the fearsome weaponry that ended the war seemed less scary. An article announced groundbreaking potential for atomic power in domestic life. It found its way into department store advertising, like the "Atomic Flash" sale on fur coats at Miller's. While 70 percent of Americans had never set foot on an airplane, people talked openly of a day when man would walk on the moon.[1]

Americans had more in their savings accounts than the entire national income of 1932. Multiplied by three. In the Depression they'd had no money, and in the war years nothing to spend it on. Now, businesses like Southern Bell ran ads apologizing for not meeting demand.

Housing was especially scarce, but once developed would be easier to own than ever before. Athens Federal Savings advertised the new fixed mortgage, with rates dropping from 6 percent to 4 percent and from prewar terms of three to five years to twenty years, "or perhaps even longer."

"Home Again!" The *Time* magazine headline above soldiers in a Pullman car gave movie mogul Samuel Goldwyn an idea. More than fifteen million people had come home or were on their way—that's a lot of movie tickets! He ordered a script about returning veterans.

What would they call this new movie? Someone proposed *The Best Years of Our Lives.* Goldwyn was skeptical. He hired Gallup to ask the public: When is the best time to be alive? The answers surprised him: "This year—right now," said one respondent. "My husband's come home from the army, I'm having a baby. . . . If I don't have any more years, this one is fine." Said another: "Oh boy, this last year will be hard to beat. Got discharged from the army, got married, got back into college."[2]

The news was filled with happy stories. Like that of Verne Tobias, introduced by mail to the sister of his friend while they served in the South Pacific. The two corresponded for three years until their well-publicized meeting. The wedding was scheduled for March 9, with *Life* magazine picking up the tab.

One soldier dropped his train ticket for the next leg of his journey home while walking to the dining car. The ticket blew and landed in the handrail on the side of the baggage car of a train miles behind him. The conductor found the ticket and wired ahead to let the station know. "Boy am I lucky," the soldier said.[3]

Jacklyn Lucas, who had enlisted at fourteen and became the war's youngest Medal of Honor winner at seventeen, returned to high school. He slept in his car before learning that arrangements had been provided for him.[4]

Russell Horton was one of four GIs making headlines for wanting to marry a German and bring her home. "You can't put love on a political basis," said Horton. "It's nature. You can fight nature for fifty years, but you won't win. I'm going to have my Trudy." If Americans and Germans were getting married, maybe anything was possible.[5]

The census estimated "a big jump in the birth rate," from the 1946 population of 140 million to five million more by 1950. The

Department of Agriculture advised farmers to plant ten million more acres.[6]

Hitler's charred remains had been found. He had dragged the world into a war where tens of millions had lost their lives, but now there was peace, and this was all that was left of him. His cohorts were on trial for war crimes or hiding for their lives.

Tennessee Wesleyan College was quickly building housing for new students. Twenty GIs were expected in the spring, among the first of 2.3 million veterans to start college over the next five years.[7]

Business leaders formed the Athens Chamber of Commerce. The heads of Proffitt's Department Store, Athens Plow, Ketron Department Store, M&N Food, McSpadden Furniture, and Harrod's Thrift Market founded the new organization, hoping to boost the local economy.

A new city bus would carry passengers for ten cents, a welcome change from walking. Only 139 cars had been built in America during the entire war.[8]

Chuck Redfern embodied the postwar optimism of McMinn County. He'd served as a marine combat correspondent in the South Pacific and publisher of his battalion newspaper. In civilian life he wanted to try journalism with fewer explosions. He interviewed with the *Post-Athenian* to serve as the first broadcaster on their new radio station, WLAR, which would go live in the spring. He was told when he took the job: "These are friendly folks, but they take their religion and politics very serious." Redfern, an Illinois native, jumped at the chance to live in Athens and raise his family there. He wrote an introductory column for the *Post-Athenian:*

"For the life of me I just can't see how this community, with its friendly people, can fail in anything it sets its heart to. In the service I didn't have an opportunity to save many pennies, but every single one that I have, I'm going to invest in this community. I'm buying stock in a spirit, and I like it. However, if I'm wrong and go broke, I can always say, thank God for my brother Orem, he's always been broke."[9]

Throughout McMinn County there were special church services for GIs. A newspaper column marked the discharge and arrivals of veterans, along with a summary of their service and how long they had been away (usually years). They had every reason to believe they had returned to an honored place in society.

The world in the opening days of 1946 seemed wondrous, especially to the war weary. But history does not offer permanent happy endings. Some are short. Others are long. And some are illusory.

Verna Gregory of Athens traveled to Fort Oglethorpe, Georgia, to receive a posthumous Bronze Star for her son. Dorothy Sykes, also of Athens, had held out hope every day for the past year for her husband, declared missing in action. He was now confirmed dead in Germany.

And then there were the men who did make it back. Paul Weeks woke up screaming in the middle of the night and terrified his young family. Carl Anderson Jr., talking to his little sister, watched a roach crawl by, and nearly grabbed and ate it out of instinct. He had weighed eighty-eight pounds when freed from a German POW camp.

Nearly half of the GIs believed the war had changed their lives for the worse. Another 6 percent knew that their lives had changed but weren't sure how. Only 24 percent said that it had made their lives better. Fifty-two percent of those who hadn't served said the war had not changed their lives, while a majority of the rest said that it had changed their lives for the better.[10]

Eleanor Roosevelt, speaking to one thousand war brides in London, said, "Just remember that what you do not see is very hard to imagine, and try to be patient."[11]

The county court met in a "short session" and reelected Paul Cantrell as chairman. Some of the older people in attendance remembered these meetings stretching for hours with multiple ballots. Now they picked a chairman, vice chairman, county attorney, and county engineer as fast as they could vote.[12]

The trial of George Spurling for the murder of Earl Ford was continued again, until July.

Bill White was shocked by the way the sheriff's men were "harassing people, abusing people." They knew which day of the month GIs received payments and stepped up arrests accordingly. "We were used to drinking our liquor and our beer without being molested," said Bill. "The more GIs they arrested, the more they beat up, the madder we got." They had hung out in bars across the country and around the world—the only place they'd had any trouble was right here at home. From the "people you were trying to save," he said.[13]

Deputies grabbed GIs right off the dance floor at the Halfway Court. Sometimes they'd pay their $16.05 fine and come right back. The joke became that the five cents was the county's share. The arrests were made for profit, but the rough "going over" that often came along with them was for fun.[14]

Sometimes deputies, lazy or efficient, depending on one's perspective, would walk into a bar and announce: "You're all drunk and under arrest." Every last patron would be loaded into police cars and taken to the jail. They began arresting passengers in vehicles instead of just the driver. Worse still were "siren bandits," law enforcement who would pull over motorists and simply rob them.[15]

Meanwhile, the deputies ignored the actual lawbreaking around them, as long as "protection payments" were made on time. "It was a big surprise," said Bill. "Liquor houses," "whorehouses," "gambling joints all over the county." All enforced by "a bunch of thugs wearing guns and badges."[16]

Pete Saulpans was a McMinn native who moved to Toledo, Ohio. He was stunned in the years that followed that nobody had thrown him in jail—or even threatened to. He had once been arrested by R. T. Bryan for "talking too much." He realized what "a dirty bunch of thugs and cut throats" ran his hometown. "Al Capone is a gentleman, compared."[17]

Tourist agencies around the country "advised motorists against stopping" in McMinn. "Some even drew a red circle on the dot on the map and wrote 'Beware' alongside of it." Visitors didn't have a chance.

The jail was an imposing fortress in downtown Athens. People would walk a block out of their way to avoid going past, lest they be arrested by a lazy deputy. The sidewalk was cracked in front of the jail, and anyone who tripped was certain to see the inside on a charge of public drunkenness. Prisoners remembered its "sickening stench," the air thick with flies, sleeping on "uncovered mattresses. . . . black with dirt," filthy blankets, "huge cobwebs," and "peeling paint." The kitchen was "a dirty, nauseating disgrace." The money not spent on the housing and feeding of prisoners went straight into the sheriff's pocket.[18]

Bill White took the entrance exam and was admitted to Tennessee Wesleyan. He hoped to learn photography and started the season on the football team. "I didn't fit in with the other students," he said. "A man that's been through all that . . . I was out of place with all them kids. They didn't understand me and I didn't understand them." Bill left school after a semester and found work at Olan Mills studios, traveling town to town and taking family photos.[19]

27

IN THE BASEMENT OF THE ROBERT E. LEE HOTEL

The term "GI" originally meant "galvanized iron." It came to stand for "government issue." Emblazoned on all kinds of gear, GI became a term for enlisted men in the army. More men had served in the army than the navy and Marine Corps combined. Thus, GI grew to be a generic term for all veterans of the late war.[1]

McMinn County was scene to a jubilant, rolling reunion, as one or more GIs seemed to come home daily. There were welcome-home parties almost every night. Spontaneous embraces happened in the streets and sidewalks as old friends saw each other for the first time in years. Happy to be alive. Happy to see their friends alive. In many cases these encounters were the first confirmation that their friends had survived. The newspapers were filled with wedding and birth announcements as GIs raced to make up for the years the war had taken.

For the most part, veterans were still in uniform. Despite their eagerness to return to civilian life, wartime cloth rationing was still in effect and these were the only clothes that fit. The *Post-Athenian* reported "few new shirts" had arrived in stores in the first three months of 1946. Shortly before Christmas 1943, Charles Quality Cleaners had been destroyed by fire, and some had lost the only nice clothes they had, which still hadn't been replaced. Jimmy Lockmiller was a sartorial standout, sporting a fashion he had picked up in the Pacific—the Hawaiian shirt.[2]

Their shared service made the GIs closer, despite years and thousands of miles apart, than they had been as students and teammates. GIs who were otherwise strangers were often more comfortable talking to each other than their own families.

Bill Grubb was happy to be back in Athens after four months in an Okinawa navy hospital. A friend invited him to join the Veterans of Foreign Wars meeting in the courthouse. Grubb thought they needed a place of their own and had an idea.

Paul Walker was the mayor of Athens and boss at the Robert E. Lee Hotel. Grubb had caddied for Walker at the country club and delivered his newspaper as a boy. He asked if they had a spot for the GIs. Walker had a room that might work—an underground space from the days of Prohibition. It hadn't gotten much use in recent years, since people could drink upstairs, and was filthy, Walker said. But it was theirs.

The VFW sold so many memberships, they ran out of forms and resorted to blank sheets of paper. Grubb found the best way to sign up a member was to say, "If you don't have five dollars one of us will pay it for you."

Local businesses chipped in to get the GIs settled: Nehi Bottling provided an icebox and soda; twelve chairs apiece came from the Evans and Quisenberry Funeral Homes; four cases of beer from the Sterling Beer distributor; and three round tables from Slim Armstrong.[3]

There, the GIs could relax and tell stories without fear of arrest by Pat Mansfield's deputies. Joseph Frye Jr. had become the most powerful man in France for a week when his unit liberated the Rémy Martin distillery in Cognac; Felix Harrod, a B-24 pilot, had been ready to crash-land in the Adriatic when his crew managed to change the engine in midair; and Carl Anderson nearly had his finger chopped off when he refused to give the Germans his wedding ring. Tom Dooley had somehow acquired a monkey, which he brought to the bars and the VFW.

But the war stories and confessions and laying out big plans for the future kept leading back to the problems they had at home.

"It wasn't really a town anymore," said Jim Buttram. "It was a jail." He'd fought his way through Tunisia, Sicily, and Normandy, and was wounded twice, all in the name of democracy he didn't have in Athens.[4]

Ralph Duggan thought it was "like Nazi Germany," run by deputies who "were nothing but a lot of swaggering, strutting, storm-troopers, drunk most of the time, beating up our citizens for the slightest reason."[5]

Bill Hamby, a captain in the South Pacific, said, "If you were on the right team, why, you could get away with almost anything. If you were on the wrong team, you couldn't get away with anything."[6]

The situation was intolerable. They were all agreed. Now what were they going to do about it?

28

"A THORN IN THE FLESH"

MARCH 20, 1946

Paul Cantrell jolted McMinn politics by announcing a campaign for sheriff. Pat Mansfield, he said, would run for his seat in the state senate. Why would a legislator with eyes on the governor's mansion seek his old job? Cantrell's family, his brothers and sisters and their children who spent Sundays gathered on the porch, were dead set against the idea. But there were home fires that needed tending, and the loss of his ticket at home would put an end to his ambitions statewide.

Cantrell had another surprise a week later. He was dropping Clyde Rogers, county court clerk, from his ticket. Boe Dunn, chief deputy sheriff, would run in his place.

The Rogers family were among Paul Cantrell's earliest backers. John, Clyde's father, had taken a ballot box home for lunch in 1940 and returned with a shotgun to count it in secret. In 1942 he had filled out ballot after ballot for voters claiming to be blind. Clyde, the former Etowah policeman, had sent poll watchers to the back of the room at gunpoint while he counted the ballots,

before being rewarded with a countywide office. There was another act of election fraud, one not as public, that they would
own up to before this fight was through.

Clyde had noticed Cantrell was avoiding him. Then Cantrell
asked for a meeting under the pretense of getting his signature
on court paperwork. There, he said: "I am against you, and all
for Boe Dunn."

Clyde asked for an explanation.

Cantrell said that Clyde had spoken badly of him in conversations.

Clyde asked if he had "forgotten so soon how you were
elected to the office of sheriff?"

"No, but I'm still against you."

As one newspaper put it, the Rogers family would become
"a thorn in the flesh to the machine." Clyde announced that
he would challenge Cantrell for sheriff. His campaign revealed
the machine's dirty laundry in a series of newspaper ads, giving
McMinn citizens a rare look inside their government. Clyde told
the voters that he wasn't running for revenge, but "because I feel
that you are completely exasperated with one person rule and
that you believe in fairness to all." He pointed to the heavy tax
burden, a $5.5 million budget, and the need to float high-interest
bonds just to keep the schools open. Clyde argued that Cantrell
had personally collected $109,104 during his six years as sheriff.
And Mansfield, after only three and a half years, had put $98,906
in his pocket. Clyde said that he had refused to turn over taxpayer
money to fund the machine's campaign, an act that contributed
to his being dropped from the ticket. He promised to limit himself to a five-thousand-dollar salary.[1]

Clyde acknowledged that some of the same bad practices

predated Paul Cantrell. "However," wrote Clyde, "we thought we were electing a man to office in 1936 who would make some changes." Instead, the sheriff's office and its deputies pocketed $335,291.50 in ten years.

"I make a confession to the citizens of McMinn County, one of which I am not, in the least, proud nor boastful," wrote Clyde. "Mr. Cantrell was elected to the Sheriff's office ONE WAY. My father and I can answer that publicly or privately because we put him in office and power and also he offered either of us any position that we desired."

If asked—and they were—here is the story John and Clyde Rogers told: It was the election of August 1936. John had been officer of election at a polling place in Etowah. At lunchtime he invited the judges and clerks to his house; free meals at the height of the Depression were seldom declined. They took the ballot box to an empty room in the Rogers home and watched as he locked the door. When they were done, he unlocked the door, took the ballot box as everyone watched, and brought it back to the polling place. Clyde Rogers had been hiding in the closet with a stuffed ballot box, and made the swap while everyone was eating. The officials brought the stuffed box back to the polling place. Democratic voters were told to wait until after lunch to cast their votes.[2]

"We have just ended World War II," wrote Clyde, "in order to have freedom from oppression and dictatorship. If we allow our present administration to remain in power we are not ending Hitlerism in McMinn County.

"When has it been the policy of Democrats to allow ONE MAN to say who the candidates are to be in our elections? I ask the question, are the Democrats of this county going to allow such people to remain in power?"[3]

Speaker George Woods chaired the "largest crowd ever to attend a Democratic convention" at McMinn High School. Cantrell and Rogers were placed in nomination for sheriff. Clyde was booed and hissed and defeated 669–95.

Jim Buttram, Shy Scott, Felix Harrod, Les Dooley, and other GIs went from informal conversations to formal meetings on challenging the machine. The wealthiest man in town wouldn't help—Paul Walker, his son-in-law, was the mayor of Athens and owed his spot to the machine. A retired state supreme court judge, one of the most respected men in town, said he couldn't get involved. Pastors, with a couple exceptions, "assured the boys they were with them," but they couldn't act on account of "members of the Cantrell machine in their congregations."

The young GIs were undeterred. They connected with Ralph Duggan and Major Anderson, and slowly the opposition came together. They didn't tell their wives. They didn't tell their parents. They were concerned about their personal safety. Phone communications were conducted in code. They met in secret—in barns, in offices, at people's houses—never in the same place twice. "It got to the point where decent citizens were not safe on the streets if they had said anything against the Cantrell organization," said Buttram.[4]

29

THE BALLAD OF OTTO KENNEDY

Sheriff J. P. Kennedy of Monroe County was a scrupulously honest lawman, a regional rarity in East Tennessee. "Absolutely fearless, and always cool headed," Kennedy "enjoyed the reputation of always getting his man." Even criminals found him hard not to like, as he wouldn't steal from them or beat them up. It was a tough place to police—the kind where a newspaper editor, critical of bootleggers, found himself doused in the gasoline he used to clean type and set on fire. Kennedy had been shot twice in his time on the job.

On March 18, 1930, Kennedy took in a school play with his family and went to bed early. He was heading to Chattanooga the next morning to follow a lead in a burglary investigation. The phone rang at 2:00 A.M.: someone had broken into the Madisonville Grocery. Kennedy rushed to the store and approached from the back. The first gunshot hit him in the right shoulder. Another tore "a great hole in his left breast." He died instantly.

The official story was that store manager Albert Jenkins had arrived shortly before Sheriff Kennedy, and mistaking him for the burglar, shot him. The Kennedy family never believed it.

Otto Kennedy was J. P.'s oldest son. The Kennedys were fully Irish, but his narrow forehead, hairy arms, and facial features gave Otto a Mediterranean look. He was the foreman at a Michigan tin factory, and married to Myrtle, with a daughter named after his wife. Otto returned to Sweetwater to bury his father and stayed to look after his family's interests. First up, stopping his father's enemies from completing their victory by installing one of their own as sheriff. The county court, controlled by Democrats and hostile to Kennedy, insisted on picking his replacement on the day of his funeral. Otto and his brother Bull were at the meeting with their preferred candidate for sheriff—their mother, Esther. The court picked a Democrat, as expected. As the meeting ended, Tom McMurray, the local high school principal, insulted Esther and her recently deceased husband. He quickly found himself on the ground. A "free for all fight" broke out in the courtroom. Otto and Bull whipped anyone with something to say, and a few of the court members who had voted against their mother for good measure.

The Republicans nominated Otto for sheriff in the upcoming election. He was a committed member of the party—a trait he insisted on in his daughters' suitors. But he wasn't a natural candidate. He and his brother had just gotten the better of a fight against a crowded courtroom, but was terrified of speaking in public.[1]

Poll taxes were required for most people to vote: for a dollar, they would be issued a receipt, which would serve as proof of eligibility to cast a ballot on Election Day. Elections were often determined in advance by which party paid for the most poll taxes. The Democrats had paid the poll tax for 1,950 voters. The Republicans shocked everyone by paying for none. Emerson Luther, county Republican chairman, had been given the money for 2,700 poll taxes, and never bought any. Had he kept the money out of greed? Worse than that, it was rumored he had taken money from the Democrats to purposely throw the election. The Republican nominees for office withdrew, knowing it would be impossible to win. Except for Otto. He appealed to voters of both parties, pledging "strict economy," to "absolutely eliminate fee grabbing of any character," hire "capable, honest, and high type men," and cap his own salary. Democrat Tom Crow won, 3,161 to 1,449.[2]

Otto moved his family to McMinn County. He worked as a bail bondsman and opened up Essankay Tires in downtown Athens. He was approaching forty when the war broke out, and had a young second daughter, Billie Bea. With rubber heavily rationed, Otto went to work at a nearby defense plant. Otto considered politics a matter of life and death—as had literally been true in his father's case. He had worked on the sheriff campaigns of Boling Shoemaker, Joe Taylor, Abe Trew, and Claude Hutsell, rising to the chairmanship of the county Republican Party.

Billie Bea Kennedy, age eight, had the run of their farm outside Athens. Wandering into the barn, she was surprised to see Daddy sitting at a table with strangers and to be ordered out as soon as she entered: "Go home, Billie. Now."

Jim Buttram and the planners of a veterans' ticket had come to see Otto. The last thing they wanted was to divide the opposition.

Otto agreed. The Republicans would formally endorse a GI ticket. "Anything to beat the machine." And it wasn't like people were banging down his door to run. Hell, they were scared just to show up for meetings. "I'll give you the complete support of the party," Otto said, "and it'll be your show if you win."[3]

30

"YOUR VOTE WILL BE COUNTED AS CAST"

> The ticket is officially labeled the "Ex-serviceman's Cleanup Ticket for McMinn County." It might go places.
>
> —Nashville Tennessean, *May 19, 1946*

The GI ticket was ready to go public.

An ad in the *Post-Athenian* called on all ex-servicemen and women, "regardless of creed or color," to attend a GI mass meeting at the courthouse for Thursday, May 9, 1946. The purpose was to nominate candidates for office. "If you are interested in cleaning up McMinn County, and the return of good, clean, honest and efficient government, don't fail to attend."

Over 300 veterans answered the call, presenting proof of military service at the door. Major Carl Anderson served as chair. He stressed, as did the other speakers, that the movement was "nonpartisan and nonpolitical," and would "solicit the votes of all peoples and parties interested in good government for McMinn County."

The floor was opened for nominations. Anderson, Otto, Duggan, Buttram, and others had approached potential candidates. Many declined on account of the high risk and long odds.

Sergeant Knox Henry, who had spent forty months in the Army Air Corps, and was wounded in a jeep wreck in North Africa, was nominated for sheriff. Henry, thirty-three, married with one child, had recently bought a filling station in Athens.

Major Frank Carmichael was the pick for trustee, the treasurer and tax assessor for the county. Carmichael, twenty-nine, had been working his family farm outside Etowah since coming home from France.

Captain Bill Hamby was nominated for circuit court clerk. Hamby, also twenty-nine, lived in Athens and worked as a building supply salesman.

Sergeant George Painter, thirty-two, selected for county court clerk, had been wounded at Okinawa and was recently married. He manufactured chenille fabric in Etowah.

Captain Charlie Pickel, nominated for register of deeds, was fifty-two, an infantry sniper from World War I who had been badly wounded, and worked as a carpenter in Englewood.[1]

Each candidate made brief remarks as they were nominated, sounding similar notes of "unity and cooperation."

Henry, Carmichael, Hamby, and Painter looked like matinee idols. Young, but proven in war. Pickel, a generation older, brought ballast to the ticket. There were two from Athens and two from Etowah, with a fifth from Englewood. Henry and Pickel were Republicans; the others, Democrats. None were from families that had been especially political.

A twenty-eight-member GI executive committee would lead the campaign. It included the candidates, as well as others like

Felix Harrod, Shy Scott, Les Dooley, and Ralph Duggan. It was similarly balanced by political party and geography. And while the military that won World War II was segregated, the GI executive committee was not.[2]

Ralph Duggan, age 37, was the oldest member of the committee aside from Charlie Pickel. The son of the last Republican sheriff and by far the most politically experienced of the GIs, he had concealed his chronic kidney condition in order to join the navy. Duggan focused on the message—creating content for print and radio advertising—and served as the "final word on any problem."

"Big" Jim Buttram was hired as the full-time campaign manager. A natural leader, he was captain of the football team and May King. Six feet, two inches tall and 220 pounds, he had served in the Ninth Infantry Division for thirty months, from North Africa to Sicily and mainland Italy to France, and had been shot in the leg on the push to Cherbourg. His campaign management experience was limited to his girlfriend's bid for homecoming queen at McMinn High. But she had won.

Asked about his party affiliation, Buttram said: "I don't expect to ever commit myself to vote any straight party ticket all the way down the line." Jim had been named "Most Independent" by his classmates at McMinn County High in 1942. This was true for many GIs, many of whom weren't old enough to vote when they had left for war. "We was just a bunch of GIs, you know?" said Bill White. "We was independent."

The GIs were able to raise around eight thousand dollars. Most of it came anonymously from businessmen who were tired of being shaken down, overtaxed, harassed, and seeing the potential of their community limited by the machine's corruption.[3]

The McMinn County Republican Party endorsed the GI ticket: "we believe that the young men selected by the convention of ex-servicemen who fought against oppression abroad will continue their fight for honesty and decency at home."[4]

Still, nobody "gave us a 10 percent chance of winning," said Bill Hamby, GI nominee for circuit court clerk.[5]

WLAR, the first local radio station, owned by the *Post-Athenian* and run by Chuck Redfern, went live four days after the GI convention, with Redfern belting out "The Sheik of Araby" in a 3:00 A.M. test. Apologies were made to anyone who might have inadvertently heard the broadcast or had their radios damaged by Redfern's rendition. WLAR provided a valuable new medium for the GIs.[6]

The GIs were used to missions and maps. McMinn County was home to 2,971 farms, which would be divided by sector and canvassed. They formed "combat teams" and "combed these Blue Ridge Mountain foothills like they'd never been combed before—even by revenue men."

The five candidates set out on the trail every day, "sunup until after dark," along with Les Dooley and other GIs. Frank Carmichael bought a 1932 Model B Ford for the campaign. He received a warm reception from everyone he met—even people with county jobs told him he had their support. By the end of the campaign "there was hardly a voter in the county who hadn't met some of the candidates personally."[7]

The novelty of an all-veteran challenge to Paul Cantrell attracted media attention. A reporter from *The Tennessean* thought the GIs "radiate[d] confidence and display[ed] aggressiveness."

Every "county road" was posted with placards, "regardless of its remoteness." Volunteers dropped campaign leaflets out of a Piper Cub airplane. They mounted loudspeakers on trucks and drove the streets of town.

The GIs knew the people were with them. Their biggest task, they thought, was convincing them that they could make a difference. Their message hammered home the promise, whether it came through radio or newspaper or fell from the sky: "Vote GI. Your vote will be counted as cast."[8]

They opened a campaign headquarters downtown, across from Otto Kennedy's Essankay Tire. "GI Headquarters Phone 787," read the sign. There it was, a tangible, prominent challenge to Paul Cantrell and the leadership of McMinn County in downtown Athens.

An old farmer in coveralls stood in the entrance of Athens Hardware and looked across the street. "I thought it was all talk till I saw that sign," he said. "It's not talk anymore. I'm with 'em all the way."

Jim Buttram could be found inside wearing a crisp white shirt with the sleeves rolled up and black pants, smoking a cigarette with one hand and greeting visitors with the other. "Be sure to vote—what we need most of all is your vote!"[9]

31

"DO YOU THINK THEY'RE GOING TO LET YOU WIN THIS ELECTION?"

> The Machine in McMinn County, which usu-
> ally controls elections in adjoining counties, has
> gained a reputation for being tough.
>
> —Nashville Tennessean, *July 19, 1946*

A sudden blast rattled the new Athens city bus. The spare tire un-
derneath had burst in the extreme summer heat. The passengers
were shaken but unharmed, relieved to learn of the accidental
source of their scare. The summer of 1946 would be remembered
for its tension and sudden explosiveness.[1]

Phones rang in the dead of night at the homes of GI supporters. Somehow the ones with whispered threats were less scary
than the ones with total silence. Menacing postcards appeared
in the mail. "I don't suppose there was one of us who wasn't
threatened," said Buttram. Knox Henry was threatened on three
occasions. In case he didn't get the message, a deputy clubbed one
of his friends in the street, right next to him. Before the votes

were counted, Henry would have to survive a serious attempt on his life.

Deputies roughed up GIs caught putting up posters. The sign was stolen off the front of GI headquarters and destroyed. An all-GI meeting was held to discuss the harassment and violence.

Bill White was there. He felt everyone was being naïve.

"Listen," said Bill. "Do you think they're going to let you win this election? Those people been taking these elections for years with a bunch of armed thugs. If you never got the guts enough to stand up and fight fire with fire you ain't gonna win."

It went over badly. "Naw, we don't want to do that," said one GI.

"You better do it or you're wasting your time," said Bill.

"Well, Bill, I'll recommend you to organize to keep them from taking the election," said Buttram. He hoped this would distract Bill and give him something to do.

"That suits me," Bill said. He promised to organize a "fighting bunch." Buttram thought Bill's approach would get people killed and divert from the real work of the election. He felt as though Bill and the few people who agreed with him were his opposition, as much as Paul Cantrell.[2]

Nothing else mattered if the GIs couldn't get poll tax receipts for their voters. A state law exempted GIs who had rendered thirty days of military service in 1945. All they had to do was to verify their service with the trustee's office, which would record their names in a book and issue a receipt that they would turn in with their ballot (a bill to repeal the poll tax for all veterans had been voted down the previous year by Paul Cantrell and seven of his colleagues on the senate elections committee).[3]

A group of GIs went to the courthouse for their receipts. Trustee John Kennedy, a Democrat running for reelection on Paul Cantrell's ticket, told them there was one receipt book for ex-servicemen and it was at Etowah City Hall. They would have to come back another time.

Jim Buttram called Trustee Kennedy: When will your deputy return with the book? Kennedy said he wasn't sure.

Buttram drove to Etowah City Hall. Sure enough, no sign of the deputy trustee or poll book. He returned to the office and typed a letter to Kennedy, which was published on the cover of that afternoon's *Post-Athenian*, protesting the unfair treatment of veterans who simply wanted to vote. "Next time please give us notice of what your deputy is doing," he wrote, "if you know."[4]

On Saturday, the poll tax book for veterans was in the trustee's office. GIs gave their names and service information, and the deputy trustee wrote out a poll tax receipt with the GI's name on it. Then something unusual happened. The deputy erased and rewrote their names, an act that made the receipt subject to challenge on Election Day.

"I can't see any use for so much misspelling," Buttram wrote Kennedy, in a letter he had published in the *Post-Athenian*. He called for new receipts to be issued and for fixed hours to register voters before the deadline. Buttram offered GI volunteers if the trustee's office wasn't up to the task. "I hope you will be more accurate in the future," he wrote.

The GIs bought ads to remind everyone of the upcoming deadline: "Everybody is talking GI. Everybody wants to vote GI. But you can't vote unless you buy your poll tax receipt on or before June 3, 1946. Spend a buck where it will do the most good. Buy your poll tax receipt."[5]

There was a line outside the trustee's office when the deadline passed. The next day Trustee Kennedy announced there had been 8,970 poll tax receipts, and 836 ex-serviceman's receipts. Of this number, the GIs felt they had 3,500 supporters, and the machine had paid for 4,600. But many GI supporters had told them to save their money: "The Democrats send them to us every year." The machine was paying the tax for people who were going to vote against them.

Voters over fifty were exempt from the tax, and so eleven to twelve thousand total votes were expected. The 1944 sheriff's race had drawn fewer than five thousand. It was an incredible show of faith in the political neophytes.[6]

The GIs thought the challenge would be buying the poll tax receipts. It turned out they also had to keep them. Veterans continued to be arrested without cause, and now "their poll tax receipts [were] taken and not returned."[7]

One of them was Charles Parris, who had been carrying a number of receipts for himself and others. He went back and told his story to Jim Buttram and the GI executive committee. Parris agreed to go on WLAR and describe what happened. Later that night three deputies arrested him and his father. "You're a liar," said Deputy E. J. Wofford. "You never had a poll tax receipt." Deputy Carl Swafford told him that he would be changing his statement. "If you don't change it, your school days are over." Both deputies had their hands on their guns.

Parris was told to show up at Athens City Hall at 7:00 P.M, less than an hour later. He and his father were scared for their lives, so they went. They were met outside by the same armed deputies and Police Chief Hub Walker. Four carloads of deputies were parked in front of the building. The deputy trustee and

Justice of the Peace Bill Etheridge had prepared a statement recanting his story. They told Parris to sign it. Mayor Paul Walker stood and watched from across the street. Two days later, Parris went back to the GI committee and told them what had happened. He offered to go back on the air and denounce the forced statement. No, he was told. It was not worth risking his life or his father's life. "Let the matter rest."[8]

The GI radio ads took aim at the fortune Pat Mansfield had made in public service: "Don't you think that $108,000 in four years is a lot of money to pay to the sheriff's office? Vote GI: your vote will be counted as cast."

Mansfield's draw would be worth more than $1.4 million today, and this was just the money on the books. In 1938, after two years as chief deputy, Mansfield bought a house for $2,750. In 1946 he bought a home for $10,125, which he paid off seven months later, and spent $2,000 to upgrade.

In another broadcast the GIs asked: "Do you believe that every vote voted in an election should be counted as cast? Do you believe that open gambling houses should be operating in McMinn County? Do you think that the voters of McMinn County owe Paul Cantrell anything more? Do you believe that three terms as sheriff, four terms as chairman of the county court and two terms as state senator should satisfy Mr. Cantrell? Should a man be chairman of the county court and also sheriff of McMinn County? Do you believe that any man seeking public office should be forced to get the blessings of any man before being permitted to run? Do you think the sheriff of McMinn County should make more money than the vice president of the United States?"[9]

The machine remained silent in the face of these attacks. Only Boe Dunn so much as put up a campaign poster. Reporter

Cleveland Smith of the *Knoxville Journal* noted "very little hand-shaking and get to know the voters work . . . by the Cantrell clique."

"We don't mind if they don't speak now," said a GI. "They're going to have to forever hold their peace, soon." But the machine's failure to respond was an ominous sign—it meant they didn't plan on winning at the polls.

Mouzon Peters of the *Chattanooga Times* thought the machine stayed silent because nobody would believe their denials. Peters merely had to walk around and ask where he could find gambling or liquor: he was directed to various restaurants, pool halls, and one full-on casino with a big crowd around a dice table. On the wall was a business license.[10]

The Tennessean interviewed Paul Cantrell and found him "quite unconcerned about the outcome": "We hope there'll be a quiet election and that everybody will keep their temper," he said.[11]

The GIs held their first public rally on June 14, a "small but enthusiastic gathering" at Englewood High School. Knox Henry and the other candidates "were almost tongue tied at first." None of them had experience with public speaking, but they talked sincerely about the differences between the community they'd grown up in, the one they'd fought for, and the one they'd come home to.

Jim Buttram delivered a "rather spirited" speech. He said that the nonpartisan candidates were clean, and would take no extra money from taxpayers other than their salaries. "The principles that we fought for in this past war do not exist in McMinn County," he said. "We fought for democracy because we believe in democracy but not the form we live under in this country."

Fred Hutsell spoke next. Fred was one of the older GIs, to whom the rest looked for guidance. Born in 1909, he would not have been drafted, but joined the navy anyway, serving almost the entire war aboard a tank landing ship, thirty yards longer than the football fields he had dominated as a college all-American. He had served in both the Atlantic and Pacific theaters. Hutsell was a math teacher at Tennessee Wesleyan and at ease before an audience. He pointed out that the McMinn County clerk made more than the vice president. He asked "every man to vote and get as many others to vote as possible. Stay at the polls after you vote to see that your vote is counted correctly. Many GIs spent from two to five years in the army fighting for what they thought right and it won't hurt any of us to take one day off to see that the things they fought for come true here at home."

The GIs rallied again six days later at Niota High School.[12]

32

THE FOURTH OF JULY

Bruner Kyle, age twenty-seven, had served nineteen months with the army in Europe. He finished his shift at the mill at 11:00 P.M., walked two blocks from his home in Englewood into a cornfield, placed his pistol to his right temple, and pulled the trigger, just before the Fourth of July.[1]

Post-Athenian editor Neal Ensminger wrote in his Independence Day column: "Eighty odd McMinn County boys won't be here to participate. Yet it is our belief that those four score men would want us to celebrate the Fourth. That is what they believed in and died for. But don't forget them. They are the invisible marchers that will be in the Grand Parade. They will be here on the Fourth if we don't forget them."

Major Warren Giles, a former regimental intelligence officer who had helped plan D-Day, was the grand master. The parade route stretched for two miles. The Southern Soda Shop jeep was "loaded with bathing beauties, and we do mean beauties." It was "roundly applauded" and greeted with "wolf calls." The Hammer Supply float had the same idea, a "big green truck packed with gorgeous girls." Likewise the Pilot Club float, a giant canoe, rowed by "two beautiful maidens."

A truckload of Boy Scouts "whooped" and "yelled." There was the Lions Club float with a king and queen, a 1914 Ford, and Chuck Redfern with the team from WLAR in a truck filled with hay.

But the "longest and loudest cheers" of the day were reserved for the VFW. Members wore full uniforms at the request of the parade planners. Their float reenacted the raising of the flag over Iwo Jima. "Those boys look just exactly like the picture," wrote a reporter. "Those fellows are regular statues. They don't bat an eye."

Competitions for prizes followed the parade: mule races, bicycle races, three-legged races, sack races, tug-of-war, jitterbug, "old time string band," hog calling, horseshoe pitching, largest family in attendance, and ugliest man.

At 1:00 P.M. there was a patriotic address in the courthouse square.

The Strand Theater hired Dub "Cannonball" Taylor, a prolific Western actor, to be on hand all day. The GIs had watched him on that very screen in movies like *Both Barrels Blazing* and *Rough Ridin' Justice,* running off outlaws and riding into the sunset, and enjoyed getting the chance to meet him in person.

For the GIs, it was their last break before the election.

33

"THE VOTES AND HEARTS OF McMINN COUNTY"

A week after the Fourth was another celebration—the "GI Democratic Barbecue" at McMinn High, with beef and pork for twenty-five hundred, "a big time for all," and the state comptroller in town to support the team. The "GI Democrats" had been hastily thrown together to back the machine. Headed by a county employee, it promoted the fiction that both sides had significant support among veterans.

Cantrell and George Woods assured the audience that the Democratic Party would win in a landslide. Woods thanked the crowd in advance—he had no opposition in the primary or the general.

GI George Melton wandered over to the barbecue out of curiosity while T. B. Ivins, circuit court clerk, was speaking. The GIs, he said, "are just a bunch of kids." Melton left in disgust and wrote an op-ed to the *Post-Athenian*. Ivins should be ashamed, he argued. It "takes more than just a bunch of kids to win a war." Fighting overseas made them "realize the freedoms which we love and cherish," he wrote, and if the young men could win the war, they were able to lead the peace.[1]

Ivins gave the kind of response that made the situation worse. "I did refer to them as BOYS, but not KIDS," he wrote.

The GI candidates took out separate ads over a course of days to introduce themselves to the public. Bill Hamby, circuit court clerk nominee against Ivins, wrote in his: "Dictatorship in McMinn County will be a thing of the past."

Frank Carmichael, candidate for trustee, held nothing back: "We didn't think much of Hitler's way of doing, that's why we fought him. But upon coming home we find that our county government is following in Hitler's footsteps. McMinn County is controlled by a Himmler, Mr. Paul Cantrell, and a few Gestapo agents, who, through various means have gained control of all phases of the government of McMinn County. These people do not have the interest and desires of the people at heart. All they want is more power to build up that which they have already gained by intimidating, coercing, and stealing at the polls."

On a practical level, Carmichael promised to keep the trustee's office open until 5:00 P.M., so that working people could do business with the office, and to remain open during the noon hour. He promised to keep the poll tax book at a fixed location, to hire a deputy who was a disabled war veteran, and to mail notices of tax delinquency before attempting to collect.

Knox Henry promised that "under no conditions" would he accept more than his lawful salary and that his deputies would do the same. "Any man who wants to oppose me two years from now will have a fair chance in that election. I will not allow my deputies to use force and fraud. . . . I believe in true democracy and honesty in elections and McMinn county is going to have decency and honesty."[2]

Those sentiments were well and good. But the greatest barrier to victory was a fair election. Congressman Jennings advised Ralph Duggan to get as many people as he could to write Attorney General Tom Clark, insisting on the prosecution of Woods and Mansfield for violations in the 1944 election.[3]

Jim Buttram wired the attorney general: "Civil rights here no longer exist." Woods and Mansfield were sending out fraudulent absentee ballots, he wrote, and for years people have been denied the right to witness the vote count. One hundred and fifty GIs co-signed Buttram's SOS.

Jennings had a message of his own for Clark: "if there was bloodshed in McMinn this year, it would be on [his] head."

Buttram also wired Governor McCord: "Paul Cantrell has stated that the highway patrol will be under his control on Election Day and will do all that is necessary for him to win. We ask that this outrage not be perpetrated." There was no response.[4]

McCord was in Chattanooga campaigning for a second term. A reporter asked about the potential for Election Day trouble. He said there was no need for the FBI or any outside observers. "We are going to have an honest election." *The Tennessean* wrote that this was the same governor who pretended not to know that his campaign was funded with kickbacks from state employees and moonshiners. Another newspaper asked the governor whether McMinn County deputies would be arrested for assaulting GI poll watchers. He refused to answer.[5]

John Rogers knew it was coming. Ever since his son Clyde had fallen out of favor with the machine. Especially after they told the story of how they had stolen the 1936 election. Paul Cantrell would retaliate. It was a question of when and how.

John was at the stockyards outside of town, carefully inspecting cattle as people bought and bargained around him. He saw Deputy Minus Wilburn and state patrolman Cecil Strader approach.

"John," said Wilburn, "I'm going to take that motherfucking gun off of you!"

"You son of a bitch, you think you are!" John responded. Wilburn and Strader overpowered John and arrested him. They took the $562 in cash he had with him to buy cattle.

Seven staring deputies greeted Clyde as he arrived at the jail to bond out his father. John was released, but they kept his gun and money.

Leota Murphy, daughter of John and sister of Clyde, heard what had happened. She called Addie Cantrell, Paul's wife, "and told her what she thought about the arrest of her father, and a little bit more what she thought of the Cantrell machine."

Her husband, Bill Murphy, was behind the counter at the Gem Drugstore on a business call. Murphy was known for having a heart of gold—for selling drugs at cost or forgiving the debts of families in need.

Leota stood weeping at the door over her father's arrest. A car pulled up in front of the Gem. Two men got out and ran toward the pharmacy. "Bill," said Leota, "you've got company." It was the Rucker brothers. They barged into the store and walked toward Leota. Bill pleaded with them to leave his wife alone. William Rucker pulled a gun and pointed it at Bill. Bill realized he wouldn't be able to duck in time. He twisted his body. The bullet struck his shoulder instead of his chest, exiting just to the left of his spine.

Sheriff Mansfield defended the Rucker brothers. They had gone into Murphy's store, guns drawn, he claimed, and shot the pharmacist while he was on the phone—in self-defense. They were serving a warrant against Leota Murphy for "public profanity," said Mansfield, for her phone call. The *Chattanooga Times* reported that the warrant was never served, "if it ever existed." In any event, the *Times* wrote, "The Cantrell Machine in McMinn County, after a decade of political racketeering, has become reckless in its desperate attempt to retain control of county government."[6]

Times reporter Mouzon Peters was sent to McMinn: "Talk to ten or a dozen people around town. Find out how they feel about the McMinn County political situation and how they're going to vote." Mouzon walked up to farmers and businessmen and found them all supporting the GI ticket. Surely this was a random accident? Mouzon walked around the block and found ten more, and sure enough, the machine had a better showing: "Seven of them were also anti-Cantrell," he wrote, "and three declined to comment."

"The machine may win the election," said one businessman, "but it won't win it with the actual votes." Another agreed: "The machine can steal it, but they can't win it."

"Isn't Cantrell popular?" Mouzon asked, a fair question about an elected official undefeated for ten years.

"Hell, there's not a man on his ticket who could get fifteen hundred votes in an honest election," said one man.

The GIs "are for the right kind of government," said a farmer. "They'll get my vote." He lowered his voice as a policeman walked past. "Can't afford to let just anyone know how you feel about things here," he explained.[7]

Cleveland Smith from the *Knoxville Journal* had a similar

experience. People tensed up when asked about the election and stared off into space. They whispered, "The GI ticket will win if the votes are counted as cast."[8]

The GIs held their final rally on July 27. Tepid crowds had greeted their initial efforts. Why get on the wrong side of the machine if the GIs were going to lose? But now they looked from the stage at more than a thousand voters. Jim Buttram said that the war for democracy had moved from foreign soil to McMinn County. Now "it was up to the individual voter to continue the fight our armies fought against foreign dictators by fighting local dictators so that McMinn County might have a free and democratic government."[9]

Reverend H. L. Love was the next speaker. As a pastor he couldn't endorse any candidate. But as a chaplain at war, he said, he had seen many boys die without complaint for democracy in other countries. It was up to them, the audience, to continue that fight. "If you do not vote as your conscience dictates then you have sold your citizenship and do not deserve to be citizens. It is the responsibility of each and every person to preserve our most cherished possession, liberty, or forever lose it."

The candidates were introduced. The crowd stayed long after the speeches to shake hands and wish them luck next week. Jim Buttram knew they had "won the votes and the hearts of the people of McMinn County."[10]

Duggan asked Woods for the absentee voter list. Woods accused Duggan of acting for Congressman Jennings, and said the only way he would ever see the list was with a court order. Woods adopted a "sanctimonious attitude" and said that he had been the "soul of honor" as election commissioner. Why won't Jennings "let me alone?" Woods asked.

"He knows you are a crook," said Duggan, "and ought to be punished for what you have done."[11]

That night, Frank Carmichael and Bill Hamby stood watch at the courthouse, waiting for the absentee list to be posted. It never appeared. George Woods told *The Knoxville News-Sentinel* that he'd put it up himself, and that Carmichael and Hamby might be responsible for its disappearance.

Fred Hutsell was as tough a guy as the GIs had on their side. One night he'd heard a group drinking and making noise outside his classroom. He walked toward them and rolled up his sleeves. The group started laughing at him. The math teacher? What was he going to do, call the police? Fred said no, he would not be calling the police, but they might want to. The group ran off. The former boxer stood guard at the courthouse on Monday for the updated absentee list.

Sheriff Mansfield, as chairman of the election commission, posted the list. Paul Cantrell said: "What's this—another sale notice?" Fred felt Cantrell was trying to distract him. "This rain will help the crops, won't it?" Cantrell asked.

Minus Wilburn grabbed for the list and tore it down before Fred could stop him. Woods denied this to the newspaper and claimed the list was up when he left. *The News-Sentinel* called Paul Cantrell. "I have no comment to make," he said, "not a word."[12]

JULY 30

Cleveland, Tennessee

Officers J. J. Hensley and Alvin Barger had the make, model, and license plate for the car they were waiting for and pulled it over on sight. Billy Lingerfelt and Doyle Brown presented McMinn County deputy sheriff credentials.

"What are you doing with all that whiskey?" asked one of the officers, referencing seventy-two pints in the back seat.

"That's election whiskey," said Lingerfelt.

Brown claimed to be along for the ride and said he had no knowledge of the whiskey or its intended use.

They were released on a fifty-dollar bond for illegal transporting.

Reporters got wind of the arrest. Mansfield denied they were his deputies: "I have a record of every deputy sheriff on my staff and everybody in McMinn County knows who my officers are."

Where did they get deputy commissions bearing his signature?

"I am making a thorough investigation and intend to find out," he said.

Mansfield made an additional statement when Brown and Lingerfelt arrived in McMinn. He claimed that neither had a deputy's commission on them, and therefore they couldn't be his.[13]

The sheriff felt threatened enough to buy a newspaper ad, dismissing the liquor bust as "last minute tales and rumors . . . flying thick and fast."

"Billy Lingerfelt and Doyle Brown ARE NOT NOW AND NEVER WILL BE DEPUTY SHERIFFS UNDER ME." In a separate ad on the same page, he urged everyone to vote, and assured them they "will be protected at any and all times during the exercise of your constitutional right."[14]

Lingerfelt was an automotive junkie who frequented garages and dealerships. He had mentioned his Tuesday whiskey run at the Dooley family dealership. Les Dooley had a friend on the force in Cleveland, which made for a perfect place to stop Lingerfelt's car. Dooley drove out and met with his friend in person, giving him all the details he'd need for the arrest.[15]

The final GI ad offered a "$1,000 REWARD!" like a Wild West wanted poster for information leading to an arrest for fraud. That meant: voting in the name of another (living or dead), voting more than once, buying or selling a vote, removing ballots from a polling place, or stuffing a ballot box. They promised prosecution to the fullest extent of the law against "any person, HIGH OR LOW."[16]

34

THE DARK CORNER

It's your right, privilege, and duty to make your choices from among candidates for all public elective offices. As free men and women, we also urge all qualified citizens to go about the exercise of their rights, duties and privileges as they see fit in an orderly peaceable manner. Vote election day. Watch how your votes are counted if you so desire—that, too, is your right.

—*Daily Post-Athenian*

AUGUST 1, 1946

7:00 A.M.

The morning was "clear and bright" as Mink Powers opened his downtown Athens garage. Across the street the Old Tellico train arrived on time. Three or maybe four people would get off on any given day. But today it was one man after another after another. Mink tried to keep count. There must've been more than thirty.

All morning, "silent, suspicious, blue jeaned farmers and shirt sleeved townspeople" watched a parade of cars drive into town, with out-of-county and out-of-state license plates. They all had one thing in common: they were armed and wore badges.

Chuck Redfern didn't expect violence. He walked to WLAR that morning and was surprised to find three "tough looking" deputies on the corner with guns on their hips. Well, maybe there will be some trouble, he thought.

Sheriff Mansfield had sixteen permanent deputies and another twenty to thirty men who were deputized when needed. Along with the state police, this had been more than enough to take previous elections. But today the town was flooded with deputies from Polk and other counties, municipal police, state police, prison guards, and even prisoners, including one who was released early from a rape sentence to work the McMinn election. All told, Pat Mansfield had put together "at least 250" armed men. Reporters described: "Burly bullies with sidearms"; looking "drugged"; "cold and arrogant" eyes, "hard as those of a band of Nazis." Athens resembled "a state of martial law."[1]

Athens had three polling places in the center of town: the waterworks utility offices, the trustee's suite in the courthouse, and the Dixie Café. The election brought out the "largest crowd anyone could remember."

Eager men and women backed up half a block from the waterworks, waiting for the polls to open. The courthouse corridors were full. It looked like 150 voters lined up in front of the Dixie Café.[2]

The giant tally board appeared outside the *Post-Athenian*. Blank for now.

The marquee above the Strand Theater advertised *The Dark*

Corner, starring Lucille Ball. The title comes from an analogy used by her character's boyfriend, a hard-boiled private detective, who, framed for murder with all the odds against him, said he felt trapped in a dark corner, badly beaten by unseen hands. People bought tickets to see the movie throughout the day, to kill time, or escape the sweltering heat. The marquee also listed an upcoming film, *Gunning for Vengeance*, a Western where the Durango Kid saved the town from a vicious band of outlaws.

The day's newspaper was a mishmash of global significance and local arcana: the crew of an army transport smiled from the front page for having survived a diphtheria outbreak; an arrestee in Brewton, Alabama, listed his profession as "burglar"; a ninety-eight-year-old bride shared her secret for snagging a seventy-five-year-old husband and attributed her longevity to ninety-three years of "tobacco chewing." There were no indications of the next day's headlines. No hint that the local news of the day would make international headlines tomorrow.

Erwin White was the officer of election for Precinct 3 in Etowah. Two years earlier he'd grabbed the ballot box and raced across a busy street to the Cantrell Bank Building with two housewives in hot pursuit. This year they decided to save a step and hold the election inside the bank. Bud Evans, a GI poll watcher, asked to see the ballot box to ensure it was empty. Evans, a Purple Heart recipient, was arrested and dragged from the polling place. White then opened the box. It was empty.[3]

Neal Ensminger, the *Post-Athenian* editor, drove with Chuck Redfern to the bank to see how the election was playing out. "Behind every teller space was an armed officer," Chuck said. Neal suggested they go get some cardboard and make signs so everyone knew they were press.

"Neal," said Chuck, "I don't think they care. Let's get out of here."[4]

9:00 A.M., POLLS OPEN

The GIs issued a statement over WLAR: "Go to your precincts, vote and stay around all day to hear who wins. This is not old Germany. Hitler is not telling you how to vote. Don't be bothered by any scare campaign that Cantrell's henchmen may try. You will be safe at the polls and your vote will be counted as cast."[5]

Their signature pledge sounded increasingly like false bravado. Jim Buttram went to the Athens polling places to see for himself. Deputies were clustered at every entrance, "so thick a voter can hardly get in." Only a few voters were admitted at a time and the lines remained long. Deputies hovered over the voters as they marked their ballots. Buttram ran into a reporter and complained that Mansfield had broken his word: "The sheriff said he would not have armed deputies at the polls."[6]

Buttram updated Congressman Jennings, who sent an urgent telegram to the attorney general: the GIs had been "TERRORIZED, JAILED AND PUT OUT OF POLLING PLACES. CITIZENSHIP HELD AT BAY BY ARMY OF ARMED DEPUTY SHERIFFS AT POLLING PLACES IN MCMINN COUNTY. CITIZENS APPEALING THROUGH ME TO YOU FOR PROTECTION OF THEIR RIGHTS."[7]

Bill Seldon couldn't wait to vote that morning. Seldon had been drafted into the army from that very square, deployed for thirty months, and saw Europe from the inside of a Sherman tank, fighting in the Battle of the Bulge. He was an enthusiastic early backer of the GI ticket. He went to the secret meetings and public rallies, and donated some of his mustering-out pay to the campaign. "Now we can vote, we can make a change, and we can decide who is going to run our government," he thought. He'd heard "all sorts of rumors about what might happen" at the polls, "most of them unpleasant." Seldon's own mother was at home, afraid to vote. But he had confidence in the GI poll watchers. And then he walked into the courthouse.

There was an armed sheriff's deputy standing just past the door. Seldon walked up the stairs past another deputy on the landing. At the top of the stairs he saw a third armed deputy. Seldon could see all three making eye contact with one another. He walked into the trustee's suite to vote and wondered for the first time whether his ballot would count.

J. B. Collins of the *Chattanooga News–Free Press* sat in his car and scribbled furiously on his notepad: ". . . electric tension generated by one of the most spirited political campaigns . . . appeared near the snapping point as polls opened at 9 o'clock this morning . . . Townspeople stood in quiet, whispering groups on the street corners . . ."

Collins looked up to see a group of officers surrounding his car. "Name, address, and your business here," they demanded.

He told them.

"Can't take any chances with strangers," they said, walking away. Collins went back to writing: "Everyone speculated on 'when the fireworks will begin.'"[8]

9:30 A.M.

The downtown Athens crowd watched as twenty armed deputies raced from the jail to the courthouse. One of them was dressed "like a character from a Western movie."[9]

Walter Ellis, GI poll watcher in the courthouse, had protested all morning, as people were allowed to vote who weren't on the list. Deputy Frank Walker, officer of election, ordered him arrested. Ellis was led away from the courthouse in handcuffs. The crowd demanded to know what law he had broken. "A federal one," said a deputy.[10]

Buttram went to the jail to post bond for Ellis. The deputies refused. Felix Harrod arrived at the courthouse to serve as poll watcher shortly thereafter. He quickly learned that protesting was pointless and would only land him in a jail cell with Walter Ellis.[11]

This was the scene as Bill White arrived in town. GIs huddled outside headquarters banging on the door. Jim Buttram let them in. Buttram looked despondent. He held up the telegrams he'd sent the governor and attorney general. That day he received a response from Theron Caudle, an assistant attorney general, acknowledging his July 22 telegram, and declining to take any action because it was a local election.[12]

"They already started knocking our boys in the head and putting them in jail," said Buttram. "They're taking this thing. They've got armed deputies at every polling place. This thing's lost."[13]

"Now, Jim," Bill said, "this thing's just getting started."

"Bill, you're going to get me killed." The election fraud hotline rang furiously in the office. "You're going to get us all killed."[14]

Bill assessed the situation. Nothing was going to happen without more guns, more bullets, and more GIs. Bill had gotten around twenty men to agree to help defend the polls that day. It wouldn't be nearly enough.

The GI executive committee, which had rejected the possibility of violence, eventually adopted a "Fair Election Plan." GI poll watchers and election officials were to bring a whistle to call for help and a flashlight in case the polling place went dark. They were to hide a gun near their polling place—in their car or somewhere nobody could find it. At closing time, if they were kicked out or forced to stand back, they would retrieve their guns and return with a demand to view the count. Mansfield's Election Day army put an end to these plans.[15]

3:00 P.M.

Tom Gillespie was a hardworking farmer, beloved in the community, and as kind a man as you could find in the Friendly City. At age sixty, he still preferred to ride his horse to town. As the grandson of people who couldn't vote, he took his own rights seriously. As on every Election Day, he appeared at the office of the Athens Waterworks. Tom presented his poll tax and marked his ballot for Knox Henry and the GI ticket.

Deputy Windy Wise stood between Tom Gillespie and the ballot box. "You can't vote," he said.

"Why's that, Mr. Wise?"

"Nigger, you can't vote here today."

Tom insisted that he had the right to cast his ballot.

Wise punched him. He wore brass knuckles, as if doubting his ability to hurt an old man. Wise shoved him outside the door onto the sidewalk.

Then Tom Gillespie stood up. And he walked back into the polling place. He folded his arms and leaned against the wall, letting everyone know that he wasn't going anywhere.

"Damn you!" said Wise. "I told you that you were not voting in this damn precinct today!" He whipped out his gun wildly and pulled the trigger.

Confusion and silence followed. And then Tom Gillespie's

shirt turned red with blood. He leaned against the wall for support.

"Get that nigger out of here," shouted Wise.

The tense crowd outside had braced themselves all day. The gunshot set off a round of anxious speculation. Their curiosity turned to fury as deputies dragged Tom Gillespie from the waterworks. The deputies waved their guns to keep the crowd at bay. Sam Lane, Tom's brother-in-law, had come a long way to town to cast a ballot. He left when he learned what had happened: "I don't want to have to vote under pistol fire."

Radiomen Allen Stout and Frank Larkin arrived from WROL Knoxville to broadcast Election Day news. Their first stop was the jail for an interview with Sheriff Mansfield. It was interrupted by deputies carrying a bloodied Tom Gillespie. "What do you want us to do with him?"

"Take him to the hospital," said Mansfield, who resumed the interview as though nothing had happened.[16]

Walt Hurt of *The Knoxville News-Sentinel* went to the jail seeking comment on the Gillespie shooting. A red-faced deputy stepped up to him and yelled: "Get out of here! When we have anything for you we'll let you know."

Hurt asked for the deputy's name. The deputy offered to have him "thrown out or locked up." Hurt declined.[17]

3:15, PRECINCT 12, DIXIE CAFÉ

Dixie Café advertised "good sandwiches" and "courteous service." Neither had been on offer.

Bob Harrill was the GI election judge and Les Dooley the poll watcher. People had voted without poll tax receipts all day. Some had cast multiple ballots. Others were clearly underage.

Deputy Minus Wilburn was the officer of election. He accepted every ballot so long as he knew how it was filled out. A man showed up without a poll tax and Wilburn took his ballot.

"Now wait a minute," Harrill said.

"Damn you," said Wilburn. "You been giving us trouble all day." He drew his club and cracked him over the head. And again until he hit the ground. Once Harrill hit the ground Wilburn kicked him in the face and continued to beat on him.

Dooley stood up and felt guns in his ribs from two different deputies. Wilburn looked over at Dooley. "You want some of this?"

"No," said Dooley. What could Dooley do? He had one arm and a whistle to blow in case of emergencies. And then what? Anyone who responded would get killed.

Wilburn had worked himself into a rage. He tried to pull out his gun. It snagged in his holster. He tugged at it harder. Repeatedly. Dooley thought it would go off and kill Harrill on the ground.

Wilburn finally finished his beating. Two deputies took Harrill—bleeding and unconscious—to the jail.

John Peck, a young reporter for the *Post-Athenian,* went to the jail to check on Harrill. A deputy punched him in the jaw, "knocking him flat on the grass." A week earlier, Peck had taken Mouzon Peters from the *Chattanooga Times* to a nearby bar for whiskey, where a lively craps game was in progress on a green felt table. The resulting article was a huge embarrassment for the sheriff's office. This was their first chance for revenge.

Chief Deputy Boe Dunn picked him off the ground. "John, I'd rather have given you fifty dollars out of my own pocket than have that happen. Don't ask who hit you. Things are white hot now. But I'll give you my word of honor that he will apologize to you tomorrow."

Peck returned to the newspaper to talk to publisher Lowell Arterburn. "I've got to get my daddy out of town before he hears about this," said Peck, "or he'll get his gun and come downtown and get killed." Arterburn understood. Peck left to get his dad out of the county.

Dr. Foree showed up at the jail demanding to see Bob Harrill. He was told to leave. Foree refused. He pushed past the deputies into the jail and found Harrill. He dragged his body out of the jail and brought him back to his hospital. A deputy had stolen Harrill's wallet, with money and the pictures of his baby he'd carried while serving in Europe.

Minus Wilburn decided there had been enough voting at Dixie Café. He and the deputies blocked the door using two-by-fours. Wilburn pointed a gun at Dooley and ordered him to a back room in the café, stocked with empty beer bottles. "Sit. Don't move."

The deputies opened the ballot box and began counting votes, a landslide for Paul Cantrell, to hear them tell it. Dooley sat on the floor, worried about his friend, wondering if he'd get out alive, the dishonest vote count ringing in his ears. Was this what he had given his arm for?[18]

The entry to the Dixie Café was in an alley. Deputies blocked off both ends with cars and stood guard in case anyone didn't get the hint. People watched, their "faces grim." It was happening again. Just like it always had.[19]

Sweet Pirkle, a young woman active in the GI campaign, ran into one of the nicest ladies she knew, who had a son that was also involved. With GI supporters arrested, roughed up, hospitalized, and shot, Sweet asked whether her son was okay. "They'd better not harm a hair on his head," said the woman, who lifted her shirt just enough to display a gun. Many of the women still downtown were there out of concern for husbands and sons. And like Sweet Pirkle's friend, they were armed.[20]

Tom Gillespie's sister raced to Foree Hospital. "You can't see him right now," said Dr. Foree. "He's being x-rayed." She pushed past him to see her brother. The bullet had struck him in the shoulder and he would survive. As she sat with Tom, she could hear Dr. Foree on the phone with someone in Nashville: the situation in Athens was spiraling out of control and they needed to send in the National Guard. She could tell that whoever he was talking to didn't take him seriously.[21]

Stella Vestal and five other women walked through downtown Athens to the waterworks. Her husband, Holland, had come home from the last two elections with stories of being chased away from the count. She gathered a group of her girl-friends to see if they could do better. Their plan was to meet in the center of town and vote near closing time. Then they would hold their ground and insist on their right to witness the count. Surely these thugs wouldn't threaten women? Stella and her crew voted without incident. And then stayed.

"Get out!" shouted Carl Neil, game warden and officer of election.

"We have a right to watch you count the ballots," said Stella.

"Go on, get out of here."

Ed Vestal, her son, was the GI election clerk. He had been a platoon commander in the Pacific, a combat engineer with two Purple Hearts over thirty-four months' service, and part of the Japanese occupation force. He was not about to let some machine flunkie like Carl Neil disrespect his mother. Shy Scott, GI election judge, physically held him back, as both of their lives depended on it. There were six armed men and only two of them. Windy Wise had just shot Tom Gillespie for a lot less.

"You better be careful what you say," said Stella, "or you'll cause my baby to fight." Stella, watching her son's reaction, knew that to stay would get him killed. She led the group out of the waterworks and back across the street to the courthouse square. They were the last voters of the day.[22]

Frank Larkin and Allen Stout from WROL had finished their interview with Mansfield and walked over to the courthouse. They asked the deputy at the door if they could watch the ballot count.

"Wait until it's time to close the polls and see," he said. A moment later, he announced, "The polls have closed." The door slammed and they heard it lock. Upstairs, poll watchers Felix Harrod and Tom Dooley, and GI election clerk Reed Shell, were ordered to stand away from the count. Felix tried testing the deputies, standing up, looking at what they were doing, but he couldn't stop them from "reading the ballots the way they wanted to." Backing off, he knew this wouldn't be the end of it. He "waited for the fireworks" to go off.[23]

4:00 P.M., OFFICIAL CLOSING TIME

Armed men walked into the Calhoun School and handed Deputy R. T. Bryan, officer of election, two packets of marked ballots. Bob Johnson, the GI poll watcher, was forced to stand back during the count. Same for Roy Jack at the Etowah Schoolhouse, who walked out rather than listen to a fraudulent tally. He was the only poll watcher allowed to leave of his own accord.[24]

The ballot box at Precinct 3 was placed in a sealed vault at the Cantrell Bank Building. They'd count it whenever and however they wanted. The GIs from that polling place drifted to Precinct 2 at the Etowah Library. Frank Carmichael, GI candidate for trustee, had been there all day. Frank's brother Earl, the GI election clerk, was observing a slow, tense, but so far fair count on the second floor. On the first floor were roughly forty deputies. The GIs had the building surrounded, ready for any attempt to hijack the election. The GIs in Athens had been badly outnumbered and had been run roughshod all day. At the Etowah Library, with significant numbers on both sides, nobody was eager to start the shooting.

Deputies tried to clear the Niota School at 4:00 P.M. The crowd refused to leave. Their numbers swelled until nearly eighty Niotans stood together demanding their right to watch an honest count. The deputies decided they wouldn't count at all. The crowd wasn't having that, either. The only way those deputies were getting out of there was to count the ballots, as they were cast, and to do it now, as required by law. Knox Henry crushed Paul Cantrell, 696 to 249, with similar results all the way down the ballot. The hometown of Harry Burn, deciding vote for woman suffrage, had achieved a fair count in McMinn County.[25]

Back in Athens, Sheriff Pat Mansfield walked out of the jail and jumped into a car "loaded" with deputies, followed by Chief Deputy Boe Dunn and a second carload of men. "I don't need any outside help," Mansfield yelled. "I have several hundred—get that right, several hundred—deputies and we'll keep the situation here under control." He and his men "sped away."[26]

At the waterworks, Carl Neil ordered Shy Scott and Ed Vestal to sit away from the count. A crowd of hundreds stood across the street in the courthouse square. Through the clear plate glass of the waterworks they could see what was happening. There was a "roar of anger."

Charles Scott Sr., Shy's father, yelled from across the street: "Come on out. We don't want you boys alone in there with those gangsters."

"If we can't see the ballots, there's no point in staying," said Shy Scott. He and Vestal stood and began to walk out.

"Men, if you have to kill 'em, kill 'em," said Carl Neil. "Don't let 'em out."

"Sit down, you're staying right here," said a deputy, aiming a gun at them.

4:55 P.M.[27]

Mansfield and his deputies pulled up in front of the waterworks. Charles Scott and Jim Buttram walked up to Mansfield's car in the hopes of freeing Shy Scott and Ed Vestal. Buttram put his foot up on the running board of Mansfield's new maroon Dodge. You can have the ballot box, Buttram said. Let us have our men back.

"Are you trying to tell me how to run this election?" asked Mansfield. "You go over and get them yourself if you want them."

"You wouldn't want me to get shot, would you?" asked Buttram.

Deputy Clarence Moses was seated in the front passenger seat. He pointed his .38 at Buttram's face. "Buttram, I ought to shoot you right now. You're the son of a bitch who started the whole thing."

Buttram had two Purple Hearts and realized that he had

never been closer to death as when that deputy aimed the gun at him. In the courthouse square of his hometown, before a thousand witnesses, for trying to free hostages in the midst of an election. Mansfield smacked the gun away. "I'm doing the talking."

Charles Scott had enough. "If you won't let my boy out of there and anything happens to him, you'll have to pay for it."

Mansfield grabbed his gun. "Let's settle this right now." He opened the door of his car. Buttram threw his giant frame into the door, closing it on Mansfield. Scott and Buttram ran into the crowd.

Shy Scott watched helplessly from the waterworks. He knew that his father would never stop trying to get him out. They'd try to kill him if he left. But his father would end up dead if he stayed.

Post-Athenian editor Neal Ensminger and publisher Lowell Arterburn showed up to get preliminary vote totals. They walked up to the front door of the waterworks.

"Go away," they were told.

Shy Scott had captained a B-17 "Flying Fortress" during the war, striking at targets deep into Nazi territory. A good combat pilot knows when to eject.

Shy figured his chances for escape would never be better than with two newsmen outside. And that if he didn't act now he would "never leave there alive." Scott looked right at the deputies. "Lowell Arterburn is looking at me. I don't believe you've got the guts to shoot me."

Scott shot out of his chair, used a desk as a springboard, and hit the glass door with a thud. It didn't break. Vestal was right behind him. The deputies came at them with brass knuckles and guns. Scott jumped at the door and shattered the glass, tumbling to the ground, and Vestal followed. Scott and Vestal were on their knees in a pile of shattered glass, cut and bleeding. Windy Wise was the first deputy behind them. The GIs were fast to their feet. They raised their hands to the sky and walked between parked cars across the street toward the crowd.

Windy Wise pointed his weapon directly at the back of Shy Scott.

"Oh, God, here it comes," shouted one woman.

The deputies poured out of the waterworks, including George Spurling, who had murdered Earl Ford, and joined Wise in pointing his gun at the GIs. Spurling began squeezing the trigger when another deputy "half grabbed his arm" and "gave him a half-dozen swift slaps in the ribs as a sign not to fire." They were joined by the men who had driven over with Mansfield and Dunn.

Fifteen deputies stood on the sidewalk in front of the waterworks across from an angry crowd, with Scott and Vestal in between. People shrieked and screamed and took cover. "Don't shoot," some yelled. "Kill 'em!" shouted one of the deputies. The crowd inched forward to absorb the GIs. Wise waved his gun in the air: "Get back or I will shoot every last one of you sons of bitches." Vestal and Scott expected to be shot from behind. Surprised, relieved, they disappeared into the crowd.

"Let's go get 'em," said a GI.

"No," said another. "Stay away from those .45s—let's go get our guns."

Bill White was in the crowd. He looked at the line of deputies in front of the waterworks and yelled: "Throw down your damn guns and we'll give you a fight."

One of the deputies yelled back that he'd "fight anybody"

with just "his fists." But he hung on to his gun just the same and stayed on his side of the street.

The crowd taunted the deputies: "Put down your guns and meet us man for man in the street. We'll beat hell out of you."[28]

5:05 P.M.[29]

The deputies formed two rows from the front of the waterworks to Mansfield's car. Mansfield walked calmly into the waterworks. He emerged a moment later with the ballot box: he was moving it to a safe location, he said. Flanked by a wall of deputies to his left and right, he returned to his car.[30]

The crowd had seen more than enough. They moved as if they might try and stop Mansfield. But the deputies were aiming enough firepower to kill every last one of them, and they couldn't do a thing about it.

Reporter J. B. Collins was swarmed by four deputies as he stood on the sidewalk. They grabbed his camera, including his photograph of Mansfield stealing the ballot box, and destroyed his film.

"You're under arrest."

"What's the charge?"

"We'll think of something." Collins was roughly searched at the jail. His pleas to call his wife and his newsroom were rebuffed. He was thrown in a communal cell. "What are you in for?" he asked the man next to him.

"I voted wrong," he said.

After some time a deputy came to release Collins. He handed him back his camera—minus the film. The deputy showed him the door and told him not to take any more pictures. Collins said he'd leave when they returned his wallet and watch.[31]

Two trees in the center of Athens mark the final resting place of Nocatula and Conestoga.

(Courtesy of Tennessee Secretary of State)

The grand old courthouse and its square were the focal point of social life in the Friendly City. *(Courtesy of Tennessee Secretary of State)*

The McMinn County Jail, headquarters for the sheriff, his deputies, and their prisoners.

(Courtesy of Durant Tullock)

Paul Cantrell was elected sheriff in 1936. Son of one of Etowah's most prominent families, he promised evenhanded law enforcement.

(Daily Post-Athenian— with special thanks to Jeff Schumacher for use of their photographic archives.)

Bill White enlisted in the Marine Corps days after Pearl Harbor and was part of the first American offensive in World War II.

(National Archives)

Ralph Duggan, renowned for his integrity and gentle nature, concealed his chronic illness to serve in the war, leaving behind his wife and law practice.

(National Archives)

The McMinn County machine relied on violent men to enforce their will, none more so than Minus Wilburn. At his death, his own mother said: "Now he's in Hell."

(Courtesy of Larry Eaton)

George Woods was elected to the Tennessee legislature in 1940. His "Ripper Bill" gave Paul Cantrell complete control of McMinn County government.

(Chattanooga Daily Times)

Sheriff Paul Cantrell *(left)* with Chief Deputy Pat Mansfield, who succeeded him in office. This photo was taken by Felix Harrod as a college student freelancing for the newspaper.

(Courtesy of Doug Harrod)

Boss Ed Crump of Memphis, the King of Tennessee.

(Memphis Public Library)

Congressman John J. Jennings Jr. fought tirelessly for free elections in McMinn County.

(Library of Congress)

Otto Kennedy led the opposition to the machine during the war years and never shied away from a fight—political or otherwise.

(Courtesy of Donna Cagle)

"Big" Jim Buttram managed and helped organize the GI ticket. The former quarterback for McMinn High, he earned two Purple Hearts with the Army in Africa and Europe.

(Chattanooga Daily Times)

The GI ticket: Knox Henry, sheriff; Frank Carmichael, trustee; George Painter, county court clerk; Bill Hamby, circuit court clerk; Charlie Pickel, register of deeds. They risked everything to challenge the machine. *(Chattanooga Daily Times)*

GI headquarters.

(Chattanooga Daily Times)

Bill White supported the GI ticket but thought winning the most votes wouldn't be enough.

(Courtesy of Travis Davis)

ELECTION DAY

August 1, 1946. Voters line up outside the waterworks.

(Daily Post-Athenian)

The street in front of the waterworks, minutes before the glass shattered. Left arrow indicates the polling place; right arrow Sheriff Mansfield's car, where Charles Scott Sr. pleads for the release of his son.

(Chattanooga Daily Times)

Shy Scott and Ed Vestal, hands raised in the air, leaving the water-works. They braced themselves for a bullet in the back.

(Daily Post-Athenian)

"Democracy, Athens Style." Deputies shut down voting at the Dixie Café, blocking the entrance and the alley with their cars.

(Chattanooga Daily Times)

GIs who tried to keep the election fair found themselves overwhelmed, beaten, and taken prisoner. *(Top to bottom):* Charles "Shy" Scott *(Courtesy of Ann Davis),* Bob Harrill with his head bandaged *(East Tennessee History Center),* Ed Vestal displaying his cut hand *(Chattanooga Daily Times),* and *(right):* Felix Harrod

(Courtesy of Doug Harrod).

Otto Kennedy's garage, scene of a fateful meeting after the polls closed. *(Chattanooga Daily Times)*

The national guard armory, one mile west of town.

(Courtesy of Tennessee Secretary of State)

THE FIGHTING BUNCH

Only a handful of men showed up to demand the ballot boxes and fight for them if necessary. They included *(clockwise from upper left)* Bill White, Jimmy Lockmiller, Buck Landers, Cecil Kennedy, and Millard Vincent. *(Courtesy of respectively: Travis Davis, Randy Lockmiller, Steve Landers, Judy Howard, and Leslie Coomer).*

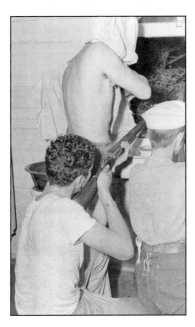

David Hutsell *(shirtless),* Ken Mashburn, and Sam Simms fire from the window of the boarding house. The identities of these shooters have never before been revealed.

(Knoxville Journal/Getty Images)

The embankment, a small hill across from the jail covered with vines, trees, and bushes, served as the principal GI position in the Battle of Athens. At the top is the boarding house where the Wilson family lived. *(Chattanooga Daily Times)*

Spectators watch the Battle of Athens. *(Chattanooga News-Free Press)*

As Minus Wilburn's in-law, Paul Weeks was the only GI willing to help keep him alive. At the moment this picture was taken, a man wearing a bag over his head snuck up behind Wilburn and cut his throat. *(Chattanooga News-Free Press)*

The deputies' cars were a constant reminder of their corruption. They were among the first casualties when the people of McMinn County took back control.

(Chattanooga News-Free Press)

GIs found boxes of blank ballots and batches of filled-in ballots inside the jail.

(East Tennessee History Center)

Deputies who had terrorized McMinn County for a decade found themselves behind bars.

(Associated Press)

AFTER THE STORM—Three tired, sleepy GI's patrol Athens streets Sunday morning, finding town quiet and peaceful after two days of looting resulting in the gun battle Thursday and Friday. Doing their rounds, the GI's found everything in order—as quiet and sleepy as themselves.

The GIs controlled the county in the aftermath of the battle. Here, three patrol the now quiet streets.

(Chattanooga News-Free Press)

The morning after. "It is one of those indelible things," said Ruly Smith. "If you close your eyes you can see it again."
(McMinn County Living Heritage Museum/East Tennessee History Center)

Windy Wise "did not arouse the friendlier instincts of the crowd." When the other deputies were released, he alone was held to answer charges.

(Chattanooga Daily Times)

THE PEOPLE RECLAIM THEIR OWN—These Americans are citizens of McMinn County. They met in this crowded courtroom in Athens yesterday and appointed a three-man governing committee to enforce the law until the nonpartisan election ticket takes office Sept. 1. Hundreds more, unseen in this picture, were unable to get into the overflowing court.

Like "witnessing a dramatic rebirth of the early days of democracy." The courtroom on the day after the battle. *(Chattanooga Daily Times)*

Over one thousand residents mobilized to defend the county against a counterattack. *(Chattanooga Daily Times)*

David Hutsell kept his commitments to his community and his girl-friend, Lillian. They would go on to be married for over sixty years.

(Associated Press)

There it was, "the showdown all had been expecting," wrote one reporter. "The deputies had made their move and the un-armed GIs had not pitched in to fight. As more and more deputies arrived and slowly moved [as] a body toward the jail it looked like the show of force was over, with the pistol toting thugs again the winners, as they had been in every election since 1936."

The crowd in the square started to break up and drift off. The GIs were frustrated but helpless: "We just aren't well enough organized and we haven't got guns"; "We haven't got a chance with this Gestapo"; "Over there we had something to fight back with."

A reporter went to Foree Hospital to interview the growing list of patients. Shy Scott was there with a bandaged head and a rivulet of dried blood down his cheek. "I won't be here ten minutes from now," he told the reporter. "I'm leaving the county until all this blows over."

Ed Vestal's ankle and hand had been slashed in the escape. He had been wounded before, by a Japanese grenade and artil-lery fire. "How did today compare to fighting overseas?" asked a reporter.

Ed thought for a moment. "Well, today it made you madder than it did over there. And it was closer range."[32]

35

THE BATTLE OF THE GARAGE

> If any shades from the Revolution are in Ten-
> nessee tonight they must be in Athens, hanging
> around that garage.
>
> —*Chattanooga Times*

5:30 P.M.[1]

Otto Kennedy was oblivious to the day's events. He'd been traveling the county with George Woods and a deputy, collecting
ballots from shut-ins.

"What do you think will happen?" asked Woods.

"If you fellas will let us have an honest count, we'll win."[2]

No sooner had Otto returned to the Essankay Tire garage than
he was beset by GIs telling him what had happened and asking
him what to do. Otto had known there'd be trouble today. He
had asked his brothers, Bull and J. P., and son-in-law, Ace Adams, to be on hand. Bull was a former professional wrestler who
had taken a judge's offer to go to war instead of prison for a fight

that resulted in a man's death. J. P. was the boxing champion of Knoxville. And Ace had been a high school football star.

Otto and his family and a garageful of agitated GIs discussed their options. None of them good. "How many of you have guns?" Otto asked. A few hands went up. It was going to take more than that. There were twelve ballot boxes: one in the jail, another inside a heavily defended courthouse, a third barricaded in the Dixie Café, a fourth in the vault in the Cantrell Bank Building, and poll watchers had been ejected at two other locations. "We're licked," Otto said angrily.

A sharp cry from outside interrupted the meeting. Some GIs poked their heads out to see what was happening.[3]

"[T]wo swaggering deputies" walked toward the garage, "badges on their shirts and holstered guns slung on their hips."

"Let's get these two men," Otto said to Bull.[4]

The crowd rumbled with anger. The deputies drew their guns, unsure of where to aim. Otto, J. P., Bull, and Ace, joined by Bill White and other GIs, were "smashing their faces and ripping their clothes" before they knew what hit them. Otto pistol-whipped a deputy in the face. They were dragged into the Essankay Garage. The GIs were lucky it had only been two. As it was, if they hadn't been taken by surprise, two could've done plenty of damage.

The crowd bayed for blood: "Kill them! Kill them!"

The disarmed deputies were tied up and thrown on a coal pile inside the garage.

Otto and the GIs had barely resumed their meeting. GI Edsel Underwood shouted that more deputies were on their way. They braced for "onrushing carloads" of men and "blazing bullets." But again there were only two, trying to figure out what had happened to their comrades. And they did, down to being ambushed, beaten, disarmed, tied, and tossed on a coal pile next to them. The group resumed their meeting.

Reporter Richard Rodgers arrived on the scene and walked to the door of the Essankay. He introduced himself to a "wild-eyed" GI demanding to know his business.

"From the *Times*? Come in here. We want you to see this." Rodgers noticed the man was holding a .38. Inside he saw the four prisoners.

A GI came to the front door and stuck his head in: "Watch out! They're going to rush us." Rodgers jumped behind a stack of tires, estimating his time at one-hundredth of a second. He heard "the loudest, most frightening, skin-crawling roar of voices" from the GIs as they prepared to face this newest threat.

Two GIs stayed inside to guard the deputies. One dared them to try and escape: "Go ahead, you sons of bitches. I'd love to kill every one of you."

The other GI told the deputies: "If those guys get in here and get me I'll kill you first."

Rodgers jumped out an open window. Back on the street he saw "the crowd had grown. The people wore expressions hard to describe, a mixture of fear and fascination. They smelled a killing and wanted to hide, but they couldn't tear themselves away."

"There were literally thousands of people" in downtown Athens, with a "curious, horrible fascination" in what was happening. The crowd ducked into storefronts and behind bushes and cars. Then and for the rest of the night, onlookers seemed to follow the same strategy: go "where you could see, but not so close [you] couldn't get away—fast."

This time the machine sent four deputies. Two were subdued

immediately. The third backed up and pointed his gun at the crowd. Otto Kennedy snuck up in his blind spot and pressed a .45 against his face. He surrendered. The fourth ran away.

The GIs decided to take the deputies out of town. They stepped outside the garage and called to the crowd. Who was willing to loan their car?

Emmett Johnson, owner of the hardware store, volunteered first. "Today I'm ashamed of my home," he said. "These gangsters have disgraced us. If the boys want my car they can have it. They can have anything. [We] should have started cleaning up on these crooks a long time ago."

The deputies were loaded into four separate cars.

"Are you guarding the election now?" asked a man in overalls. "You boys ain't very tough once you lose your guns," said another.

"Did you ever watch mob spirit mount?" GI Harry Johnson asked a reporter. "It's awesome."

A line had been crossed. For nearly ten years the deputies had done whatever they wanted to whomever they wanted. What had been the consequence? People complained. They wrote letters. A handful of henchmen had some small legal difficulties. Only one had seen the inside of a jail. Now seven deputies had been roughed up and robbed and were being held prisoner. More justice had been meted out in those frantic minutes than in the previous ten years.

The seriousness of the situation dawned on Otto Kennedy. "Let's get out of here," Kennedy said to his brothers and son-in-law. "We don't want to have no part of this." Bill White followed Otto to his car and tried to get him to stay. "We're going to go out and see if we can't get some more ammunition," Otto said, "some more men."

"Well, okay," said Bill.

Bill and the other GIs treated the deputies to a drive along the country roads of McMinn. They marched the captives into the woods, made them take off their clothes, and tied them to trees. Some got whipped with a hickory stick. The GIs headed back to town, leaving the deputies behind.[5]

36

"DEMOCRACY, ATHENS STYLE"

Les Dooley, Ed Vestal, and Ed Self, another GI, arrived back at headquarters. It was quiet and looked empty. "Back here!" yelled Jim Buttram. "All hell is about to break loose," he said. He was planning to get out of town before Mansfield could arrest him for assault.

"Wait a minute," said Dooley. GIs Felix Harrod, Reed Shell, and Dooley's brother Tom were trapped in the courthouse. "We're not going anywhere until we get them out." But Buttram was done. He walked outside, where Shy Scott had pulled up in his car, and they headed for the Scott lake house.

That left the three to try and rescue their friends. But where to start? Dooley, Vestal, and Self walked to the door of the courthouse and knocked. They heard furniture move. The lock turned. Deputy Bill Bradford opened the door. They asked for the release of the GIs.

No, said Bradford. They had to stay while the count was under way. Otherwise the results wouldn't be official. But they hadn't been harmed.

The GIs insisted on seeing for themselves. Bradford agreed: go to the side door and wait. They walked around the building. The door opened, revealing an interior staircase.

The deputies were nowhere to be seen. Felix, Tom, and Reed walked down the stairs and stood on the bottom step. Why didn't they just make a break for it?

"Let's go," whispered Les Dooley. But the prisoners didn't move from the stairs. Dooley, Vestal, and Self stood awkwardly outside the door. Then Dooley looked up directly into the shot-gun barrels of William Rucker and a deputy, leaning out of a second-story window, ready to pull the trigger. Vestal and Self didn't notice. Self was about to hand one of the GIs a gun. Les Dooley ended the conversation abruptly, said good-bye to those inside, and encouraged Vestal and Self to leave with him.[1]

Allen Stout and Frank Larkin of WROL were about to break a big story: "The political powder keg of east Tennessee has exploded and violence has broken out here in Athens. Just before this broadcast, angry GIs using only their fists rounded up several special deputies and hauled them out of town."[2]

6:35 P.M.

George Hull, photographer for the *Chattanooga Times,* took a picture of the car blocking the door to Dixie Café. Knowing deputies would seize his camera, he pulled the plate, stuck it in his car, and switched in a new plate. A deputy who looked like "a horse opera character with sideburns and sidearms" walked up to Hull. "No pictures here," he boomed. "We may have to take you in."

"Never mind," Hull said. "You take my plate and I'll keep

the camera." The deputy seemed pleased with that. The city editor was, too. The photograph was on the front page of the next day's paper with the caption: "Democracy, Athens Style."

Deputies, backed up by the city police and highway patrol, removed the automobile from the front door of the Dixie Café. They went inside and came out with the ballot box. Two men with shotguns walked ahead of them. Four men with "heavy gauge shotguns" and "high powered rifles" walked behind the deputies with the ballots. "Apparently pistols," wrote one reporter, "of which several hundred were on display, were no longer considered suitable to handle the occasion."[3]

The GIs who had taken the deputies out of town returned to Essankay. Everyone stood around aimlessly. No one seemed to know what to do. Otto Kennedy had headed home. Some GIs had peeled off and done the same. The rest would follow suit if something didn't happen soon.

Bill White had never been asked to speak at a GI rally or sent out on the road as a surrogate. But he realized he needed to "light a fire under them," or it would all be over.

"Well! Here you are!" Bill said. "After three or four years of fighting for your country. You survived it all. You came back. And what did you come back to? A free country? You came back to Athens, Tennessee, in McMinn County, that's run by a bunch of outlaws. They've got hired gunmen all over this county right now at this minute. What for? One purpose. To scare you so bad you won't dare stand up for the rights you've been bleeding and dying for. Some of your mothers and some of your sisters are afraid to walk down the streets to the polling places. Lots of men, too! Because they know what happens. A car drives by in the night and shoots out your windows. If that doesn't scare you enough, they'll set fire to your house or your barn. They'll beat up members of your family and put them in jail. For no reason! Is that the kind of freedom you were supposed to be fighting for? Do you know what your rights are supposed to be? How many rights have you got left? None! Not even the right to vote in a free election. When you lose that, you've lost everything.

"And you are damned well going to lose it unless you fight and fight the only way they understand. Fire with fire! We've got to make this an honest election because we promised the people that if they voted it would *be* an honest election. And it's going to be. But only if we *see* that it is. We are going to have to run these organized criminals out of town, and we can do it if we stick together. Are you afraid of them? Why, I could take a banana stalk and run every one of these potbellied draft dodgers across Depot Hill. Get the hell out of here and get something to shoot with. And come back as fast as you can."[4]

The GIs scattered.

Harry Johnson sat through dinner feeling like a fool. Here was his wife—five months pregnant—who'd prepared a great meal. And he'd nearly ruined everything by sticking around at Essankay when trouble broke out. He'd signed up to be treasurer of the GI ticket, and that was risky enough. Now he could face charges for what happened to those deputies. Maybe even get killed! He wouldn't be going back out tonight. He had too much to lose. Paul Cantrell could have the election if he wanted it that badly.[5]

Bill White's mother and sister Betty were surprised to see him home. "Turn off the lights," he said, "get on the ground, and

stay there. I don't know if they know where I live." And as quick
as Bill had arrived, he was gone.[6]

7:30 P.M.[7]

Bill ran back to GI headquarters. The courthouse had been full of
GIs that day in May when they'd nominated Knox Henry and the
rest. Their rallies started respectably and then swelled. Now only
a handful of those who had left to get guns returned.

Bill was there. So was fellow marine Jimmy Lockmiller,
wearing his Hawaiian shirt. David Hutsell, an army rifleman,
was famous for never finishing a joke because he'd make himself
laugh too hard. Tonight he was deadly serious, standing there
with a Browning rifle he had brought from home. Sam Simms
had been a machinist's mate in the navy, one of four brothers to
serve, along with their father. He was ready to go again. Paul
Weeks was there, too. He had lost hard-won medals for punch-
ing a British officer, who wouldn't have seen Germany with a
telescope if it weren't for American men like Weeks, and Weeks
wasn't about to take any guff off him. There was Thomas Shamblin, who had served with the army signal corps in Germany;
George Rowland, an army artillery sergeant; Millard Vincent, a
mechanic in the Army Air Corps; Mack Carney, who had landed
with the army in Normandy days after D-Day; Gene Gunter, a
marine; Edgar Miller, an infantryman and Battle of the Bulge
veteran who had been home only a few days; Buck Landers, a
heavy machine gunner in the army who had shot down enemy
planes over the Pacific; Cecil Smith, an aviation machinist's mate
in the navy; Edsel Underwood, who had earned a Silver Star; and
Cecil Kennedy, who had witnessed the surrender of Japan, and
thought he had seen the end of war. Ken Mashburn, a member of

the National Guard, had been about to fight for his country when the war ended. He was getting another chance.

They brought back shotguns, various calibers of rifle, pistols, squirrel guns, and a war souvenir German Mauser.

"We need some more firepower," said Bill. And they definitely needed more ammunition. They knew there was one place to find it.

Mink Powers, owner of a downtown Athens garage, offered to take them in his wrecker. He'd never had any patience for bullies, especially the ones who ran the county. Mink's formal education had ended in the seventh grade—his brother was being roughly disciplined by a "mean old teacher" and Mink knocked him out with a textbook. A generation older than the GIs, with a son recently returned from the navy, Mink couldn't wait for the boys to get home to challenge the machine. He had served in the State Guard during the war and been at the GI convention.

Several other drivers offered their cars. The caravan pulled up in front of the national guard armory, a white brutish building one mile west of town. Some of the GIs had served in the guard, while others had attended wrestling matches and magic shows there, giving them some familiarity with the layout. Mink Powers's two-ton truck emptied out and the GIs demanded the keys from Sergeant Perly Berger, the armory caretaker. "You won't find them in my pocket," he said.[8]

The group hurried into the strong room. Jimmy Lockmiller took two .45 Colt revolvers. He figured they'd be easy to conceal under his Hawaiian shirt. One lucky GI grabbed a Thompson submachine gun. There were plenty of .30-caliber M1917 rifles. And, most important, ammunition. They draped themselves with bandoliers of bullets, took everything they could carry, and drove back to town.[9]

The GIs had opened their headquarters with such fanfare—a sign of their political viability a block from the courthouse. They had passed happy days there, answering encouraging phone calls and greeting enthusiastic supporters. Now here they were, divvying up guns and ammunition. A group of GIs came in to tell them that the sheriff's men were converging on the jail, where the ballot boxes from the waterworks and Dixie Café were taken.

Then Bill White and the fighting bunch walked out of headquarters for the last time. They made a right on Jackson Street, past the First National Bank, and the waterworks with its shattered glass door, on a sidewalk stained with the blood of Shy Scott and Ed Vestal, who wanted nothing more than to witness an honest count. They walked past the *Post-Athenian* building, with its giant blank tally board. Had it been any other county in America, they'd be watching that tally board filled in, precinct by precinct, recording a landslide for the GIs. They crossed Hornsby Street and stopped in front of Tennessee Wesleyan College. A reporter noted them "milling around in the center of the street," draped in ammunition, carrying guns. They were waiting for last light to make their move on the jail.

Walt Hurt of *The Knoxville News-Sentinel* walked up to them. "What is your purpose here?" he asked.

"We just want to see an honest election," said one.

"A fair count," said another.

Hurt roamed the neighborhood interviewing people on the street. One person after another told him that they had feared violence for years. He walked up to a house near the jail and talked to two women on the porch, a homemaker and schoolteacher. They fretted about their relatives in the crowd. "At least he knows how to use a rifle," said one.

"I guess there is no other way," said her friend. "You have to fight fire with fire."

Hurt noted women in the street, "wringing their hands . . . wives, mothers, and sweethearts . . . their sorrow and fear was genuine and one you'll remember."

Grandfathers, fathers, and uncles of the boys drove around hoping to convince them to come home, "dreading what might happen. They and their wives for years have known this situation down here would some day come to a head."

One woman told Hurt: "I guess most of us older ones had lived through it so long we had just grown helpless about it. A great many of us never voted. We simply felt there wouldn't be any use."

Not everyone expected a fight. "There won't be any trouble tonight," said one man. "Come back four years from tonight and we'll show you a clean, orderly election. These are mostly kids gathered tonight. They haven't any real leader yet."

Hurt agreed that no one seemed to be in charge. Yet he detected "a deadly seriousness about them." By now he'd been watching Bill and the GIs for nearly an hour. Resolute. Armed. Waiting for sunset. "They didn't appear to have increased their ranks much," he wrote, but "their ranks hadn't thinned any either. And there was no less purpose evident than when we had first questioned one of them an hour earlier."[10]

Cleveland Smith of the *Knoxville Journal*, himself an army veteran who had landed on Normandy Beach, noted a GI "carrying his rifle on his shoulder like he did in combat, his thumb hooked in the trigger guard, the way he did when he moved into battle."[11]

His *Journal* colleague Ed Harris was also on Jackson Street, observing "a group of men who bled and had buddies die for the exercise of their voting privilege. These men had been taught during their military days that one of the things they were fighting a war for was for the sacred privilege of voting in a free country, and for voting for whom they pleased. You understood from them all they wanted was a chance to vote and to make certain their votes were counted.

"The men were not drinking. The crowd was strangely sober. You'd think it'd be a drinking crowd, but this one was one that appeared to have a serious motive and meant to carry it out." It was like the "electrifying spark you feel just before a kickoff at a championship football game."[12]

Allen Stout resumed his broadcast at 8:30 P.M. Frank Larkin would leave their impromptu studio in the courthouse square and race back to report what was happening to Stout, who would tell listeners throughout the region: "The crowd is converging on the county jail at this time. But no violence has been reported. Everyone here acts as if they are waiting for a time bomb to explode. That may happen. All women have just been ordered off the street."

8:45 P.M.[13]

The sun disappeared from the horizon and the light was fading. Whatever lines had been crossed, the one between Jackson and White Streets was something else altogether.

Bill White knew he could get arrested. He knew he might be killed. But he had already made that decision—to fight even though he could die. And from his perspective, he'd made it with a lot less of a personal stake. He had joined the marines just steps away at the old post office, which now stood between him and the jail, and swore to defend America against all enemies. "If it was worth going over there and risking your life, laying it down, it was worth it here, too," Bill said. "So we decided to fight."[14]

Edsel Underwood had won a Silver Star in France. Grenades were falling and killing men all around him. "Determining the source of the grenades but with no knowledge of the enemy's strength," Underwood "leaped a hedgerow and disposed of enemy soldiers who had been inflicting casualties upon his company." That was the key to understanding their decision. They were stepping into the unknown at significant risk. But they had done it before.

The boardinghouse facing Jackson Street sits on a little hill. In the backyard is an embankment, thirteen feet high, covered with trees, vines, bushes, and tall grass, overlooking White Street, roughly even with the second story of the jail. The GIs moved quickly around both sides of the house through the backyard and to the embankment.

Reporter J. B. Collins watched "shadowy, armed figures . . . moving to a hillside opposite the jail. They took position and waited."[15]

One hundred and twenty feet away from them was the jail, a massive brick fortress that looked like a haunted house, headquarters of the McMinn county sheriff. It seemed out of place among the colorful storefronts, the grand old courthouse, and its shady square. For years, people had gone out of their way to avoid the building and the people inside.

Kenny Wilburn, Minus's fourteen-year-old son, was sent by his mother to bring his father home. He'd never worked this late on Election Day and she couldn't figure out what had happened. Kenny walked alone, oblivious, on White Street between the embankment and the jail.

"Bring those boxes out and there won't be any trouble," someone yelled from the GI side.

An answer came from the jail. "You're going to have to come get them."

"That's what we're going to do."

Kenny ran into the jail and found his father. "Lay down on the floor," Minus told him.

"Why don't you call the law?" someone shouted from the jail.

"There ain't no damn law in McMinn County!" someone yelled from the embankment.

Enough talking, Bill thought. He pulled back the bolt on his rifle.

"I heard a bolt click," came a voice from near the jail. The deputies outside scrambled to get in.

Chuck Redfern was on the air in his studio across from the courthouse: "You're listening to WLAR, the *friendly* voice of the *Friendly* City." Gunfire exploded in the background and was carried on the airwaves to homes across the county.[16]

THE GUNS OF AUGUST

> Shortly after 9pm tonight the little town of
> Athens rolled back its pages fifty years and re-
> verted to wild west tactics, as gunfire climaxed
> a hectic day at the polls.
>
> —*Daily Post-Athenian*

Lowell Arterburn thought the first blast sounded like a volley, "as if the shots were fired at a command." The first to hit the jail shattered a second-story window; the rest were broken in the opening seconds.[1]

The "crowded streets and sidewalks instantly . . . changed into mass disorder. Women and children screamed and ran for cover, stumbling, crawling, running into doorways and alleys, hiding behind ash cans, automobiles, telephone poles. Men, some cursing, some praying aloud, followed them." J. B. Collins ran into the entryway of a clothing store, "half kneeling, half crouching," crammed with a dozen other people.

Ella Eaves, fifty years old, fell and hit her head on the sidewalk. The first injury of the battle.

Both sides were now firing almost simultaneously, "Flashes stabbing through the darkness as carbines, shotguns, pistols, and an occasional submachine gun went into action."[2]

Edgar Miller was hit by a buckshot blast to the face and chest. Miller had fought Hitler's army and come away with nothing but frostbite. Now he was on his way to Foree Hospital. He planned to return to the fighting the second he could.

Bill Grubb, an army pilot who had found the VFW a home in the Robert E. Lee Hotel, was scouting for ammo to bring back to the GI position. He had been skeptical of the decision to fight, but once it was made, he was going to do everything he could to see the GIs win. He worried that they wouldn't all survive: "Go through all the war and get home and get killed in your own hometown," he said. "That'd be sacrilegious in a way."[3]

Athens "rattled to the roar of Tommy-guns, rifles, and pistols" and the "blunt blast of shotguns mingled with the sharper crack of rifles and the whine of ricochets."[4]

Millard Vincent carefully moved near to Bill White. "Bill," he said, "the light down there in front of Bill Cate's beer joint needs to be knocked out. They can see too much." Bill took it out with a single rifle shot. Millard pointed to another light down the street. Bill missed the first shot and shattered it with the second. The jail was now in darkness. Millard thought that "it was fun, in a way."[5]

Bill was taken by the surreal nature of the scene: the familiar sounds of combat, ones he never expected to hear again, that seemed so out of place amidst the familiar sights of home.

"The jail was a gray blob . . . outlined in the twinkling of gun bursts fired from the windows." The deputies were responding with revolvers and the occasional shotgun.[6]

The battle could be heard inside the courthouse. Felix Harrod could tell the guns from the sounds: "Carbines, .45s, rifles, Thompson subs, and one that sounded like an old .30-caliber machine gun."

Felix, Reed Shell, and Tom Dooley decided to test their captors and stood up to leave. Deputy Frank Walker, officer of election, told them that he couldn't guarantee their safety. Even if Walker let them out of the room—and nothing indicated he would—there were twenty deputies on the lower floors of the courthouse who might not be willing to lose their hostages.

The courthouse deputies "became very congenial," threats notwithstanding. It was a delicate balance—keeping them as bargaining chips, but showing courtesy that might be remembered if things went south. Felix could hear them calling the jail for guidance.

Felix thought of the people he'd known growing up who made the ultimate sacrifice, only for him to be held prisoner in his own town. One of his best friends from high school football had eaten raw cabbage for two weeks to make weight for the Air Corps, only to be shot down early in the war. Tommy Amburgy, another friend who Felix considered Athens's "all-American boy," had died with his submarine shipmates in the Sea of Japan. Felix could hear his parents calling to him from the street outside.[7]

"It seemed as if the whole world had exploded," thought Allen Stout. He took shelter under a desk. "A stray bullet is just as deadly as an accurately aimed one if it hits you." With that he resumed his broadcast: "The people are running, some are yelling, and we don't know what the activity is," he whispered. "The increase in the shooting just started as we came on the air. There are certainly scurrying of feet and the excited voices of the people as they move over towards the firing line. Perhaps they, too, had heard the rumor that an attack was about to be made."[8]

Between the GI position and the jail was a row of the deputies' cars. Windows and windshields were shattered by bullets; tires and doors were punctured. "I don't know where they got all these guns," thought one reporter, "but I know where they learned to use them so well."

Les Dooley had planned a hunting trip earlier in the summer and couldn't find enough ammunition in the stores of Athens. He made the drive to Asheville, North Carolina, where he had finished the war as the manager of the Grove Park Inn, helping soldiers transition to civilian life. The resort's shooting range had plenty of ammo, and he took home enough to justify the long drive. Now he drove up to Hornsby Alley with all the ammo he had and brought it to the GI position.[9]

Chuck Redfern's WLAR was heard throughout downtown: on a speaker outside the station a block away, and on every car radio, like watching a baseball game while listening to the play-by-play.

The GIs carefully fanned out under fire, "climbed rooftops, took up positions in the shadows of buildings and encircled the [jail] from the windows of adjacent buildings." A reporter wrote: "Along the streets could be seen small groups of the attacking forces, racing through the shadows to replenish ammunition supplies and to improve their firing angles." They shot from "behind walls, parked cars, and from one alley which leads to the jail." They were doing what they'd learned in training and what some of them had sharpened in combat: putting their target in a crossfire.

"I saw three veterans moving into the firing position together," wrote another reporter. "They stood along the brick wall in the dark. They spaced themselves, laid down, and began firing single shots into the windows of the jail. Their war experience sticks out all over them."[10]

George Woods was the most senior machine official away from the jail when the shooting started. He raced across the county line to Benton and the home of Burch Biggs. "We have to have help," he said. "An armed mob has Paul Cantrell trapped in the jail. And I'm afraid they're going to kill him."[11]

The GIs may have made it look easy not to get shot. But it wasn't. Charles Underdown had been given a farm exemption during the war. He hadn't been trained in battle tactics, but he showed up with his brothers to help free their brother-in-law, Howard Thompson, a GI who had been jailed earlier in the day. Charles found himself with bullet holes in both pant legs of his overalls and a battle-ending wound to the hand.[12]

Reporters frantically dialed the number for the jail. The *Knoxville Journal* got Sheriff Mansfield on the line.

"I can't talk anymore," he said. "There's mob violence here at the county jail. Things are too hot here now," he said, hanging up.[13]

Mansfield made a phone call of his own: "Otto, your boys are shooting at the jail." He told him that he could either come down and handle them himself or that he would do it for him.

"You're gonna have to go ahead and get 'em," said Otto, hanging up.[14]

Deputy Clarence Moses was constantly changing positions, with bullets coming in "thick and fast." Young Kenny Wilburn found a place behind a brick wall and stayed there. "Glass kept falling and falling," he said. "Bullets would hit the plaster and it kept falling."[15]

Jack Brown was "scared to death," lying on the floor of his cell lamenting the drunken bender that had gotten him arrested the night before.[16]

Wendell Phillips of Tampa, Florida, had no clue what was happening. Two months earlier he'd been arrested for burglarizing a service station. Now there was all this shooting. I wish they would just go ahead and try me, he thought.[17]

A deputy walked back to the cells that held GI prisoners Walter Ellis, Bud Evans, and Howard Thompson: "Help is on the way from Fort Oglethorpe, the state highway patrol is coming in, and the state guard will be here. We'll have everything under control."[18]

Ellis, arrested early that morning at the courthouse, thought "confusion reigned over the entire scene." The prisoners were in the back of the jail—as far from the fighting as they could get. The deputies were not so lucky. Their "moanin' and hollerin'" filled the building.[19]

Thelma Wilson lived in the boardinghouse on Jackson Street with her four children, aged one, six, nine, and eleven, waiting for her husband to return from the war. He was staying in the army and only days away from returning to move them to their next station.

A man had come to her door at 3:00 P.M.: "Let me in, they are going to kill me."

"No, you cannot come in here," said Thelma. "I have four

children. You will have to go someplace else." It was the type of
hot day that screen doors were made for. Instead she bolted and
closed the main door. She'd heard the GIs walking along the sides
of her house to the embankment in her backyard. Thelma heard
the demand to bring the ballot boxes out of the jail, followed
by machine gun fire, "the whiz of a bullet," and glass breaking.
It had pierced a wall of her house and exited her open window,
shattering the window of the post office. Thelma gathered her
children and went to her bedroom at the front of the house. They
lay on the bed. The phone rang.

"Are you all right?" It was her friend Zella Pickens.

"We're on my bed."

Thelma and her children lay flat on the floor at the urging
of Zella's husband. The children were terrified. Thelma prayed
for their safety and didn't want to let the kids see how scared she
was. The phone rang again. This time it was her landlady. She
was coming to get her out. Thelma and her children walked to
the front door and were escorted to the ice-cream parlor across
the street. One-year-old Rose was in her underwear. Jean and
Donna were in their pajamas. Jim had no shirt or shoes. Thelma
wore a jumper dress with no blouse.[20]

David Hutsell, Ken Mashburn, and Sam Simms moved from
the embankment to the boardinghouse, followed by a *Knoxville
Journal* reporter. The kitchen window looked right at the jail.
Hutsell stood with his T-shirt wrapped around his head to avoid
being photographed, while the other two knelt in firing positions. They pointed their three rifles out the window and opened
up on the jail.[21]

Chuck Redfern came down from his studio to the GI position

for interviews: "I ain't had so much fun since Guadalcanal," said Bill White. "We're going to have a brighter tomorrow."[22]

Jimmy Lockmiller felt a sharp pain in his back that sent him to the ground. Here it is, he thought—he'd been hit with a bullet, probably a ricochet. Bill looked down at him. "Get up, Jimmy, you ain't shot." A bullet had blown off a piece of the retaining wall on the side of the embankment and sent it flying toward his back.

Reporter Cleveland Smith watched a GI fire five shots into the jail. He turned to Smith and said: "We're going to keep those deputies in there until they give us an honest count of those ballots." Smith thought "The veteran talked like he meant it."[23]

The fighting slowed down. Both sides were lazily "swapping shots back and forth," like tired boxers in late rounds. The GIs were running low on ammunition. The men in the jail had all they were going to get. Both sides had found secure positions where they could fire with minimal exposure. It was a stalemate.

Two men appeared on White Street. Each had a gun in his hand.

"Hey, where are you going?" Bill yelled from the embankment.

"We're going to help our friends in the jail." It was Deputy Pug Fagg and Pryor Crowe, one of Burch Biggs's gunmen.

"That's the wrong place for you fellas to be," Bill said.

"Who in the hell do you think you are?"

"You take one step off that curb toward the jail and you'll find out who I am."

Bill grabbed a double-barreled shotgun from the ground

between him and Edsel Underwood. Pug was a large man, around 260 pounds, and Bill sprayed him with buckshot as soon as he stepped off the curb. He fell to the ground. Pryor Crowe tried to run and Bill fired a shot in his direction. It ricocheted and hit him in the rear. He kept running while Pug lay on the ground. But Crowe was about to pose a greater threat to the GIs outside the jail than in it.[24]

Tom Raines was J. B. Collins's editor at the *News–Free Press*. All day he'd been getting calls with increasingly crazy details, including his reporter getting jailed and having his film destroyed. He decided to drive to Athens himself. Raines found Collins squatting near the GI position on the embankment. He was disappointed. "I thought you said something was going on up here. I haven't seen a thing, it's quieter than church . . ." A bullet struck the tree just over his head, causing leaves to fall around him. He joined Collins on the ground.[25]

Allen Stout resumed his broadcast for WROL: "No one knows how many are injured," he whispered, "but the crowds are mad. It is one of the greatest dramas in our time. The office here is in total darkness, and the people on the street below are talking loudly, and laughing—not because they are glad, but a nervous, hysterical laugh.

"The men are armed with all kinds of firearms, as you know by the shots." Bang! "See, there's another one," followed by a burst of gunfire. "The people are now carrying searchlights, flashlights on the street. I believe the battle has subsided . . . but then again it broke out . . . and then Frank Larkin, our news editor, was nearly caught in the crossfire on the street. How many are injured, we do not know, but there have been injuries."

WROL advised Stout and Larkin to get out of town for their own safety.

"We don't dare take a chance," Stout said. "We're not on the air, are we?"

"No, you're not on the air."

"Tell Mrs. Stout I'm all right, but it's like a damned civil war outside. It wouldn't be safe to leave. Cars are filled with armed men, and they're cruising the highways even out of the city. We're safer planted here. They don't know we're here, and we'd be taking a chance by trying to leave."

"Well, you know what's best," replied WROL. "If you think you're safe. But don't endanger your lives any more than you can help."[26]

The Etowah Library was filled with deputies and surrounded by GIs. A fair count continued on the second floor. Frank Carmichael was outside. The son of Horace Reynolds suddenly aimed a rifle at Broughton Biggs, who had permanently injured his father at a polling place two years earlier. Frank grabbed the barrel and pointed it down.

You're "about to get a lot of people killed," he said. All it would take was one shot for a close-range battle between two groups of heavily armed men. Frank shuddered to think what would've happened if he hadn't stopped him in time.

Roe Rucker, officer of the election, walked outside to talk to Frank. If there was any shooting, he said, he would kill his brother Earl Carmichael first, followed by the GI poll watcher.

"If you kill them," Frank said, "everyone in the library will die. Keep counting the votes as cast and no one will get hurt."

Rucker was heavily drunk. "A drunk policeman is a dangerous man," Frank thought. To say nothing of a drunk Rucker brother on Election Day.[27]

The Chattanooga-to-Knoxville bus pulled into the downtown Athens station. The door opened as the shooting resumed. "Oh, hell!" said the driver. The bus pulled out of its space and drove away as fast as it could.[28]

It was easy to forget there was an election under way. Five of the smaller precincts completed their counts. Allen Stout read the first results over the air: "Sheriff's race, Cantrell 725, Knox Henry 1,620 . . ." The margins were similar down the ballot. It confirmed what the GIs had long believed: a fair count would give them the keys to the county in a landslide.[29]

A deputy yelled from the jail: "We have three [GI] hostages and will shoot them if the attack is not called off."

The GIs responded by firing into the jail. None of the hostages wanted to be the reason the mission failed. And everyone knew that if the deputies made good on their threat, they would never leave the jail alive.

Horace "Biscuit" Farris was superintendent of the Brushy Mountain Prison Camp and a major in the National Guard. He'd served as a Democratic election judge at the Cantrell Bank Building, where the ballot box was safely in the vault. He raced to the jail when he heard there was trouble and snuck in during a break in the shooting. Farris phoned Adjutant General Hilton Butler of the National Guard in Nashville and asked for help. A .30-caliber bullet hit his thumb as he held the phone and entered his jaw, sending him to the floor. His wailing through the night was the only indication that he was alive.

Butler could hear the shooting in the background. The line went dead. It was time "to quit investigating and start moving," he thought. Butler announced that he was mobilizing the Sixth Regiment of the National Guard "in connection with election violence in McMinn County." The I and K Companies and the machine gun and chemical company of Chattanooga were alerted, as well as units from "Clinton, Lenoir City, Sweetwater, Harriman, Cleveland and South Pittsburg." He did not activate the Athens unit.[30]

Springer Gibson of the *Chattanooga Times* arrived on the scene just before midnight. There must've been a hundred rounds of gunfire in the first five minutes, he thought. He watched the fire coming from the embankment and the roof of the power company on Jackson Street behind the main GI position. "Volley after volley" of gunfire flooded the windows of the jail.[31]

Lowell Arterburn's phone kept ringing at the *Post-Athenian*. It was the United Press, Associated Press, *New York Post, Atlanta Constitution, Washington Herald,* and *Chicago Tribune.* What's going on over there?[32]

MIDNIGHT

Constable Bryant Sharp had tried to make a break for it at the beginning of the battle. He was shot badly in the leg and spent the next three hours in the no-man's-land in front of the jail. His leg was "bloody and ragged," his "bone smashed to pieces," but he managed to get to Foree Hospital.[33]

Cecil Smith, one of the GIs, met him there, knowing he'd need a blood transfusion. It required them to sit arm to arm with a tube connecting their veins. Regardless of their politics, Cecil did not want his neighbor to die and was willing to go through this painful procedure to save his life. Is he going to die? Someone asked. "Hello no," said Dr. Foree. "I got to him too quick."

"I don't know what happened," said Sharp. "Thank God I am out of it."[34]

Phones had been disturbing the quiet in homes throughout East Tennessee. Men climbed out of beds, searched for their uniforms in the dark, and made their way to their local guard units. Like the members of Company M, in Cleveland, who lined up outside the stone armory. One by one they reached the window, where they were handed a rifle by Supply Sergeant Walter Bidwell. They were getting ready to deploy for Athens.[35]

Mink Powers, who had been monitoring the radio, came to the GI position and went up to Bill: "They're mobilizing the National Guard. They're on their way in here."

"Well, where are they at now?" Bill asked.

"They're down by Cleveland. What are we going to do about it?"

"We're not going to do anything about it. We're going to keep shooting here until we get those ballot boxes and get those people out of there."

"They'll be in here in an hour or two."

"I hope in a couple hours we'll win this thing."

Mink sounded the alarm, telling the other GIs on the embankment.

"Look, Mink," said Bill, "I want you to keep your information to yourself. You're getting these boys jittery about the National Guard. We've got seasoned veterans here doing this fighting. They can fight a whole lot better than the National Guard."[36]

Over three hours of shooting, and the jail was standing firm with the ballot boxes against the GIs. Their guns could keep them in the jail, but they couldn't get them out. Something would need to change, and with the National Guard on the way it had to happen soon.

Bill Grubb returned with gasoline from Knox Henry's filling station and a wick from Johnson Hardware, whose owner quietly opened his inventory to the GIs.

The GIs made Molotov cocktails in glass bottles and threw them at the jail. These "fire torches" fell short and burned out, failing to do any serious damage. They were going to need a bigger blast to put an end to this.[37]

Ken Mashburn came over to Bill White. "Bill, we know where there's a bunch of dynamite out in the old county barn." The county owned a supply of dynamite for use in clearing roads or blasting stumps and stones on county land.

"If we can make some homemade bombs," Bill said, "we can get these people out of here quicker." Mashburn left with Cecil Kennedy and Gene Gunter, who'd been hit with buckshot in the foot.[38]

1:00 A.M.

Four hours into the shooting the public had a good sense of where they could safely view the battle. Around a thousand people watched from the courthouse square. "Buckshot sang through the trees, the crowd panicked," but as "the hours went on, most returned to form a lively sideline of spectators."[39]

Others were content to listen to Allen Stout or Chuck Redfern. They "crouched in cellars at their homes or bolted their doors and hid under furniture as stray shots ricocheted through the streets."[40]

38

THE NIGHT WATCH

Fifteen miles from Athens a plot was in place to put an end to the GI cause. Over the line in Monroe County a car drove the quiet main street of Sweetwater. Then it circled again. Two more cars appeared, along with a truck, and the caravan drove down the main drag. The cars turned sideways without warning and blocked off the road. Four carloads of gunmen walked into the James Monroe Hotel. Where was Knox Henry, they demanded? The posse was led by the Polk County deputy Pryor Crowe, who had been hit with buckshot when he'd tried to enter the jail. But it wouldn't matter what happened at the jail or with the ballot boxes if the GIs didn't have a candidate. Paul Cantrell would be the next sheriff.

Knox Henry was warned by an anonymous telephone call that there was a threat on his life and that a gang of deputies were on the way. He made it out of the house in time and headed for Sweetwater. Henry gave up any hope of winning the election and shifted his focus to surviving it.

Buck McDaniel had spent a lot of time thinking about duty. He'd joined the army to fight Germans. But before he could, he'd found himself in the gardens of a French castle, on a twelve-man firing squad aiming at a hooded figure tied to a stake. Their target was twenty-four-year-old American Eddie Slovik. Slovik had refused to fight—some said he was too scared to hold a gun straight—hoping to join numerous others in military prison for the same offense. None of the firing squad believed in what they were doing. They were all right out of basic training and "all we knew to do in the army was to take orders," said McDaniel. It was Slovik's misfortune that the army was looking for an example. Ironically, his superiors reconsidered what this would mean to the men in uniform and country at large, and kept it secret. General Eisenhower personally approved the execution of Eddie Slovik, the only American to die for desertion between the Civil War and today. Slovik weighed heavily on Buck's mind—he'd never spoken to anyone about it and wouldn't for years. He told himself that his gun had fired the blank. And he was sure he'd tell the army brass "to go to hell" if they asked him to shoot another scared young man. Buck McDaniel found work after the war as a night policeman in his sleepy hometown of Sweetwater. On an otherwise uneventful shift he got the call.[1]

The deputies banged on the doors of the James Monroe Hotel and searched for Knox Henry room to room. Guests were roused from their sleep and pulled from their beds, their faces scrutinized, their rooms searched for any signs of the GI candidate. The businesses on Main in Street Sweetwater were all on one side of the road, across from the train station and tracks. If they wanted to search every building in town, they would find him eventually. Buck McDaniel stood guard over Knox in a darkened city hall. They sat there with the lights out waiting for the deputies to figure out where they were. It was scary and dangerous, but it was what Buck McDaniel had signed up for.

Blocking Main Street and harassing every patron at the hotel turned out to be a good way to get the town's attention. Led by the mayor, men converged on city hall carrying guns. On the one hand, the deputies could figure out where Knox Henry was. On the other, a growing group of armed citizens were prepared to do what it took to stop the deputies from turning their town into the scene of a killing.

The enthusiasm of the murder party dimmed. They left Sweetwater. Knox Henry had dealt with threats and harassment and had some idea of what he was up against. But he seemed genuinely surprised that it had almost cost him his life. "They were going to kill me," he said in disbelief.[2]

America was in rebellion from the moment of its existence, and the spirit remained in its DNA. Other uprisings, such as Shays' Rebellion and the Whiskey Rebellion followed. None had succeeded. Nobody on White Street had set out to triumph where rebellions had failed. But the battle raging in downtown Athens was about to enter its final phase.

Jackson Street, behind the main GI position, had taken on the feel of a block party. Women brought lemonade and cookies to the GIs. People cheered as they prepared to take the conflict to the next level:

"Hoopee!"

"Get 'em, GIs!"

"They asked for it!"

Ken Mashburn returned to the GI position carrying dynamite in a wooden suitcase. "Come out in the street with your hands up," the GIs yelled from the embankment. "Turn the GIs loose within fifteen minutes or we'll dynamite the jail," someone yelled. The threat led to an "ominous quiet" over the crowd.

"Don't do it!" a woman screamed. "I've got a boy in that jail." The rest of the crowd loved it.

A man could be heard near the site of the battle, loudly reciting the Lord's Prayer.[3]

2:45 A.M.[4]

WROL cut in for an update: "We take you to Allen Stout, somewhere in McMinn County. Come in, Allen . . ."

The first stick of dynamite was tossed across White Street toward the front of the jail, where it exploded. There was the soft sound of glass shattering in the distance. Everything went silent.

Stout continued: "Ladies and gentlemen, suddenly a hubbub of activity is taking place here. One of the loudest explosions we have heard since the firing started . . ." The second dynamite blast landed near the first. ". . . There's another one. People are running, people are yelling . . ."

2:50 A.M.

But no one was surrendering. The GIs bundled more dynamite for the third toss. The blast lit up the jail.

"There's another shot. It sounds very much like a grenade or a small bomb. People are running, hurrying and scurrying. We might add that several hundred people are still on the streets here at this hour of the morning."

2:57 A.M.

The GIs threw a bundle of five sticks of dynamite to the porch of the jail. The blast was "considerably louder and brighter than the preceding three." It bounced the needle on Chuck Redfern's recording device a block away.

"The next one will be through the window!" yelled a GI.[5]

The GIs pointed their guns at the jail and fired the last volley of the Battle of Athens. "The firing has suddenly picked up," said Allen Stout, "and this may be the long-awaited attack. I'm sitting here talking as quietly as I possibly can. We'll await further developments."

There were yells from the jail:

"Stop that blasting!"

"We give up!"

"We're dying in here!"

"Quit shooting and we will surrender!"[6]

The GIs yelled out the terms: "Come out with your hands up! Come on out, you!"[7]

The scene was incredibly dark except where cars aimed their headlights. Drivers blared their horns. The crowd "let out roars reminiscent of a college football game audience during perilous moments of the third-quarter period."

One after another the deputies marched out of the jail with their hands as high in the air as they could possibly go. Some of them held guns around their fingertips. There was celebratory fire from the GI position. The deputies walked out slowly.[8]

Bill White and the Fighting Bunch disappeared in plain sight. The public had spent the night on the edge of the zone of danger and now it was gone. "Fuzzy faced youngsters with high powered rifles and elderly men with pistols and blackjacks" walked onto the jail lawn and "swarmed toward the first half dozen frightened men." There were "sharp punches in stomachs."

The deputies fled the courthouse, leaving the ballot box behind. Felix Harrod, Tom Dooley, and Reed Shell walked out.[9]

3:02 A.M.

Chuck Redfern read a statement over the air that had been given to him by a GI: "The GI election officials went to the polls unarmed to have a fair election, as Pat Mansfield promised. They were met with blackjacks and pistols. Several GI officials were beaten and the ballot boxes were moved to the jail. The GI supporters went to the jail to get these ballot boxes and were met by gunfire. The GI candidates had promised that the votes would be counted as cast. They had no choice but to meet fire with fire. In the precincts where the GI candidates were allowed watchers, they led by three-to-one majorities. The GIs are elected and will serve as your county officials."[10]

At a nearby airstrip lit by headlights, news of the surrender aborted a planned aerial attack where GIs would fly over the jail and drop bombs.[11]

Walter Ellis, Bud Evans, and Howard Thompson, the GIs jailed for trying to keep the election fair, strolled out the door as free men. Thompson had taken his duties as a poll watcher seriously and had worn a suit for the occasion. Throughout the night he had shifted on the floor of his cell, left, right, back, forth, in response to gunfire that never made it to the back of the jail. When he emerged his suit was tattered and the seat of his pants worn out.[12]

A spotlight was trained on the jail door. "Chagrined deputies, dirty and bloody," continued to file out. They were "marched through the street with upraised hands." One deputy was carried out, "so covered with blood it was impossible to tell if he were dead or alive." He was brought to a car to be transported to Foree Hospital. "Doesn't he look brave," said someone. "Doesn't he look sweet," said another. Deputy Ed Robinson was brought through the crowd toward the hospital, "bleeding profusely from a bullet wound to the side."

Reporter Tom Gilliand grew increasingly concerned. "Like animals with the taste of warm blood on their tongues the revenge crazed men leaped onto the high front porch like rising tide water, and in efforts to enter the jail literally jerked helpless hand-raised men from the doorway, shoving them mercilessly to the onrushing horde. That horde welcomed the men with outstretched hands—hands that held sticks, knives, blackjacks, and guns." By now it seemed "the whole town of 10,000 had swarmed to the jail area."[13]

Deputies shouted: "Don't kill me! Please don't kill me!"[14]

The deputies were searched for weapons. Bill White led a group of GIs who marched the deputies down to the courthouse, dragging and pushing them all the way, and paraded them around the square. Bill wanted them to get a look at the people they'd been oppressing, the ones they'd been sworn to protect. They marched the deputies back toward the jail.

The deputies' fancy cars—mostly 1942 models, the last made for domestic use before the war—had been a constant, visible reminder of their corruption. Now they were overturned, doused with gasoline and oil, and set on fire. "Anything that would break on the cars was broken. Anything that could be pulled off, or cut, or torn, or just bashed to hell, was a fair target." The first car set upon was turned to "smashed junk" in "a matter of minutes."[15]

Gilliand followed the first group of GIs into the jail. It was pitch-black inside except for an occasional flashlight or headlight from outside, and he slipped in a puddle of blood. There were deputies who had been too scared to come outside crawling on the floor. One wrapped his arms around a GI's leg and begged for help.

The intermittent light reflected "dirty faced men and boys ripping apart mattresses, flinging tables upside down, and destroying anything they could get their hands on." There were gunshots inside the jail—the conquerors had not yet processed that it belonged to them now.

"Beds and furniture were broken and overturned. Debris was scattered all over." In the backyard of the jail was a coal pile that had been used as a springboard over the barbed wire fence. Dozens of deputies had escaped. Only thirty were left at the time of the surrender, less than half the number they had started with.[16]

Windy Wise, who had shot Tom Gillespie, was beaten in front of the jail until "he fell in the street prostrated." He was picked up and punched and kicked and cursed. The GIs took turns: "Now you hit him." Blood was pouring from his "eyes, ears, mouth, and forehead."

A man leveled a rifle in Wise's direction. Reporter Cleveland Smith grabbed his shoulder. "Don't shoot, you might kill some women or children." The rifleman was grabbed by several other men and disarmed.[17]

Chuck Redfern watched a deputy escape up the alley by the church. A GI pursuing him aimed a rifle at him from ten yards off. And pulled the trigger. It was a miracle it didn't go off, thought Redfern, who prevented him from firing a second shot.[18]

The crowd yelled: "Turn 'em loose and let's see how fast they can run"; "Let's hang them—who's got a rope?"; "We should machine gun the whole crowd." Shots were fired in the air.[19]

J. B. Collins thought he was about to witness a massacre. Minus Wilburn had blackjacked Bob Harrill earlier in the day. Paul Weeks took personal responsibility for him. Not because of any warm feelings, but Minus's brother was married to Paul's sister, and he didn't want to spend holidays hearing about how he let him get killed. Weeks, looking rumpled, with his shirt half untucked after the six-hour battle, grabbed Minus by the arm and led him across the jail lawn. A man wearing a paper bag over his head came up behind them. The assailant grabbed Minus's hair and cut hit throat from one side to the other. Minus held his hand over the bleeding wound. "Please take me to the hospital," he told Weeks. He was able to speak and ultimately survive because the attacker hadn't sharpened his knife. Weeks walked Minus the three blocks to Foree Hospital. There was a trail of blood on the sidewalk from the jail to the hospital that had been building throughout the day. Weeks arrived to find the doors locked. He banged on the door, left Minus outside, and headed back toward the jail.

Dr. Foree, whose list of patients continued to grow, made an emergency call for plasma from the Knoxville Hospital.[20]

3:45 A.M.

Claudia Duggan was barring the door to her house. She had let her husband join the navy after Pearl Harbor, but she was not about to lose him in some riot downtown. Ralph Duggan insisted that he had to try and stop what was happening. Neither could convince the other. Duggan picked her up, as gently as he could, and moved her out of the way. And sprinted to town.

Duggan watched the disordered violence all around him. He jumped up on top of a deputy's overturned car. "Quieten down, men," he shouted, waving his hands. He was interrupted by rifle fire.

"Men—listen to me!" Duggan yelled. "Men, you've gained your objective." The crowd quieted a bit.

"At ease, men!" Duggan shouted as loudly as he could.

"Let's kill the bastards!" someone yelled.

"Men, listen to me!" Duggan shouted.

"He's right, men, listen to him," said Lowell Arterburn, standing nearby.

"Let's don't commit murder," Duggan said. "I am not a murderer and I know all of my good friends here are not murderers. We've had a hard fight to get these men out. Let's put these men in jail and treat them a damn sight better than they treated us. We're not beasts. We mustn't do anything here that we will be ashamed of. When the state patrol or the home guard or the National Guard come here in the morning, we'll show them that everything is all right. Let's don't spoil the fruits of the victory now. And when they do come in the morning—we'll dictate the peace terms."

The crowd cheered their approval. There were more shots, but they were celebratory, somehow "no longer ominous."

The deputies were filed back into the jail. As they did, the lights flickered and came on as power was restored to the building. The deputies—now inmates—"were led to their cells with rifles prodding their backs."[21]

Gilliand went back to the room where he'd slipped in blood. As he struggled to stand he looked up at the wall, directly at a "neatly lettered sign which read: 'Let Us Live Together and Love One Another.'"[22]

There were ballots all over the jail. Stacks of ballots, "nearly all" marked for Paul Cantrell. The check marks and x's looked as though they were made with the same hand. The ballot boxes were found opened in a cell with boxes of blanks nearby.[23]

There was a "tremendous roar" and "great cheer" from the crowd as the GIs walked the ballot boxes toward the courthouse, where they would be placed under armed guard. "Down with Cantrell, down with the deputies," someone yelled. Someone started singing and the rest of the crowd joined in. "God Bless America . . . land that I love . . ."[24]

There was no sign of Paul Cantrell or Pat Mansfield. And no guesses from the deputies, despite aggressive questioning. Ralph Duggan found a handgun in the jail. Engraved on the handle: "Sheriff Paul Cantrell." Duggan kept the gun and, when his son was old enough, gave it to him as a gift.[25]

On the tally board outside the *Post-Athenian* someone wrote, "GIs Win."

T. B. Ivins, circuit court clerk, emerged from the Etowah Library. He approached Frank Carmichael and shook his hand. "Congratulations."

"I didn't know I had won," said Frank.

Deputies on the first floor indicated they wanted to leave. One at a time, and unarmed, said Frank. Could they come back for their guns? Later, individually, it was decided.

Inside, the deputies conducting the election gave up. Count the ballots however you want. Frank insisted on continuing the count and getting an accurate record. It was what the campaign had been about. Knox Henry had beaten Paul Cantrell 612–455 in Cantrell's hometown of Etowah.[26]

4:00 A.M.

George Woods was in Chattanooga at the state office of public safety. He had been trying to find an open phone line into Athens and succeeded in getting an answer at the *Post-Athenian*. Ralph Duggan came in to take the call. What would it take to get the violence to stop?

Duggan told him. Woods agreed and dictated a statement for the newspaper: "As a member of the McMinn County Election Commission I will concede that the GI candidates have been elected." This was read in the courthouse square and greeted by "a great shout."[27]

Les Dooley was driving home after one of the longest days of his life. He noticed Deputy Clarence Moses, who had somehow avoided being jailed, in the car ahead of him. He watched as Moses pulled up to Foree Hospital and went inside. Dooley found him lying on a table under a sheet. Dooley grabbed him, dragged him out the door, and took him to jail. After everything he had been through, he was not about to let Moses get away.[28]

Day "broke with a dull, gray dawn and the first rays of the morning sun looked down upon a battlefield reminiscent of other conquests."[29]

7:05 A.M.

The *Post-Athenian* received a telegram: "On behalf of my brother, Paul Cantrell, I wish to concede the election to the GI candidates in order to prevent further shooting." It was signed "Frank Cantrell."

Armed veterans stood guard at the jail and courthouse. Patrols marched up and down the now silent streets. Small groups of GIs raided houses looking for escaped deputies. And up and down those same quiet streets, "a few scattered American flags fluttered in morning breezes."[30]

39

"GROPING BACK TO NORMALCY"

I was interested in knowing what went on in
Athens that made ordinary young men go out
to kill or be killed for the sake of politics.

—*Thomas O'Neil,* Philadelphia Record

It was a good thing I organized a bunch of men
who wouldn't run or who didn't mind busting
a cap on you.

—*Bill White*

FRIDAY, AUGUST 2, 1946

To Lowell Arterburn, publisher of the *Daily Post-Athenian,* fell
the task of arranging, with little sleep and frayed nerves, the most
important edition of his newspaper. The banner headlines read:
"GI Claim Election to Office—Issue Statement," "Woods Con-
cedes GI Victory," and "Athens Is Battleground Thursday." The

left-hand corner was reserved each day for Arterburn's musings, under the headline "The Friendly City."

"Around midnight," he wrote, "we were prepared to remove our headline over this column and bow our heads in shame with citizens of McMinn County. As this is being written shortly after four o'clock this morning, you will notice the heading is still over the column. It remains an expression of hope—that Athens and McMinn County will become just that."[1]

Governor McCord and Ralph Duggan had a tense conversation on the phone. McCord insisted on sending in state police. No, said Duggan, that was not happening. Duggan explained that the people of McMinn were running the county.

"Mansfield is still the legal sheriff," McCord said.

"Don't be ridiculous," Duggan said. "Mansfield wouldn't be allowed in Athens." He told McCord that they had won the fight by themselves, as their appeals to him had gone unanswered, and they would take care of themselves now.[2]

Otto Kennedy took his eight-year-old daughter, Billie Bea, to White Street. "I want you to come back here and see," he told her. "I want you to see it all." Billie Bea, who had spent the night at her grandmother's ("Where my parents always took me when they couldn't figure out what to do with me"), hadn't been able to find her shoes, so Otto carried her. They walked into the jail, where the deputies were still behind bars. "Never get fixed up in politics," said one.

Everyone was in town, it seemed. A massive crowd on White Street milled about smashed-up and burned-out cars, staring at a jail that had been "pitted and scarred" by bullets and dynamite blasts. People spoke "in whispers." Ruly Smith was six years old. "It is one of those indelible things," he said. "If you close your eyes you can see it again." Henry Stamey, a young man on crutches, surveyed the wreckage. "They really gave it to them," he said.[3]

John Henry was thought to be the only man to have covered the war on five continents. He was the first to interview the pilot of the *Enola Gay* after Hiroshima, and was there for the Japanese surrender on the USS *Missouri*. Now he was covering a battle in Tennessee for the International News Service.

He interviewed Bill White, a "strapping Second Marine Division veteran." What was it like last night?

"Just about like a show in the Pacific," Bill said.

"Where did the dynamite, rifles, shotguns, and automatic weapons come from?" Henry asked.

"Just showed up," Bill said.[4]

There were reporters everywhere and everyone seemed to be giving interviews. Otto Kennedy told the *Chattanooga News–Free Press:* "It's a shame such a thing happened in Athens, but it's the only thing that could be done to prevent something worse from happening. All we want is to get this mess cleaned up and get back to normal under democratic government."[5]

Ralph Duggan told a reporter he "had done what he thought best for the people of his county, but he did not wish to be publicized for doing it, or at least he did not wish his picture to be used."[6]

"I've never been so happy over anything for which I should feel sorry," said one woman.[7]

Reporters on the ground felt the community "groping back to normalcy, like a sleeper trying to shake off a long, bad dream," or "a man who has dreaded a leg amputation, but who is glad and almost happy when it's over."[8]

A widow who lived a block from the jail said she was "most amazed Friday morning when someone told me there was all that fighting. Why, I thought they were shooting fireworks in celebration."

Bill and the others were in the kitchen of the jail when Ralph Duggan came in. "Boys, listen," he said. "You broke in the armory out there and got all those guns. You wounded a lot of people, you blew up a lot of these cars. They're going to be in here trying to prosecute you, but if you don't say anything, they can't find out who did it."[9]

This warning was the first layer of dirt over the story of the Battle of Athens. Some of the men never spoke of it in public; some never said a word even to their families. David Hutsell spent nights as an old man at the Elks Lodge, listening quietly to people who weren't there tell stories of the battle. He told his daughter that while he didn't want credit, it was a shame that Bill White never got the recognition he deserved. Even Bill, who agreed, didn't speak publicly for twenty years.

Duggan was not wrong when he said that these men, who had kidnapped sheriff's deputies, robbed the armory, fired thousands of rounds downtown, burglarized the county barn, and then dynamited the jail, might be in legal jeopardy. The attorney general in Washington had already announced an investigation. But part of Duggan's warning, undoubtedly, was that the men who were good enough to do the fighting were not deemed fit to represent the town to the public.

Thelma Wilson returned home with her children after a night at her in-laws.' Three bullets had gone through two walls and landed in the chimney. Another had hit a water pipe in the bathroom. Her house was filled with water and cigarette butts.

People had walked in and out like it was "Grand Central Station." Her son's photograph appeared in newspapers, scooping piles of shotgun shells in a bucket.[10]

Knox Henry was at the jail, "confident, thankful, and tired." There were men reconnecting telephone lines, cleaning up glass, mopping up blood, and starting repairs.

Fred Puett told a reporter, "[We] have been living under a horse and buggy government and this is an atomic age. It's a mighty funny thing, but all these boys in that fight—the leaders, I mean—were in my old high school civics class. We used to discuss the machine rule of Pat Mansfield and Paul Cantrell in the classroom. I would say that they've passed their examination."[11]

Mouzon Peters of the *Chattanooga Times* went to the jail and interviewed Windy Wise. Wise, who posed for a photograph, looked comically patched up: a giant bandage over his eyes and another covering his right cheek and curving around his nose. Seeing Wise "did not arouse the friendlier instincts of [last night's] crowd," Peters wrote.

"No hard feelings," Wise said. "I don't blame the boys for wanting to get in a few licks at me. I had it coming."

"How do you feel?" Peters asked.

"Man, I hurt all over."

"How did it feel here in the jail during the bombardment?"

"It wasn't much fun. I can tell you that."

"How did Paul Cantrell and Sheriff Mansfield stand up under the shelling of the jail?"

"They were plenty nervous, especially Paul. He started talking about surrendering long before we actually did. He said to me, 'Windy, if I give up to them boys they'll kill me.' I told him, 'Hell, Paul, they're going to kill you anyway, and if they break in here they'll kill all of us.'"[12]

The deputies were released at 9:55 A.M.—escorted by GIs through a parting in the crowd outside. All except for one. Ralph Duggan walked up to the bars of a cell that Windy Wise now had to himself. "We are going to send you for as much time as we can get," he said.

Reverend Bernie Hampton, a "straight talking preacher" and former cop, encouraged the crowd to go home. "Don't spoil victory," he said. And they did—"melted away like a cake of ice in the hot August sun," per one reporter.[13]

Congressman John Jennings was euphoric. He mocked the attorney general's call for an investigation. I guess he was "dynamited out of" inertia, said Jennings. *The Tennesseean* asked the Department of Justice what they had done with Jennings's evidence from the 1944 election, which included one thousand affidavits of voter fraud. Still "studying the material," they said.[14]

One of the first national reporters to arrive was Thomas O'Neil, political editor of the *Philadelphia Record*. "It is impossible to find anyone willing to say a decent word about the old regime," he wrote. "The old gang were a bunch of thieves," said a "prosperous businessman." "They should have been driven out long ago. But don't quote me. They may get back—and I have to make a living."[15]

A sound truck rolled through the streets of Athens announcing a 3:00 P.M. meeting at the courthouse. The Ministerial Association was asked to spread the word to their congregants.[16]

People from "all walks of life" flooded the courtroom, with "standees packing the aisles and jamming and lining the walls." The people of McMinn County had overthrown their government. There were no federal or state or local laws in place. Except for maybe one: a sign on the wall read "$5 fine to spit on floor." It was a good place to start. Richard Rodgers of the *Chattanooga Times* looked at the sign and thought: "These people were there to make that regulation and all other laws of civilized people valid again."

Harry Johnson Sr. opened the meeting: "For some reason or other the sheriff's force is not around," he said. Someone needed to be in charge.

The U.S. marshal had made his way to Athens and was in the room. He suggested asking Governor McCord for help.

"The governor did not see fit to step into the picture last night," said Harry. "Let's leave him out of it." The room "shouted with laughter and applauded."

Harry nominated three people to lead the county while it sorted out the future: Major Carl Anderson, businessman J. P. Cartwright, and Reverend Bernie Hampton of Keith Methodist. "Is it your will to elect a governing body to rule this county until a formal government can be set up?"

There was applause and shouts:

"Yes!"

"Now that those crooks are gone, let's have some order around here."

"Let's be our own bosses."

The slate of three was selected by acclamation.

"We want to bring back decent government," said Major Anderson.

"We will serve you," said Reverend Hampton. "If you need us for anything, come right away." He "promised to make the county once more a decent place in which to live."

Richard Rodgers felt he was witnessing "a dramatic rebirth of the early days of democracy," something out of a movie.[17]

The commission set up shop in the courthouse. Cartwright busied himself with a press release, writing and rewriting, finally tearing it up and telling a reporter: "Just say we're going to keep the town straight."

Hampton told the press: "We want no further stain on the names of Athens and McMinn. Our mission is to restore peace and you may say that things are getting quiet right along."

"Athens is quieting down by the hour," Rodgers wrote.[18]

There had been Cantrell and Mansfield sightings in "almost every part of East Tennessee and north Georgia." Another rumor was that the GIs held Paul Cantrell at an undisclosed location, "where he is dictating a confession of his acts while boss of the county and city governments there."[19]

A gaggle of reporters went to the hotel room of a man in Nashville, who had signed in with the last name "Mansfield."

"I have no comment, absolutely none," said the man, closing and locking the door. Was that him?

No, said a reporter who knew Mansfield. But it looked like his brother.[20]

Paul Cantrell left Athens in a hearse. But not the way he might have suspected. He had managed to escape in the chaos and confusion that surrounded the liberation of the jail and appeared at the Quisenbery Funeral Home. Marcus Quisenbery was not a supporter by any means and certainly not keen on hosting the target of an angry mob. But Cantrell and Quisenbery were members of the Free and Accepted Masons, Blue Lodge Chapter, and members of this brotherhood were bound by ancient rites to give succor to one another. Quisenbery drove Paul Cantrell out of Athens in the back of his hearse. Cantrell made his way to his wife's hometown in North Carolina, where she and their daughters had fled the night before.[21]

Pat Mansfield made it to Chattanooga with a fraternal appeal of his own. He appeared at the Hamilton County jail with a leg full of buckshot and asked for "protection."

"No one can be admitted without first having some charge placed against him," he was told. He was, however, welcome to sit in the lobby, "and steps would be taken to protect [him] if necessary."[22]

40

FORT ATHENS

The three-member commission has pledged itself to restore law and order in this bullet blasted county.

—*Chattanooga Times*

If ever there was a political keg of dynamite, it's in Athens tonight.

—*Philadelphia Record*

SATURDAY, AUGUST 3, 1946

The Mayfield Dairy milkman walked up to the porch of a house. Another empty milk bottle. Another note: "Out of town, no milk until further notice." Lots of people gone suddenly with no date of return. This is going to be bad for business, he thought.[1]

The gambling joints had thrived by paying a machine that could no longer protect them. Major Anderson directed raids that were carried out by more than seventy GIs. Throughout Saturday they visited "every establishment" known to have illegal betting: the Dinner Club, Vincent's Café, Rock Inn, Edna's Sandwich Shop, Russ's Café, Frank's Place, and the home of Cowboy Moses. The GIs seized punch boards, slot machines, and gaming tables. The gambling devices were smashed against the wall of the jail for everyone to see. "We cleaned up the dirty politics here," Duggan told a reporter, "and now we're cleaning up the stepchildren born of politics."[2]

"The GIs have brought the closest thing to perfect law enforcement the town has seen," wrote one reporter after conducting interviews.

Chuck Redfern was one of the volunteer jailers. The first two arrestees under the new regime were GIs, on charges of drunkenness, an example of the intended impartiality of the new guard. Chuck escorted one of them into the jail. He had nearly left when he realized his pistol was missing.

"Chuck," said the inmate, holding his gun between the bars, "never walk in a jail with a prisoner and carry a weapon. He may take it away from you." He handed him back his gun.[3]

The Knoxville News-Sentinel posted an article with the headline: "Sheriff Set for Return, Hears Athens." The reporter claimed to be repeating what he'd learned on the street: "McMinn County today remained quiet, but there was a tenseness as reports were heard that Sheriff Pat Mansfield and deputies might 'attempt an invasion of McMinn from Polk County' tonight."

The news was read over the radio and everyone with guns was urged to report to the courthouse. Word spread like wildfire and armed men flooded into town. Bill White and a small group had made the decisive stand on Thursday. But many more were ready to protect what they'd won. One truck appeared with two men in the cab and twelve in the bed, "all armed with shotguns or rifles."

Reverend Hampton made a speech to the impromptu army: "The call that went out was just to alert you and not to alarm you," he said. "We are expecting no trouble and hope there will be none." But "we want to be ready." Around fifteen hundred people had arrived in downtown Athens by 5:00 P.M., carrying "every kind of weapon imaginable."[4]

GI headquarters became an arsenal. People who didn't have a gun waited in line for hours to be issued one. Guard posts were established around the jail and the courthouse. A woman holding a .22-caliber rifle stood in front of the Robert E. Lee Hotel. "I'll use it if I have to," she told a reporter.

David Hutsell, who had traded fire with the jail all night from the window of the Wilson house, was there, in full army uniform. He kept his commitment to his sweetheart, Lillian, and his community by strolling "down the street with a shotgun on one arm" and his girlfriend on the other. A photo of their unusual date night made it in newspapers across the country. They would soon be married, and were together until her death in 2009.

Around seventy-five sharpshooters took positions on the rooftops of the courthouse square. GIs "patrolled the streets" as Athens took on a "frontier appearance, with hardware on every hip," ranging from ".22's to automatic shotguns, German Lugers, and Army .45's" all "very much in evidence."[5]

An elderly woman told a reporter, "If they try to come back into town now they'll get hit harder than they did Thursday night."

Dent Dodson, fifty-six, sat on a bench outside the courthouse with his fourteen-year-old son, who seemed to be enjoying himself. Both had rifles.[6]

Bus passengers stopped in Athens "were startled and baffled by the appearance of young veterans carrying weapons, some of them walking set posts in slow, military gait."

"Is this Fort Loudoun?" asked a passenger.

"Hell, no," said the bus driver. "This is Fort Athens."[7]

The GIs mapped out supply lines and ammunition dumps and even evacuation routes for the wounded depending on where the invasion struck. Military roadblocks and checkpoints were set up at every entrance to the county. Around two hundred people manned the one on the border with Polk County. All incoming cars were searched for weapons. Lila Butler, a teacher from Galveston, thought it was a stickup, and sped at the checkpoint. She stopped after the bullets started. The confusion was settled and the GIs treated her "very nicely."[8]

Ralph Duggan had a message for the press in case Mansfield was listening: "Sheriff Mansfield will never serve another day as sheriff of McMinn County. We have 1,500 men, ready to shoot it out with him if he attempts to return. The good citizens of McMinn County will not tolerate Mansfield again."[9]

By 7:00 P.M. "the waistband or belt that lacked a pistol, or the shoulder a rifle, was a rarity." An hour later the mood was "grim." No conversation, "no gossiping, only waiting."[10]

Two highway patrol cars with six men pulled up in front of the Robert E. Lee Hotel. The crowd moved toward them, "tightening, a silent irresistible force."

Les Dooley walked into the crowd and they moved for him. "Back to your posts, men." Dooley had gotten the troopers a reprieve, and he told them to take it. They pulled out of town almost as soon as they had arrived, "a message to the governor of Tennessee from the men of Athens." [11]

The state police chief "denied reports that they had been escorted out of town by representatives of the new government."[12]

It was decided that Felix Harrod and Tom Mayfield would fly a reconnaissance mission with the AT-6 plane that Tom had brought home from the navy. If they saw an invasion force, they would fly over the courthouse and Felix would fire his revolver two times. They took off from a field, watching the unusual scene on the ground from the sky. There wasn't a single car on the road to Polk County. Nobody was headed to McMinn County from any direction.[13]

George Painter, GI candidate for county court clerk, decided he was going to Burch Biggs's house to ask for himself. He arrived with a group of armed veterans. Biggs came to the door.

"We heard you were going to join Pat Mansfield and pay us a little visit in McMinn County," Painter said.

"Do you think I'm crazy?" Biggs asked.[14]

Reverend Hampton appeared in downtown Athens around 10:00 P.M. "Go home, please," he begged the crowd. There would be no counterattack tonight. Or any other night. The men began to demobilize.[15]

SUNDAY, AUGUST 4

"Three tired, sleepy GIs" patrolled the streets of Athens. "They found everything in order—as quiet and sleepy as themselves." People returned to civilian pursuits. "Some went to church and others went fishing."[16]

One GI told the *Chicago Tribune* that "there would be no further violence." Unless Mansfield came back to town. He might "get roughed up a bit."[17]

At churches across the county, people were "thankful that the battle of the ballots was over, thankful that no one had been killed in the jail fight, thankful that gang rule was no longer the code of officials, thankful that the voice of the people could again be heard." They "chatted freely and fearlessly as if a strange new freedom had been cast into their laps."

A reporter at one church took note of "a clean cut, athletic GI who had Thursday night used his bare fists on a gun totin' thug [and who now] marched by the side of his pretty little wife, pushing his baby in a stroller before him as he took his place in church," and "a clear eyed chap who had called in sniper fire on the jail," and a man who had overturned a car and now "carried a laughing little child down the church steps to the nursery."[18]

Reverend Hampton's service on the commission didn't excuse him from his Sunday sermon. "I am prouder of my community today than I have been at any time since I came here," he said. "I believe God's hand guided many of those who participated in this little revolution. We should give thanks to God because the bloodshed was no worse. I am praying that we will lay aside these methods and depend upon a new order based upon love." Hampton had stirred up major controversy the week after Pearl Harbor with a sermon titled "Who Is Our Neighbor?" In it he said he still loved the Japanese and the Germans. How much more was it true of the people who lived in McMinn?[19]

Newspapers carried a list of Thursday's many injuries: from Tom Gillespie, "shot at a voting booth," and Bob Harrill, black-jacked by Minus Wilburn, to a number of GIs with buckshot wounds from the battle, to the deputies who were shot inside the jail or beaten in the aftermath, everyone had survived the Battle of Athens.[20]

Governor McCord returned from a week's vacation at Monteagle to a telegram from Mansfield: he was tendering his resignation due to the "state of insurrection" in McMinn County, and called for the appointment of Knox Henry to the remaining twenty-seven days of his term.

McCord alerted the press. "I hope this is the end of it," he said. It wasn't. McCord was dogged by questions about what he did and failed to do. Why hadn't he taken steps to keep the peace on Election Day? Jim Buttram told *The Tennessean,* "I stayed on the wire about a month trying to get help."

There had been no "official request from any official of McMinn County," McCord said. "It's over, isn't it?" he asked. "It worked out admirably."

Why did he send in the National Guard against the GIs? They were simply alerted, he said, "in case such a request should come." One headline summed up the press's skepticism: "That's His Story." Another was less circumspect: "The facts don't square up."

McCord was contradicted by his own head of the National Guard. General Hilton Butler said the Guard was converging on Athens from two directions: "Before we could get there," he said, "the situation was restored." The Guard shouted for joy when ordered to turn back. They might well have joined the fighting in Athens had the battle continued—but on which side?[21]

41

GLORIOUS VICTORY

> GI CANDIDATES SWEEP TO GLORIOUS
> VICTORY
>> —Daily Post-Athenian, *August 5, 1946*

MONDAY, AUGUST 5

10:00 A.M.

There was a car for every parking space within three blocks of downtown. The courtroom was filled with rows of happy GIs. Shy Scott sat in the front with a bandage over his eye. Bob Harrill wore an even thicker bandage around his head but was smiling big. More than forty reporters from across the country were there to witness the scene.

Herman Moses, vice chairman of the county court, presided over the meeting. Moses had originally joined the court through the Ripper Bill. He had been in the jail on Thursday night, was lightly wounded in the shooting, and had spent the rest of the morning in a cell with the deputies.

R. A. Davis was the first to address the court: "I have received a communication from Frank Cantrell, who asked me to submit his resignation of Mr. Paul Cantrell as justice of the peace, chairman of the county court, and any other county offices he may hold." It was accepted.

A committee was formed to audit the county's finances. The former chief deputy, Boe Dunn, was removed from his office as coroner for "fraudulent and corrupt practices" on Election Day. Harry Johnson Jr., treasurer for the GI ticket, was appointed as his replacement.

Jay McAmis, the first chair of the county court under the Ripper Bill, proposed that Knox Henry fill Pat Mansfield's unexpired term. The motion was approved unanimously.

George Woods, Speaker of the Tennessee House of Representatives, secretary of the election commission, and county purchasing agent, walked into the room under GI protection. Woods had arranged for Otto Kennedy to meet him north of Cleveland on Sunday evening and bring him into Athens. Woods had not left his side since. He nervously chewed a cigar.[1]

Woods and Otto formed a quorum of the election commission. They sat at a table with the ballot boxes in front of them. When no one could find the keys to the ballot boxes, Otto improvised by shooting the locks off. Woods motioned to certify the results of the ballot boxes where the count had proceeded fairly. Otto seconded the motion. The final result was read to the room: for sheriff, Knox Henry, 2,230. Paul Cantrell, 1,244. There was a "loud cheer" and "wild applause." The results were similar all the way down the ticket.

"I am certainly glad to be back here and to do my sworn duty as a good citizen," Woods said. "I am a good loser." He shook hands with the victorious GI candidates as he handed them their certificates of election. They were nearly blinded by dozens of flashing cameras.

"Your shirttail's out, Frank," someone yelled at Carmichael when he stepped up to receive his certificate of election. Everyone laughed, Frank included.[2]

Ralph Duggan stood up to speak. "As you know, we have had much bitterness here the last few days. That was bad and we hope such a thing will never happen again." Woods "has come here at considerable risk to himself and I want him treated with politeness and courtesy. I don't know about everybody else, but I think it's time to settle down to work and business here in Athens and McMinn County."[3]

With Knox Henry as sheriff, the three-man commission, the revolutionary government of McMinn County, disbanded. Reverend Bernie Hampton, whose time in office spanned seventy-two eventful hours, said in parting: "the most important thing is to carry on now in an orderly way . . . keep our victory clean."

Otto Kennedy said it was time "to forget the past and start out anew under the new government."[4]

Knox Henry was sworn in at 3:00 P.M. in the office of the county court clerk Clyde Rogers. He wore a broad smile and a wide tie that didn't quite reach his belt. Mrs. Clyde Rogers, deputy clerk, smiled just as big. In the past few months, her husband had been dumped from the ticket; her father-in-law roughed up, robbed, and arrested; and her brother-in-law shot at his drugstore. It seemed like a different world than the one they were living in now.

"We have accomplished what we started out to do," Henry said. "We've broken the grip of the political machine that has ruled McMinn County for ten years without regard as to the wishes of the people in how their government was to be run.

"When I say we, I mean the other GIs on the nonpartisan cleanup ticket and the citizens of McMinn County who helped us win the battle. We regret that the gunfight at the jail had to happen. . . . Our only alternative was to use force." But "there will be no trouble of this kind at the next election. Any person who can qualify for an office may run with the full assurance of an honest election and the people will have nothing to fear when they go to the polls on Election Day.

"There will be no 'fee grabbing' by my deputies—we want tourists to travel through McMinn County, instead of intimidating them as has been the practice. We really intend to have a clean, honest government—one run on the best principles we know—of the people, by the people, and for the people."

In his first official act as sheriff, Knox Henry pinned a star on his new chief deputy, Otto Kennedy. Otto, who had led the opposition to the machine during the war years, finally had a chance to bring professional law enforcement to his county. The kind his father had given his life for.

Sheriff Henry and Chief Deputy Kennedy needed an entirely new team of deputies, well respected, honest, and tough. They had one man especially in mind—Bill White. No sooner had Knox pinned a star on Bill White than the three of them went out together on raids against the moonshiners who had enjoyed the machine's protection—in the woods near Vincent's station or at a house in South Etowah, there was so much to clean up.[5]

One of the New York reporters, a twenty-five-year-veteran

journalist, sent his wife a postcard. On it, he wrote: "I am in the most wonderful part of our country. Truly I mean it. I wish that some day we might find a place in this section to reside."[6]

The Tennessean praised what "has happened in the beautiful little city of Athens in McMinn County," which "undoubtedly has awakened a thrill of pride throughout this machine-ridden state. Make no mistake. The McMinn County veterans and their supporters had first won their victory at the polls. Then they fought, with their bare fists and such weapons as they could seize, to protect their election from the theft attempted by force of arms before their eyes. This was no 'riot'—unless Bunker Hill was a riot." The "Boston Tea Party of Tennessee [caused] by a decade of election corruption and thievery, has stamped upon a brutal farce it had determined to endure no longer." The battle was "what always has happened where men not born of a craven race have been pushed too far by tyranny."[7]

The *Philadelphia Record* asked: "What else could they do? The Constitution of the United States says 'the right of the people to bear arms shall not be infringed.' In Tennessee nearly every man and boy and many women know how to use a pistol, shotgun, and rifle. Nearly every home has at least 'a lawn gun' for potting squirrels, rabbits, birds, and other intruders. It seems reasonable to assume the Founding Fathers were thinking of more important things when they wrote the Constitution—perchance that the time might come when the bullet might be necessary to protect the ballot."

Not everyone was convinced. Another editorial in the same newspaper pointed to Athens, Alabama, where the same week a white mob had attacked members of the black community. "Lawlessness begets lawlessness," they wrote.

The *Detroit News* editorialized: "Shame on Athens, Tennessee!" and condemned its citizens' lack of patience and faith in democratic institutions.[8]

Syndicated columnist Robert Ruark found it hard to sympathize with the "armed mob in Athens, Tennessee, even though the mobsters apparently had cause for indignation." He thought such "violent action" could easily "run free in the wrong direction. He also objected to the use of "GI" or "veterans" in the news coverage, calling it an attempt to excuse their behavior. "A guy running around with a loaded gat is no less a rioter because of his war record."[9]

Lowell Arterburn wrote a letter to the editor of *The New York Times* in response to a critical editorial: "I lived in New York for a time while obtaining one of my three degrees (M.A., Columbia). My first requirement in selection of newspaper property was that its location must be in a place in which my wife (Helen M. Richards, M.D.) and I could live happily and enjoy all those things that go toward making life worth living. Athens was selected. At no time have we regretted our decisions."

Arterburn included a copy of his coverage so that they could understand what was happening. "We're cleaning up a bad situation here—one some of you people do not have the guts to do in your own back yard."[10]

But the most important word belonged to the most popular woman in the country—Eleanor Roosevelt, who made the battle the subject of one of her regular columns: "We may deplore the use of force but we must also recognize the lesson which this incident points for us all," she wrote. People must be able to determine their fate at the ballot box in a fair election. Ultimately, Americans would not accept living under tyranny. "The decisive action which has just occurred in our midst is a warning, and one which we cannot afford to overlook."[11]

Many of the machine's leaders left town. Minus Wilburn moved to Polk County and joined Burch Biggs's crew. There was no sign of the Rucker brothers, only their shot-up car in Etowah. They had gone to Ohio, where they stayed for years, a decision that almost certainly saved their lives.

Minus Wilburn searched for the man who had cut his throat for the rest of his life. He didn't search long. Three years later he and his cousin Buddy were driving home after a few drinks. They were both sober and Minus seemed perfectly fine. Suddenly, he lost consciousness and drove straight into a filling station, killing him. Buddy was certain that someone had drugged his drink.[12]

Walter Martin, division supervisor of the state Department of Conservation, got a curious call. It was the game warden, Carl Neil, phoning in his resignation from "an undisclosed point." Martin told him that he had already written him, demanding his resignation. Neil said that he was selling his things and moving his family to California.

The VFW and American Legion adopted resolutions demanding the resignations of city councilmen and county court members who owed their offices to stolen elections. Mayor Paul Walker of Athens said that he would not quit under pressure. He did exactly that after his window was shot out, leaving the city recorder and street superintendent as the only remaining officials in Athens. In all, twenty-eight elected officials resigned. Every deputy sheriff and police officer was replaced.[13]

Windy Wise pleaded guilty to felonious assault in the shooting of Tom Gillespie. He was given a sentence of one to three years and paroled after one year. George Spurling was convicted of the murder of Earl Ford, and sentenced to fifteen years and a day behind bars.[14]

The formation of the Good Government League was announced. The league would hold town halls and forums to discuss and recommend policies to improve government. "We hope to set up an organization that 25 years from now will be demanding the same good government practices," said Harry Johnson.[15]

Ralph Duggan was tasked with drafting a statement of principles. The league was for judges trained in the law, salaried law enforcement, limits on the power to deputize, and adopting a council-manager form of government; it was against the poll tax. More than eight hundred people showed up to its first meeting. George Kennedy, a reporter for the Washington *Evening Star,* was in attendance. Afterward, Cliff Ingram, a GI, gave him a ride to his hotel. "When people in New York, or Americans abroad, used to ask me where I came from, I used to explain that it was a little city, halfway between Knoxville and Chattanooga," said Ingram. "From now on I'll just tell them that I came from Athens, Tennessee."[16]

The VFW decided to keep its scheduled dance for Friday, exactly one week to the day from the liberation of the jail. The Ray Kinney Orchestra, featuring ukulele and string guitar and a chorus of Aloha Girls, played at the Athens armory starting at 8:30 P.M. They renamed the event "The Big VFW Victory Dance."

In the days that followed, Pat Mansfield told the press his side of the story. He and Boe Dunn, his former chief deputy, had made it to Cartersville, Georgia, where Pat had grown up. "How many people could have changed from lifelong friends within a few hours," Mansfield said, "into a bloodthirsty mob yelling for our lives I will never understand if I live a thousand years."

Mansfield claimed that the GIs used "young boys" as shields and that no shots were fired from the jail. "We certainly didn't want the blood of a single one of these children on our hands," said Dunn.

"Why, I could have killed dozens of my fellow citizens," said Mansfield, "but the very thought of such a thing was so revolting, I would not fire myself, nor would I permit my deputies to do so." Two years later Mansfield told an interviewer that he'd ordered his men to fire but over the heads of the GIs.

Mansfield suggested the election had been stolen, and that people assured him that he was "the most popular citizen of McMinn County."

Mansfield said that things were going great on Election Day until he "suddenly lost control." He'd been called to a disturbance at a polling place caused by Shy Scott and Ed Vestal. He claimed that he had impounded the ballots in the county jail "until calm had been restored and their count could go forward in an orderly and legal manner."

"I'm through with politics for good," Mansfield told *The New York Times.* "It'll sure mess you up sometimes. I'm going back to railroading."[17]

Paul Weeks responded with an op-ed in the *Post-Athenian.* "You will excuse us, won't you Pat, while we go somewhere and laugh up our sleeves?" He asked Mansfield if he'd seen the photographs of Scott and Vestal's "disturbance." "You know, your deputies didn't capture all the photographers and films that day." As for the jail refusing to fire, "Guess all of those boys still picking buck shot out of themselves dreamed the whole thing." Paul expressed regret that Mansfield had not said these things before he came home to clean out his house. "Goodbye, Pat. Hope you like Georgia." Mansfield lived in Atlanta for the rest of his life.[18]

A *Life* photographer went to Cantrell's house to try and get a picture. "I do not know when he will be back," his wife said pleasantly. "No, I can not say where he has gone. I am just thankful I am not a widow."[19]

On August 21, Paul Cantrell was spotted at the Hermitage Hotel in Nashville, wearing a brown suit, sporting a "day's growth of beard," and appearing "highly nervous." He was asked to comment on the battle, but declined. "I'm in the gas business," he explained. His new venture would pipe natural gas to Chattanooga and Knoxville.

"Is it a trade secret how you got out of that jail?" asked a reporter.

"It's a military secret," he said.

Burch Biggs entered the lobby and ignored Cantrell. Members of the press tried to coax them into a joint interview or photograph. Biggs refused.[20]

Ed Crump felt an incredible backlash from the battle, one that ultimately broke his reign over the state. Crump took out half-page ads throughout Tennessee: "I have never been in McMinn County—have never met the Cantrells. I didn't know who was running for office over there." The Associated Press called the Crump machine "pathetic" for trying to wash its hands. "For 10 years the Cantrell machine took the elections in McMinn and played with Boss Crump in all his statewide enterprises."[21]

42

UNKNOWN SUBJECTS

Judge Sue Hicks charged the grand jury with investigating every possible crime arising from the election: the break-in to the armory, the firing on the jail, the election fraud, the overturned cars. With the exception of Windy Wise, there were no indictments. People were ready to move on.[1]

An investigation by the Tennessee National Guard found "no evidence that the armory was entered or that anything used the night of the riot belonged either to the state guard or to the federal government." They knew this was untrue, of course.[2]

C. McAfee McCracken, special agent in charge of the Knoxville office for the Federal Bureau of Investigation, received a message from J. Edgar Hoover in Washington, to investigate a crime committed by "UNKNOWN SUBJECTS":

THEFT OF WEAPONS FROM ARMORY, ATHENS, TENNESSEE.

YOUR OFFICE IS CAUTIONED TO EXERCISE EVERY PRECAUTION TO

PREVENT BEING EMBROILED IN DISPUTES ARISING FROM HEAT OF

ELECTION ACTIVITIES. YOU SHOULD ALSO DETERMINE IF AMMUNI-
TION OR GUNS MISSING FROM ARMORY. KEEP BUREAU ADVISED
OF ALL DEVELOPMENTS.

Agent McCracken joined a long list of unfamiliar faces that appeared in Athens. He interviewed Supply Sergeant Perly Berger, caretaker of the armory. A "truckload of young fellows came the evening of August 1," he said, "and demanded the keys to the strong room." Berger said he didn't get a good look at any of them.

Major Anderson told him "he really did not know just what had happened to the guns, whether they were actually stolen or taken from the Armory during the political riot." Anderson promised that if he learned anything he would report it to the FBI. "He was as much concerned about the missing firearms from the armory as anyone."

Captain Charlie Pickel, company commander in the Tennessee State Guard and newly elected recorder of deeds, said the "weapons could have been missing anytime from inventory in May, 1946, to August 7 or 8, 1946."

What about ammunition? the agent asked.

"Expendable and no record of amount used is kept," said Pickel. McCracken recorded the disappointing answer in his notes.

Sheriff Knox Henry "advised that he had no idea whatsoever as to what happened to the weapons or when they were taken from the Armory." Why didn't he report the theft to the FBI? "He wanted to keep it quiet hoping that the weapons would turn up in Athens."

The agent interviewed Chief Deputy Otto Kennedy. Did he know who went to the armory to get the guns?

No, he said, and he "did not want to know."

The agent contacted U.S. Attorney James Frazier. Frazier told him that "prosecution would be improbable, even [if] it was determined who the individuals were that took the guns from the Armory."

McAfee concluded his findings:

In view of the political nature of this occasion and in view of the fact that there are no logical leads as to the whereabouts of the missing guns in this case, no further action is being taken in this matter unless advised to the contrary by the Bureau, and the case is being closed upon the authority of the Special Agent in charge.

-CLOSED-

"We thought we were going to be prosecuted," said Bill White. "The only reason we didn't was because the sentiment of the public was behind us."[3]

43

"LET US LIVE TOGETHER AND LOVE ONE ANOTHER"

John McKay of Etowah charged at the oncoming Germans and shook hands. Seconds earlier, at 11:00 A.M. on November 11, 1918, the Germans raised white flags in surrender, bringing the Great War to an end. Now the men who had been trying to kill one another embraced and celebrated surviving the greatest catastrophe in human history. McKay had served with two of his brothers, one of whom did not live to see the war's end. Now he would return, along with eighteen hundred others, to McMinn County to get on with life. [1]

If only the political leaders had a fraction of the magnanimity of those who fought. The old men who signed the Treaty of Versailles ended the First World War and ensured their children and grandchildren would fight another.

The first Germans to learn the terms rushed to telephones to convey the news to Berlin, yelling in such hysterics that eavesdropping French spies could barely make out what they were saying. The long treaty was unnecessary, said one. "Germany surrenders all claims to its existence" would have sufficed.

Herbert Hoover, in charge of feeding Europe, was woken at 4:00 A.M. by a messenger bringing the complete version of the treaty. He wandered the streets of Paris, unable to sleep, thinking "the consequences . . . would ultimately bring destruction."

The American secretary of state thought the treaty "immeasurably harsh and humiliating."

"I am grieved beyond words," wrote Jan Smuts, representing South Africa, "that such should be the result of our statesmanship."

Germany lost 13 percent of its territory and 10 percent of its population. John Maynard Keynes, adviser to the British delegation, advised that Germany might be able to come up with ten billion dollars in reparations. Anything more would cause a revolution. The allies settled on thirty-three billion.

Adolf Hitler launched his career in politics by mesmerizing Bavarian beer halls condemning "the peace of shame."[2]

The people of McMinn County, a world away, were pulled into the war that was the result. They returned from that war and fought the Battle of Athens. Having brought free elections to the county and ejected the machine, they had nothing to gain by vindictiveness and everything to lose.

Billie Bea Kennedy went to a birthday party three weeks after the battle. Otto called his wife: "Don't let Billie leave" her friend's house. "We have word that the thugs are coming back." Myrtle hurried to the party, but Billie was gone. With tears in her eyes and her hair in her hands, Myrtle raced home, where she found Billie, perfectly alright, wondering what was wrong. It was one of many false alarms in a community that remained tense. For six months Otto's family stayed outside while he entered the house and stayed in the house while he started the car.[3]

Paul Cantrell returned to Etowah. Otto Kennedy showed up at his house shortly thereafter. He asked to borrow his famous bird dogs to go hunting. Cantrell agreed, on one condition. "That you let me come with you." Kennedy accepted. And the former rivals went armed into the woods. In another era the warring factions might have cemented their new relationship with a family marriage. Otto Kennedy and Paul Cantrell settled for a regional variation, and bred their bird dogs together. Cantrell's was named "Lady Feegrabber."[4]

Cantrell's grandson, Paul Willson, remembered walking the streets of Athens with his grandfather years later. "Daddy Paul," he said, "do you carry a gun?"

"No, Baby Paul," Cantrell said, using his nickname for him, "I have no need to carry a gun."

Paul Willson, a beloved and respected member of the community, recalled that the most important relationships in his life outside of his family were with men who had been part of the GI ticket and the Battle of Athens. Willson considered Bill White a personal friend to the end of Bill's life, in 2006.

Ann Davis, daughter of Shy Scott and the former mayor of Athens, considers Mintie Willson, Paul Cantrell's daughter, to be a second mother to her. She still spends Thanksgivings at Mintie's house. Shy Scott had signed a contract in the weeks after the battle to play himself in a movie version. But he and others decided that reconciling the community was more important than fame. A visitor to Athens today would have no doubt that it was the right decision.

At Tennessee Wesleyan College Pop Wilburn, Minus's son, introduced himself to a new freshman, Billie Bea Kennedy.

Could they be friends despite what had passed between their parents? "Sure," Billie said, "that'd be fine."

"I liked him," she remembered. "We were just people."

If the people of McMinn County could come together after all that had happened, there is hope for everyone. "The real story of the Battle of Athens is about reconciliation, thankfully," said Paul Willson.

The fall elections of 1946 featured record turnout and saw major victories for GI allies: Rhea Hammer became mayor of Athens, Shy Scott was the leading vote getter for alderman, three-man-commission member J. P. Cartwright replaced Paul Cantrell in the state senate, and John Peck, secretary of the GI ticket, won George Woods's seat in the House. Mansfield and Woods, who had won the Democratic nominations for those offices on August 1, withdrew. "They know they couldn't be elected dog catchers," said Buttram.

Frank Larkin, who had covered the Battle of Athens with Allen Stout, wrote an article on McMinn County for *The Knoxville News-Sentinel* on the one-year anniversary. He found "so much improvement over the old that there can be no comparison." The "wide-open bootleg joints, so apparent under the Cantrell machine, have disappeared or they are very quietly operating undercover." Weekend arrests dropped from seventy-five to a hundred down to fifteen.[5]

The hackberry tree over Nocatula died and the oak that covered Conestoga followed, like the lovers who couldn't live without each other. The people of Athens planted a hackberry seed and an acorn in the same place, where two tall, intertwined trees stand to this day.

Knox Henry won reelection in 1948. The Democrats took out a full-page ad to thank him for his fairness: "Every vote cast in the August 5th election was counted for whom cast where it was cast without friction and all the election officials worked in harmony, peace, and friendship to see that every voter voted as he or she desired and that his and her vote was counted for the candidate it was cast for."

Gordon Browning, defeated as governor in 1938 for defying Ed Crump, regained his old job after the 1948 election, defeating Jim McCord. Estes Kefauver ran as the anti-Crump candidate for U.S. Senate and won. The Associated Press headline said it all: "Crump Receives Smashing Defeat." It was the end of the road for the king of Tennessee.[6]

Knox Henry died in 1952, at thirty-nine, "after several months' illness." His obituary mentioned that he had first been elected in the "Battle of the Ballots."[7]

Otto Kennedy replaced him as sheriff. Otto was able to pay his own salary, his deputies, and all the costs of running the jail and housing prisoners for what Pat Mansfield had spent on food alone, in an era when the price of food was much lower.[8]

The McMinn County Jail was sold the following year for $55,700, with newspapers taking note of its unusual history, "used and abused since Civil War days," and "scene of the Battle of Bullets and Ballots." Tom Sherman, a real estate developer, tore down the building. Today the site is a parking lot for an insurance office.[9]

Ralph Duggan died at the age of fifty-one, from the kidney disease he had hidden to join the navy. His send-off in the *Post-Athenian* befitted a city father, a front-page story and banner headline calling him "one of the most prominent attorneys in the state of Tennessee."

"He swung hard for what he believed in," read the obituary, "but abided by a fair code of ethics."[10]

The GIs remained active in politics for the rest of their lives. Carroll Ross's father had been one of them, a POW at Stalag-17, who stood guard outside the Etowah Library for his right to vote on August 1, 1946. Fifty years later, Carroll was elected circuit court judge with their support, the last campaign, he believes, at which their backing was decisive. Judge Ross knew these men his entire life, knew them in their middle years and as old men.

He remembers the GIs this way: "They held good jobs and they worked hard. They belonged to the various civic clubs and demonstrated their leadership abilities in many important ways other than politics. They were active in their churches. They raised children, many of whom, like myself, were the first in their families to graduate from college. They led positive and productive lives, and they left a legacy that their families can and should be very proud of. In short, they proved themselves to be the very kind of good citizens that deserve a fair and honest government to represent them, which is all they had ever asked for in the first place."[11]

EPILOGUE

Before you go, I want to say that I hope that
our country, especially those places that are as
boss ridden as we were, will take hope from
what we have accomplished here. I think we
have shown how to clean out those dirty nests.
Anyway, we've done it.

—*Major Carl Anderson,*
The News *(New York), August 6, 1946*

Bill White had an eventful career as a sheriff's deputy. He was
shot at by a prominent doctor for trying to repossess his car,
apprehended a serial burglar who targeted post offices, tracked
down a murderer escaped from the penitentiary, seized illegal liquor hidden in the Robert E. Lee Hotel, and destroyed a
seventy-gallon still in Starr Mountain with eight sticks of dynamite. When he pulled over Lester Hickman for drunk driving,
Hickman told him that he wouldn't go alive. But the hammer

on his gun snagged in his pants, giving Bill the chance to arrest him.[1]

One night Deputy Bill White came home to his wife, Jean. He had a major proposition and wasn't sure how she was going to take it. The Tellico Lodge was for sale. It was the land where he'd hunted and fished with Grandpa Wiggins, and as soon as he saw it was available he knew that he wanted it.

"Jean, would you like to move to Tellico?"

She didn't need to think about it. They put it to a vote of their four children: girls fifteen and fourteen, and boys twelve and seven. All were unanimous.

Bill allowed the samurai sword he had sent home from Tarawa to be displayed at Tennessee Wesleyan. A group of Japanese businessmen had come to town to look at buying Mayfield's Dairy. They visited the college and read the inscription on the blade. Word spread back in Japan that the sword had turned up in Athens, Tennessee. The Japanese government made a formal request for its return. Collectors offered Bill White serious money. He wasn't interested. But he made it known that he would return it to the family of the man he'd taken it from.

In 1967, Pakaore Hashitami arrived in the United States and traveled to the Tellico Lodge in the mountains of East Tennessee to meet the man who had killed his father. He admired the polished sharkskin scabbard and gold-tipped handle of his father's sword. Before he could accept, he asked Bill to tell him how his father died. He had to know that he had lost his life honorably. Bill told him the story of Swede and the concrete blockhouse on Tarawa. Hashitami bowed to Bill, drew the sword from the scabbard, and held it over his head. Bill realized a second too late that he had given this man room to take a swing at him. Bill took a big step closer. But Hashitami had no intentions of revenge. He thanked Bill for restoring honor to his family. The sword had been with them for four hundred years. Of course, Bill said. The war was over.[2]

ACKNOWLEDGMENTS

My first thanks are to God for the opportunity to tell this story. For Dr. Hannah DeRose, my hero and wife, who saved lives every day of her pregnancy during the greatest health crisis of our lifetimes. For my mother, Anna, and sister, Cathy, who brought her considerable literary talents to bear on this book. For my in-laws, Tom and Cindy, Maddie and Billy, Alex and Phil, Sam and Jim.

Unearthing an old mystery required help from more people than I can thank personally, but here's my best shot. For the people of McMinn County, and the loved ones that remain to tell their stories, and who shared them with me, especially: Travis Davis, who trusted me with his grandfather's memory, Randy Lockmiller, Ralph Duggan, Jim Buttram, Joe Grubb, and the Vestals and Hutsells. Special thanks to Paul Willson, grandson of Paul Cantrell, a true gentleman, for his graciousness.

Historian Tyler Boyd became a valued friend, partner, and sounding board. Larry Eaton provided valuable connections and enthusiasm. Adam Martin lent advice and tech savvy. Durant

Tullock shared his deep knowledge of history. Steve Byrum, for his willingness to answer questions and give guidance, and for preserving stories that would otherwise have been lost.

Sheriff Larry Wallace and Judge Carroll Ross read the book with attention to the details of McMinn history, of which they are important parts. Kimberly Beare, Mikel Steinfeld, and Amy Durbin are part of my regular preview squad and the book is always better for it.

For the teams at the McMinn County Living Heritage Museum, Historical Society, and Tennessee State Library and Archives for all of their help, particularly Esther Nunley, Laura LeNoir, and Ann Davis. For Alex Rutherford, master of unlocking DOJ's secrets, and Geoff Gentilini of Golden Arrow Research—if he can't find a military record, it's not there.

For the wonderful people at St. Martin's Press: especially my editor Marc Resnick, for a truly enjoyable collaboration, his love of this story, and insight on how to make it better; assistant editor Lily Cronig, for making sure everything happened when it needed to, despite the author's best efforts; and Gregory Villipique, for his attention to detail.

For Adam Chromy, agent, advocate, friend.

For Laura Hanifin, for her generous assistance with finding and licensing photographs.

Writing this book reminded me that chaotic times are the rule, rather than the exception in the human experience. I am especially thankful for our friends who were there for us from a safe distance: Jon Anderson, Alex and Allie Benezra, Elliot Berke, Yvonne Cahill, Nolan Davis, Jeremy and Robyn Duda, Rob Ellman, Ashley and Connie Fickel, Tom and Ana Galvin, Ruben Gallego, James Hohmann, Justin Herman, Lee Hudson, Eric

Johnson, Amy Kalman, Randy Kendrick, Adam and Orit Kwasman, Whitney Lawrence, Heather Macre, Simer and Vicki Mayo, Danny and Bonnie Mazza, Lee Omar, Tysen Schlink, James Slattery, Jay Swart and Carol Perry, Don Tapia, Trey and Elise Terry, Jim and Kitty Waring, Katie Whalen, Justin Wilmeth, Katie McShane, Megan Wojtulewicz, Hector Dominguez, Maggie Miller, Heather Pearson, Lolita Jackson, and Vivek Nagrani. Heartfelt and special thanks to Brian Johnston and Vilert Loving.

And for you, the reader. You have made possible this extraordinary chapter in my life.

NOTES

PROLOGUE

1 Broadcast script in the William Downs Papers, Georgetown University Library; information relative to Oak Ridge was found in an Associated Press article, August 2, 1946.

2 Papers of Theodore White, Harvard University, "The Votes and Hearts of McMinn County," the original draft for this story; Theodore White, "The Battle of Athens, Tennessee," *Harper's,* February 1947.

3 Bill White, interview with Dan Henderson, Memphis *Commercial Appeal,* September 30, 1979.

1. HOME, SWEET HOME

1 *Home to War,* documentary, Bagwell Productions, 2001; interview with Bill White, Veteran's Oral History Project, Center for the Study of War and Society, Department of History, University of Tennessee at Knoxville, July 20, 2000.

2. ON THE LITTLE TENNESSEE RIVER

1   Audio recording of Bill White, from cassette tapes in the possession of the White family. Unless otherwise specified, Bill White's recollections of his childhood, time at war, and the Battle of Athens are drawn from these sources.

2   Bill White, Oral History; "James White," *Tennessee Encyclopedia*, https://tennesseeencyclopedia.net/entries/james-white/.

3   "Let me tell you about Bass" by Bridget McCurry in Joyce Green, Casi Best, and Foxfire Students, eds., *The Foxfire 45th Anniversary Book: Singin', Praisin', Raisin'* (New York: Anchor, 2011), 167–68.

4   Green et al., *The Foxfire 45th Anniversary Book*, 150.

5   Interview with Betty Lehning, sister of Bill White; interview with Jean White, Bill's widow; *Knoxville News-Sentinel*, April 21, 1968;

3. WARRIOR ROOTS

1   Thomas J. Baker Jr., "Political Violence in Tennessee: The Battle of Athens, 1946," 2 (this article, written in 1969 and never published, is in the archives of the Tennessee State Library and Archives); George Q. Johnson, "A Legend Which Centers Around Two Trees in the Heart of Athens," *Tennessee Historical Magazine* 8, no. 3 (October 1924), republished from accounts serialized in the *Athenian* newspaper during November 1922. The Nocatula story was told to the author by his grandfather, who had firsthand knowledge of the events.

2   David Hackett Fischer, *Albion's Seed: Four British Folkways in America* (New York: Oxford University Press, 1989), 620.

3   Ibid., 125.

4   Ibid., 624.

5   Ibid., 615.

6   Ibid., 618.

7   Joe Guy, *Hidden History of McMinn County* (Charleston, SC: History Press, 2007), 20.

8   C. Stephen Byrum, *McMinn County* (Memphis, TN: Memphis State University Press, 1984), 17–19, 22–23, 25, 32.

9   Byrum, *McMinn,* 18-19.

4. HARD TIMES

1   White, Oral History.

2   Various authors, *"Tennessee: A Guide to the State"* (Federal Writers' Project, 1939), 306.

3   Bill Akins, "Hard Times Remembered" (McMinn County Historical Society, 1983), 57; Frank McKinney, "Tall Tales and Unusual Happenings of McMinn County, Tennessee" (McMinn County Historical Society, 1988), 29.

4   Akins, "Hard Times Remembered" 12–14, 50, 55; Bill Akins and Kenneth Landley, *A Date That Will Live in Infamy: McMinn County, Tennessee, During World War II* (Etowah: Choate, 2011), 1.

5   Akins, "Hard Times Remembered," 17; Speeches of Franklin Roosevelt, www.fdrlibrary.marist.edu, October 22, 1932.

6   *Daily Post-Athenian,* July 3, 1936; see, e.g., *Daily Post-Athenian,* June 17 and July 1, 1936.

5. THE RISE OF PAUL CANTRELL

1   *Daily Post-Athenian,* August 7, 1946; Baker, "Violence," 3; Akins, "Hard Times Remembered," 36-37.

2   Interview with Paul Willson, grandson of Paul Cantrell; *Knoxville News-Sentinel,* undated article, August 1946.

3   Baker, "Violence," 5.

4   Ibid.

5   *Daily Post-Athenian,* July 31, 1936.

6   George Brasington, "The McMinn County, TN Election of August 1, 1946" (Emory University, thesis, 1948), 4-5.

7   Deposition of Pat Mansfield, May 19, 1951, Circuit Court of McMinn County.

8   *Knoxville Journal,* September 12, 1940; Baker, "Violence," 6.

9   *Knoxville News-Sentinel,* June 16, 1937; July 24 and 26, 1938; October 13 and 14, 1939.

10   *Chattanooga Times–Free Press,* September 11, 2016.

11   *Knoxville News-Sentinel,* July 26 and October 14, 1938.

6.   THE BEST FIGHTS OF THE SEASON

1   *Daily Post-Athenian,* August 3, 1938.

2   Ibid., August 5, 1938.

3   Ibid., August 4, August 8, and August 13, 1938; Bicentennial Edition.

7.   CIVICS AT McMINN HIGH

1   Washington Star six-part series on the Battle of Athens, by George Kennedy, August, 1946; Baker, "Violence," 11.

8.   "POLITICOS IN McMINN SPLIT OVER VOTE ROBOTS"

1   *Taylor v. Cantrell,* Tennessee Supreme Court, Tennessee State Library and Archives (TSLA); *McTeer, Detherage, Cantrell, and Williams v. Cate, Webb, Duggan, et al.,* complaint, filed July 20, 1940, Circuit Court of McMinn County.

2   *Taylor v. Cantrell,* Chancery Court petition, TSLA; *Knoxville Journal,* July 14, 1940 and August 3, 1940.

3   *Daily Post-Athenian,* August 1 and 2, 1940; Bicentennial Edition.

4   *Chattanooga Times,* October 21, 1942; *Knoxville News-Sentinel,* August 2, 1940; *Knoxville Journal,* August 2, 1940.

5   *Daily Post-Athenian,* September 22, 1942.

6   *Knoxville Journal,* August 2, 1940.

7   Ibid., August 3, 1940.

8   *Daily Post-Athenian,* August 2, 1940; February 24, 1941, and September 22, 1942.

9   *Daily Post-Athenian,* March 10, 1941; Brasington, "McMinn County Election" thesis 7.

9. THE KING OF TENNESSEE

1   United Press, August 3, 1938.

2   *Daily Post-Athenian,* August 5, 1938.

3   *Knoxville News-Sentinel,* August 5, 1938.

4   Ralph Martin, *The Bosses* (New York: G.P. Putnam's Sons, 1964), ch. 3; Charles Van Devander, "Mailed Fist in Tennessee," *American Mercury,* May 1944; election totals are from relevant Tennessee Blue Books; the story of Biggs and Cantrell's connection is from the *Chattanooga Daily Times,* July 9, 1944.

10. "FOR THE DURATION OF THE NATIONAL EMERGENCY"

1   Brian Walsh, "In Plain Sight: The Pearl Harbor Spy," *World War II Magazine,* https://www.historynet.com/in-plain-sight-the-pearl-harbor-spy.htm; Ralph G. Martin, *The GI War* (New York: Little Brown, 1967), 12. Ray Merriam, *Pearl Harbor* (Scotts Valley, CA: CreateSpace, 2012), 58.

2   *Daily Post-Athenian,* December 5, 1941.

3   Interview with Ann Davis, daughter of Shy Scott.

4   Interview with Jim Buttram, son of Jim Buttram; Jim Buttram's personal papers.

5   Condit, Kenneth, et al, "Marine Corps Training in World War II" (Washington D.C.: Historical Branch, HQMC, 1956), 155, 158, 161.

6   Akins and Landley, *Date,* 16; 1940 census.

7   Byrum, *McMinn,* 112.

8   Akins and Landley, *Date,* 53; Guy, *Hidden History,* 80–81; *Knoxville Journal,* August 2, 1946.

9   C. Stephen Byrum, *August 1, 1946, the Battle of Athens, Tennessee* (Littleton, Mass.: Tapestry Press, 1996), 21.

10 *Daily Post-Athenian,* undated, January 1942; Bill White, Oral History, 29.

11 Green et al., *Foxfire 45th Anniversary Book,* 150.

12 Ibid.

13 William Manchester, *Goodbye, Darkness* (New York: Little Brown, 2008), 120-21.

14 Richard Wheeler, *A Special Valor* (New York: Castle Books, 1996), 1.

15 Manchester, *Goodbye,* 38-39, 42.

16 Manchester, *Goodbye,* 166.

11. EVERYTHING I NEEDED TO KNOW ABOUT GEOPOLITICS, I LEARNED FROM FRANK CAPRA

1 Matthew Gunter, *The Capra Touch* (Jefferson, North Carolina: McFarland, 2012), 138-59.

2 Manchester, *Goodbye,* 120-21.

12. GEORGE THE RIPPER

1 *Tennessean,* February 14, 1941; Baker, "Violence," 7, 13.

2 *Daily Post-Athenian,* February 19, 1941.

3 Ibid., March 5, 6, 10, 1941.

4 Census Bureau and Bureau of Labor Statistics, https://www.census
.gov/hhes/www/housing/census/historic/values.html; https://www
.navycs.com/charts/1942-military-pay-chart.html; https://data.bls
.gov/cgi-bin/cpicalc.pl?cost1=56%2C886.00&year1=194101&year2
=201911.

5 Tennessee Blue Book, 1942–43, pages 205-06; North American Newspaper Wire Service, August 11, 1946, printed in *Atlanta Constitution* of the same date; *Philadelphia Record*, August 5, 1946; Baker, "Violence," 9, 13; Statement of Harry Henson, on the payroll as a deputy sheriff, who never received his salary or performed any duties, *Daily Post-Athenian,* undated; *Philadelphia Record,* August 5, 1946; Department of Justice, file 72-70-13, National Archives; *Knoxville News-Sentinel,* July 11, 1946; *Chattanooga Daily Times,* July 23, 1946; *Knoxville Journal,* July 25, 1946; *Tennessean,* July 14, 1946.

6 *Daily Post-Athenian,* September 22, 1942; *Tennessee v. Cate and*

Webb, Circuit Court of McMinn County; *Tennessean,* March 30, 1943; *Chattanooga Daily Times,* September 23, 1942.

7   Akins and Landley, *Date,* 30, 32.

13. "WE WERE LIKE YOUNG TIGERS"

1   Manchester, *Goodbye,* 77-78.

2   John Wukovits, *One Square Mile of Hell* (New York: Dutton, 2007), 37.

3   Wheeler, *Special Valor,* 34, 36–37.

4   Ibid,; Campaign overview: https://www.history.navy.mil/content/dam/nhhc/browse-by-topic/Solomons%20I.pdf.

5   Record of events, summary of events, and historical record of the First Battalion, Second Marines. Richard Johnston, *Follow Me: The Story of the Second Marine Division in World War II* (New York: Random House, 1948), 2, 20–23, 25; Manchester, *Goodbye,* 162.

6   Wheeler, *Special Valor,* 41.

14. "A MONSTROUS, SHOCKING, AND REVOLTING STATE OF AFFAIRS"

1   *Daily Post-Athenian,* October 7, 1942.

2   Ibid., May 12, 1942.

3   *Tennessee v. Cate and Webb,* February 15, 1943.

4   *Knoxville Journal,* August 1, 1944.

5   Brasington, "McMinn," 8; E. D. Paul to Jennings, August 24, 1942, Papers of John Jennings, University of Tennessee at Knoxville. All correspondence of John Jennings is from this source unless noted otherwise; *Daily Post-Athenian,* Bicentennial Edition; the story of Ivins extorting senior citizens comes from the *Knoxville Journal,* October 29, 1942.

6   John Jennings to constituent, 1942.

7   *Tennessee v. Cate and Webb,* filing, February 15, 1943; Ken Wilburn, son of Minus, described the hidden pockets and their function; *Daily Citizen* (Dalton, GA), September 21, 2008; the anecdote about Wilburn's mother comes from my interview with Raymond Wilburn, Minus's nephew.

8   *Daily Post-Athenian,* August 7, 1942.

9   Ibid., August 10, 1942.

10   Jennings to the Department of Justice, March 9, 1943; Jennings to
     J. Edgar Hoover of the FBI, June 1, 1943.

11   Walter White to John Jennings, September 25, 1942; Zeb Aldridge
     to Jennings, August 26, 1942; Judge Sam Brown to Jennings, Oc-
     tober 14, 1942; *Knoxville Journal,* August 23, 1942.

15. "HIGH, DRY, AND BARE ASSED"

1   Wheeler, *Special Valor,* 48–50.

2   Manchester, *Goodbye,* 86.

3   Manchester, *Goodbye,* 120–21; Toshikazu Ohmae, "Leading the
     Charge at Savo Island," *Naval History Magazine* 31, no. 4.

4   Wheeler, *Special Valor,* 53.

5   Richard W. Johnston, *Follow Me: The Story of the Second Marine
     Division in World War II* (New York: Random House, 1947), 36.

6   Manchester, *Goodbye,* 176.

7   Bill White, Oral History.

16. "U.S. INDICTS SIX FOR VOTE FRAUD"

1   *Daily Post-Athenian,* September 22, 1942.

2   Ibid.

3   *Chattanooga Times,* October 21, 1942.

4   Speech by John Jennings, August 3, 1946, Papers of John Jennings.

5   *Tennessean,* October 28, 1942; Frank Carmichael, *Two Memoirs*
     (self-published), 25.

6   This correspondence is in Bill White's military personnel file at the
     National Archives.

7   Affidavits of W. T. Wade, John Hicks, and Claude Hutsell, Novem-
     ber 5, 1942.

8   Affidavit of H. A. Vestal, November 5, 1942.

9   Affidavits of M. A. Barnett and H. Reynolds, November 6, 1942;
     affidavits of Eugene Torbett and Burt Vaughn, November 8, 1942,
     National Archives.

10   *Johnson City Chronicle,* October 29, 1941; *Knoxville News-*

Sentinel, February 7, 1941; interview with John Pirkle, nephew of Raymond Count King.

11   *Knoxville News-Sentinel,* November 4, 1942.

17. "COME TO THE RESCUE OF A HELPLESS PEOPLE"

1   Transcript of radio interview with Les Dooley, 1942; text of the Distinguished Service Cross award; *Knoxville News-Sentinel,* June 16, 1943; January 13, 1944; December 6, 1942; December 13, 1942; *Daily Post-Athenian,* November 30, 1942.

2   *Daily Post-Athenian,* December 29, 1942.

3   *Biggs v. Beeler,* 180 Tenn. 198 (Tenn. 1943); Martin, *Bosses,* 155.

4   Jennings to Biddle, Department of Justice file 72-70-13, National Archives.

5   Rhea Hammer to the Department of Justice, November 3, 1942, file 72-70-13, National Archives.

6   H. L. Love to Biddle, November 8, 1942, Department of Justice file 72-70-13, National Archives.

7   H. A. Vestal to Biddle, November 6, 1942, Department of Justice file 72-70-13, National Archives.

8   John Proffit to Francis Biddle, November 7, 1942, Department of Justice file 72-70-13, National Archives.

9   Frank Porter to Jennings, November 30, 1942.

10   Notes by Sylvester Meyers from interview with Mrs. George Reed, Mrs. Henry Boyd, and Mrs. J. Matthews, of Athens, TN, Department of Justice file 72-70-13, National Archives; Jennings to Assistant Attorney General Roy Frank, June 14, 1943, gives details on the three women's travel to Washington, DC; interview with Lisa Reed Lee, granddaughter of Kathaleen Reed.

11   Jennings to Clay Matlock, November 9, 1942; *Knoxville Journal,* October 25, 1942.

18. "SAY A PRAYER FOR YOUR PAL ON GUADALCANAL"

1   Johnston, *Follow Me,* 48, 67.

2   Henry Shaw Jr., *First Offensive: The Marine Campaign for Guadalcanal*

(Washington, D.C.: History and Museums Division, Headquarters, U.S. Marine Corps, 1992)

3   Wheeler, *Special Valor,* 132.

4   Johnston, *Follow Me,* 78, 81.

19. *UNITED STATES V. LATTIMORE ET AL.*

1   Jennings to Attorney General Biddle, December 2, 1942.

2   Jennings to Tom Taylor, November 11, 1941; Jennings to Attorney General Biddle, November 13, 1942.

3   Walter White to Jennings, November 12, 1942.

4   S. C. Brown to Jennings, November 10, 1942.

5   *Tennessean,* January 30, 1943.

6   Associated Press report printed in *Kingsport News,* January 26, 1943; *Tennessee v. Cate and Webb,* court filings, McMinn County Circuit Court; *Daily Post-Athenian,* January 26, 1943.

7   *Kingsport News,* January 28, 1943.

8   *Chattanooga Daily Times,* January 29, 1943.

9   Jennings to Attorney General Biddle, February 4, 1943.

10   Rhea Hammer to Jennings, April 12, 1943.

11   Johnston, *Follow Me,* 84.

12   Ibid.; Wukovits, *One Square Mile,* 47.

13   Howard Cook, *Swifter Than Eagles* (Athens: Friendly City Publishing, 1980), 144–45.

14   *United States v. Simpson et al.,* Eastern District of Tennessee, February 6, 1943.

15   Brasington, "McMinn," 9-10.

16   *Tennessean,* February 19, 1943.

17   *Knoxville Journal,* May 30, 1943.

18   Jennings to H. Reynolds, March 15, 1943.

19   Jennings to Wilbur Piper, May 22, 1944.

20   *Knoxville News-Sentinel,* January 5, 1943.

21   Ibid., January 7 and 12, and June 9, 1943; *Knoxville Journal,* January 7 and February 3, 1943.

20. "NO ATHEISTS ON TARAWA"

1 Johnston, *Follow Me,* 110; Wukovits, *One Square Mile,* 61, 77.

2 Wukovits, *One Square Mile,* 64.

3 Manchester, *Goodbye,* 219; Wukovits, *One Square Mile,* 103-04, 106.

4 Manchester, *Goodbye,* 223-24; Wukovits, *One Square Mile,* 111.

5 Byrum, "Athens," 22.

6 Johnston, *Follow Me,* 123, 128.

7 Ibid., 138.

8 Wheeler, *Special Valor,* 210.

9 *Knoxville News-Sentinel,* January 2, 1944.

21. *UNITED STATES V. WILLIAM RUCKER*

1 Affidavit of Zeb Aldridge, January 29, 1944, in the Jennings Papers.

2 Judgment and Commitment, Eastern District of Tennessee, Southern Division, National Archives Southeast, June 8, 1944.

3 Jennings to Judge Brown, June 13, 1944; *Knoxville Journal,* December 5, 1943.

4 Ibid., *Knoxville Journal,* December 5, 1943; *Chattanooga Daily Times,* June 8, 1944; *Knoxville Journal,* June 8, 1944; affidavits of Zeb Aldridge, August 3, 1943 and November 6, 1942; affidavit of Frank Cline and Tom Hayes, November 6, 1942.

5 *Knoxville News-Sentinel,* July 21, 1944.

6 Newspaper clipping in the papers of John Jennings.

7 Attorney General Biddle to Jennings, August 2, 1944; Jennings telegram to the Department of Justice, July 17, 1944; *Knoxville News-Sentinel,* June 10, July 19, July 28, July 30, and November 5, 1944; Jennings to Judge Brown, February 23, 1943.

22. FROM ATHENS TO NORMANDY

1 Carmichael, *Two Memoirs,* 1-16.

2 Byrum, "Athens," 23.

23. "I DON'T KNOW WHICH WAY IS UP"

1   Johnston, *Follow Me,* 166–69.

2   Cook, *Swifter,* 181.

3   *Knoxville Journal,* June 16 and July 11, 1944.

4   *Knoxville Journal,* July 13, 1944; letter from Commissioner Ander-
    son to his colleagues, July 31, 1944, in the John Jennings Papers;
    Woods to Anderson, August 1, 1944; unsigned and dated letter in
    the Jennings Papers; *Knoxville News-Sentinel,* July 18 and August 17,
    1946.

5   Affidavit of Horace Reynolds, August 29, 1944, John Jennings
    Papers; *Knoxville Journal,* September 17, 1944; affidavit of John
    Walker, dated page missing, John Jennings Papers; Carmichael,
    Two Memoirs, 26.

6   Affidavit of Mrs. C. E. Ballew, January 28, 1946; affidavit of M. A.
    Barnett, January 25, 1946; affidavit of Mrs. J. P. Thompson, Jan-
    uary 22, 1946; Affidavit of S. H. Newman, Jr., January 25, 1946,
    all from the Jennings Papers; *Knoxville News-Sentinel,* August 17,
    1946.

7   Election returns are from the *Daily Post-Athenian* from their respec-
    tive years.

8   *Knoxville News-Sentinel,* August 7, 1944.

9   Jennings to DOJ, May 26, 1945; Associated Press, August 3, 1944;
    Knoxville Journal, August 4, 1946.

10 *Knoxville Journal,* October 6, 1944.

11 *Knoxville Journal,* October 8, 1944; *Tennessean,* November 1, 1943.

12 *Knoxville News-Sentinel,* April 13 and 22, 1944.

13 *Knoxville Journal,* August 6, 1944; Tennessee Blue Book 1945–46,
    262; United Press report in *Johnson City Press,* April 4, 1944.

14 *Jackson Sun,* September 24, 1944.

15 Personnel records of Ralph Duggan, National Archives; Ralph
    Duggan's personal papers, in the possession of the Duggan family;
    Duggan to Jennings, November 5, 1944.

24. "KILLED IN THE SERVICE OF HIS COUNTRY IN ATHENS, TENNESSEE"

1   Ken Wilburn, son of Minus, is the source for this story. Printed in *Daily Citizen* (Dalton, GA), September 21, 2008; *Knoxville News-Sentinel,* September 27, 1944.

2   *Daily Post-Athenian,* October 2 and 3, 1944.

3   Bill White, Oral History.

25. "THE AMERICAN WAY OF LIFE"

1   Papers of John Jennings, notes for a speech, August 3, 1946; *Knoxville News-Sentinel,* September 22, 1945; *Knoxville Journal,* November 4, 1944; Jennings to Department of Justice, November 8, 1944.

2   *Knoxville Journal,* December 29 and 30, 1944; *Bristol Herald Courier,* December 30, 1944.

3   *Tennessean* and *Knoxville Journal,* January 10, 1945.

4   *Knoxville Journal,* January 19, 1945; Joe Hatcher, *Tennessean* column, undated clipping.

5   *Knoxville Journal,* February 16, 1945.

6   Ibid., August 13, 1945.

7   Jennings to Clay Matlock, April 23, 1945.

8   Akins and Landley, *Date,* 23; Kenyatta and Matthew Darby, "History of Rubber," historyofrubber.weebly.com.

9   Bill White, interview with Dan Henderson; White, Oral History.

10 White, Oral History; Cook, *Swifter,* 191–92, 194.

11 Brasington, "McMinn," 11–12; *Daily Post-Athenian,* June 21, 26, 28 and July 9, 1945.

12 Personnel records of Pvt. James Lockmiller.

13 Joseph Goulden, *The Best Years, 1945–1950* (New York: Atheneum, 1976), 40.

14 H. A. Vestal to Jennings, November 29, 1945.

15 Interview with Carl Anderson, June 19, 1948; Brasington, "McMinn," 14.

16   *Daily Post-Athenian,* January 15 and 22, 1946.

17   Goulden, *Best Years,* 31.

26. THE BEST YEAR OF THEIR LIVES

1   *Daily Post-Athenian,* January 1, 1946.

2   Goulden, *Best Years,* 1–7.

3   *Daily Post-Athenian,* January 17, 1946.

4   Ibid., February 6, 1946.

5   Ibid., January 25, 1946.

6   Ibid., January 16, 1946.

7   Goulden, *Best Years,* 67.

8   PBS, "War Production," https://www.pbs.org/thewar/at_home
     _war_production.htm.

9   *Daily Post-Athenian,* January 25, 1946.

10   Goulden, *Best Years,* 47.

11   *Tennessean,* January 25, 1946.

12   *Daily Post-Athenian,* January 15, 1946.

13   Baker, "Violence," 10.

14   Cook, *Swifter,* 182.

15   Carmichael, *Two Memoirs,* 26.

16   Bill White, Oral History; Baker, "Violence," 11.

17   Undated letter from Peter Saulpans to Jim Buttram, shortly
     after the Battle of Athens, in the possession of the Buttram
     family.

18   *New York Post,* August 5, 1946.

19   Bill White, Oral History.

27. IN THE BASEMENT OF THE ROBERT E. LEE HOTEL

1   Jonathan Lighter, ed., *Historical Dictionary of American Slang,* vol. 1,
     A–G (New York: Random House, 1994), 888–90.

2   *Knoxville Journal,* December 24, 1942.

3   Letter from Bill Grubb to the VFW, June 15, 1998, in the posses-
     sion of the Grubb family.

4   Martin, "GI War," 392.

5   Ibid.

6   *Home to War*, documentary, interview with Bill Hamby.

28. "A THORN IN THE FLESH"

1   Baker, "Violence," 4; *Daily Post-Athenian,* April 12, 1946.

2   Carmichael, *Two Memoirs,* 23–24; *Chattanooga Daily Times,* July 23, 1946, 23–24.

3   *Daily Post-Athenian,* undated advertisement, McMinn County Historical Society.

4   Baker, "Violence," 13–14.

29. THE BALLAD OF OTTO KENNEDY

1   *Sweetwater News,* May 12, 1932 and March 19, 1930; *Madisonville Democrat,* March 19, 1930 and April 1, 1931; *Knoxville News-Sentinel,* March 25, 1930; interview with Billie Bea Kennedy Heltz, daughter of Otto Kennedy, and Mary Ann Hendershot, niece of Otto Kennedy and granddaughter of J. P.

2   *Daily Post-Athenian,* June 16, 1932.

3   Baker, "Violence," 15; *Washington Star,* August 29, 1946; *Daily Post-Athenian,* April 17, 1944; interview with Bille Bea Kennedy Heltz.

30. "YOUR VOTE WILL BE COUNTED AS CAST"

1   *Daily Post-Athenian,* May 10 and August 5, 1946; *Knoxville Journal,* August 6, 1946; *Tennessean,* July 14, 1946; International News Service report, August, 1946.

2   A directory of the GI Executive Committee was found in the safe of Jim Buttram, and has never before been released to the public. The names included were: "Jim Buttram, Chairman. John Peck, Secretary. Harry Johnson, Treasurer. Shy Scott, Edgar Self, Ralph Duggan, Bill Hamby, Knox Henry, Tony Pierce, Leslie Dooley, Felix Harrod, Reed Shell, Sewell Ward (colored), Fred Hutsell, Fred Leon, Ralph Reynolds, Frank Carmichael, George Painter, Feets Jones (Hobert), Earl Carmichael, Harold Sewell, Noel Knox, A. B. Ervin, Abe Johnson, Charlie Pickel, Wayne Williams, Bob Collins,

Elroy Hampton." Of these twenty-eight men, thirteen were from Athens, seven from Etowah, four from Niota, three from Englewood, and one from Riceville.

3   *Tennessean,* August 4, 1946; *Chattanooga Times,* August 3, 1946; Brasington, "McMinn," 16.

4   *Knoxville News-Sentinel,* May 12, 1946; *Daily Post-Athenian,* May 13, 1946.

5   Bill Hamby interview, *Home to War.*

6   *Daily Post-Athenian,* May 13, 1946.

7   *Washington Star* series on the Battle of Athens; *Tennessean,* July 14, 1946; Brasington, "McMinn," 2, 15, 19; Carmichael, *Two Memoirs*; International News Service report, August 1946; Byrum, "Athens," 110.

8   *Tennessean,* July 14, 1946.

9   Ibid., July 24, 1946; Byrum, "Athens," 106.

31. "DO YOU THINK THEY'RE GOING TO LET YOU WIN THIS ELECTION?"

1   *Daily Post-Athenian,* July 15, 1946.

2   Jim Buttram's perspective comes from an interview with Jim Buttram, his son; his quote is from the *New York Post,* August 5, 1946, which is also the source for the threats against Henry and assault on his friend; Bill's perspective comes from his UT Knoxville oral history and audio recordings in the possession of the White family; the destruction of the sign from *The Tennessean,* July 24, 1946.

3   *Tennessean,* January 25, 1946.

4   *Daily Post-Athenian,* May 16, 1946.

5   Ibid., May 28, 1946.

6   Ibid., June 4, 1946; Brasington, "McMinn," 19; *Washington Star,* August 1946.

7   *Daily Post-Athenian,* July 23, 1946.

8   Parris published a full accounting in the *Daily Post-Athenian* in August 1946, shortly after the election.

9   *Knoxville News-Sentinel,* July 15, 1946; Mansfield's real estate

transactions are from a deposition found in the office of McMinn County circuit court clerk.

10   *Chattanooga Daily Times,* July 23, 1946; *Knoxville Journal,* July 25, 1946.

11   *Tennessean,* July 15, 1946.

12   Martin, "GI War," 392; Ralph Duggan personnel file, U.S. Navy; Interview with Ted Hutsell, son of Fred Hutsell; *Washington Star* series on the Battle of Athens; *Daily Post-Athenian,* June 14, 1946.

32. THE FOURTH OF JULY

1   *Daily Post-Athenian,* June 25, 1946.

2   Ibid., July 1946.

33. "THE VOTES AND HEARTS OF McMINN COUNTY"

1   *Daily Post-Athenian,* July 15, 1946.

2   *Daily Post-Athenian,* undated advertisement.

3   Jennings to Duggan, July 19, 1946.

4   *Tennessean,* August 4, 1946.

5   Ibid., July 26, 1946; *Leaf-Chronicle* (Clarksville), July 24 and 25, 1946; *Maryville-Alcoa Times,* August 1, 1946.

6   *Chattanooga Times,* July 22, 1946; *Knoxville Journal,* July 26, 1946; *Daily Post-Athenian,* July 22, 1946.

7   *Chattanooga Times,* July 21 and 23, 1946.

8   *Knoxville Journal,* July 24, 1946.

9   *Chattanooga Daily Times,* July 27, 1946.

10   *Chattanooga Times,* July 28, 1946; "Votes and Hearts of McMinn County," Theodore White Papers, Harvard University.

11   Jennings to Clark, March 13, 1946; Duggan to Jennings, December 20, 1945.

12   *Knoxville News-Sentinel,* July 30, 1946.

13   *Chattanooga Daily Times,* July 31, 1946.

14   *Daily Post-Athenian,* July 31, 1946.

15   Byrum, "Athens," 116.

16   *Daily Post-Athenian,* July 31, 1946.

34. THE DARK CORNER

1 *Chattanooga Daily Times,* August 2, 1946; White, "Votes and Hearts"; interview, Allen Stout and Frank Larkin; Otto Kennedy, audio, 1983; *Maryville Times,* August 2, 1946.

2 *Chattanooga Times,* August 2, 1946; *Daily Post-Athenian,* August 1, 1946.

3 *Daily Post-Athenian,* August 2, 1946; Brasington, "McMinn," 27; Otto Kennedy, audio.

4 Interview with Chuck Redfern, McMinn County Living Heritage Museum.

5 *Chattanooga News–Free Press,* August 2, 1946.

6 *Chattanooga Times,* August 2, 1946.

7 Telegram, Jennings to Attorney General Tom Clark, August 1, 1946.

8 *Chattanooga News–Free Press,* August 2, 1946.

9 *Chattanooga Times,* August 2, 1946.

10 The deputies' response is from Millard Vincent, in notes he prepared for a presentation on the Battle of Athens, in the possession of the Vincent family.

11 Interview with Felix Harrod, McMinn County Living Heritage Museum; *Chattanooga Times,* August 2, 1946; *Knoxville Journal,* August 3, 1946.

12 Theron Caudle to Jim Buttram, August 1, 1946, in the possession of the Buttram family.

13 Baker, "Violence," 25.

14 *Newsweek,* "Veterans: Tennessee Siege," 1946; Baker, "Violence," 25.

15 "Fair Election Plan," document in the personal papers of Jim Buttram; Carmichael, *Two Memoirs,* provides additional details of the failed contingency plan.

16 *Daily Post-Athenian,* August 5, 1946; *Chattanooga Times,* August 2, 1946; Byrum, "Athens," 129-30.

17 *Knoxville News-Sentinel,* August 2, 1946.

18 *Chattanooga Daily Times,* August 3 and 4, 1946; *Washington Star* series on the Battle of Athens; Brasington, "McMinn," 28; *Daily Post-Athenian,* August 5, 1946; *Maryville Times,* August 2, 1946.

19 *Washington Star* series on the Battle of Athens; *Chattanooga Times,* August 2, 1946.

20 Interview with John Pirkle.

21 Interview with Everett Gillespie, grandson of Tom, McMinn County Living Heritage Museum.

22 *Chattanooga Times,* August 2, 1946; Brasington, "McMinn," 29, interview with Charles Scott.

23 *Knoxville Journal,* August 3, 1946.

24 Interview with Lena Cantrell; interview with Bob Johnson; Brasington, "McMinn," 31.

25 *Daily Post-Athenian,* August 2, 1946; *Maryville Times,* August 2, 1946.

26 *Knoxville News-Sentinel,* August 2, 1946.

27 *Chattanooga Times,* August 3, 1946.

28 *Knoxville News-Sentinel,* August 2, 1946; *Chattanooga Times,* August 2 and 3, 1946; *Tennessean,* August 4, 1946; interview with Charles "Shy" Scott; Brasington, "McMinn," interview with Ann Davis, daughter of Shy Scott; Narrative Report of Mission, 303rd Bomb Group, National Archives.

29 *Chattanooga Daily Times,* August 2, 1946.

30 Ibid.

31 *Chattanooga News–Free Press,* August 2, 1946; John Wilson, "JB Collins Celebrating 100th Birthday on Sunday," Chattanoogan .com, Monday, September 18, 2017; Associated Press, August 2, 1946, reprinted in *Kingsport News* of the same date.

32 *Chattanooga Times,* Dateline August 1, 1946; *Knoxville News-Sentinel,* August 2, 1946; Baker, "Violence," 24; *Philadelphia Record,* August 5, 1946; *Knoxville News-Sentinel,* August 2, 1946; interview with Charles Scott Jr.; Brasington, "McMinn," 30; Associated Press, August 2, 1946, reproduced in the *Philadelphia Record* of the same date; *Knoxville News-Sentinel,* August 2, 1946; *Chattanooga Times,* August 2 and 3, 1946; *Daily Post-Athenian,* August 2, 1946.

35. THE BATTLE OF THE GARAGE

1   *Daily Post-Athenian,* August 5, 1946.

2   Otto Kennedy, audio.

3   *Knoxville News-Sentinel,* August 3, 1946.

4   Otto Kennedy, audio.

5   *Washington Star* series on the Battle of Athens; *Tennessean,* July 14,
    1946; Brasington, "McMinn," 2, 15, 19; Carmichael, *Two Memoirs;*
    International News Service report, August 1946; Byrum, "Athens,"
    110. *Chattanooga News–Free Press,* August 2, 1946; *Chattanooga Daily
    Times,* August 2, 1946; Bill White, audio tape.

36. "DEMOCRACY, ATHENS STYLE"

1   Byrum, "Athens," 146–48.

2   All reporting from Allen Stout comes from the original tapes, se-
    cured by John Pirkle and shared with the author.

3   *Chattanooga Daily Times,* August 2, 1946; *Chattanooga Times,* August
    2, 1946.

4   Baker, "Violence," 25. The details of Bill's speech have appeared in
    numerous places over the course of decades and remained remark-
    ably consistent. Baker's interview with White, in the late 1960s, is
    the earliest.

5   *Washington Star* series on the Battle of Athens, undated.

6   Interview with Betty Lehning, sister of Bill White.

7   *Daily Post-Athenian,* August 5, 1946.

8   Narrative of Sgt. Perly Berger, FBI interview, FBI file 62-771;
    affidavits of Sam Simms, David Hutsell, and Ken Mashburn; Bill
    White, audio. Mink's background can be found in the self-published
    memoir of his son, Harold Powers: *Prof: The Autobiography of an
    Elementary Principal.*

9   Report of FBI Agent C. McAfee McCracken, FBI file 62-771;
    affidavits of David Hutsell, Sam Simms, and Kenneth Mashburn;
    Bill White, audio.

10 *Knoxville News-Sentinel,* August 2, 1946.

11 *Knoxville Journal,* August 2, 1946.

12 Radio interview with Ed Harris, published in the *Tennessean,* August 2, 1946.

13 *Daily Post-Athenian,* August 5, 1946.

14 Bill White, interview with Dan Henderson, Memphis *Commercial Appeal,* September 30, 1979.

15 *Chattanooga News–Free Press* April 4, 1999.

16 Ken Wilburn, son of Minus, was the source. Printed in *Daily Citizen* (Dalton, GA), September 21, 2008; *Tennessean,* August 4, 1946; Martin, "GI War," 395.

37. THE GUNS OF AUGUST

1 *Tennessean,* August 2, 1946; United Press, August 2, 1946.

2 *Chattanooga News–Free Press,* August 2, 1946.

3 *Home to War,* documentary, interviews with Edgar Miller and Bill Grubb. For more on Miller's perspective, see Byrum, "Athens," 155.

4 *Daily Post-Athenian,* August 2, 1946; Associated Press, August 2, 1946, reproduced in the *Philadelphia Record* of the same date; *Knoxville Journal,* August 2, 1946.

5 Millard Vincent told this story before the McMinn County Commission on August 1, 2016, the sixtieth anniversary of the Battle of Athens, and in notes in the possession of the Vincent family.

6 *Chattanooga News–Free Press,* August 2, 1946.

7 Writings of Felix Harrod, in the possession of the Harrod family; *Knoxville Journal,* August 3, 1946; *Chattanooga Times Free Press,* July 31, 2006; *Chattanooga Times,* August 2, 1946; *Knoxville Journal,* July 29, 1956.

8 Interview with Felix Harrod, McMinn County Living Heritage Museum; *Chattanooga Times,* August 2, 1946; *Home to War,* documentary.

9 Byrum, "Athens," 152.

10 *Chattanooga News–Free Press,* August 2, 1946; *Knoxville Journal,* August 2, 1946; *Tennessean,* August 2, 1946.

11 *Washington Star* series on the Battle of Athens.

12   Interview with Jesse Ray Underdown, brother of Charles Underdown.

13   *Knoxville Journal,* August 2, 1946; *Chattanooga Times,* August 2, 1946.

14   Otto Kennedy, audio recording, 1980s.

15   Ken Wilburn, son of Minus, was the source. Printed in *Daily Citizen* (Dalton, GA), September 21, 2008.

16   *Knoxville Journal,* August 2, 1946.

17   *Daily Post-Athenian,* June 6, 1946; *Chattanooga Times,* August 3, 1946.

18   *Chattanooga Times,* August 5, 1946.

19   Ibid.; *New York Post,* August 2, 1946; *Newsweek,* "Veterans: Tennessee Siege," 1946.

20   Thelma Wilson's written account, McMinn Living History Museum; interview with Jean Wilson, her daughter, age nine during the battle.

21   Affidavits of David Hutsell, Kenneth "Ken" Mashburn, and Sam Simms; *Knoxville Journal,* August 2, 1946.

22   Martin, "GI War," 395.

23   *Knoxville Journal,* August 2, 1946.

24   Bill White, audio tape.

25   Byrum, "Athens," 153.

26   "Announcer Describes McMinn War from Darkened Room as Guns Roar," loose clipping in the archives of the McMinn County Living History Museum.

27   Carmichael, *Two Memoirs,* 36.

28   Byrum, "Athens," 153.

29   "Announcer Describes McMinn War from Darkened Room as Guns Roar"; *Daily Post-Athenian,* August 2, 1946.

30   *Knoxville Journal,* August 4, 1946; *Chattanooga Times,* August 5, 1946; *Tennessean,* August 2, 1946.

31   *Chattanooga Daily Times,* August 2, 1946; *Chattanooga Times,* August 2, 1946; UP News Service, August 2, 1946, published in the *Knoxville Journal* of the same date; *Newsweek,* "Veterans: Tennessee Siege," 1946.

32   *Daily Post-Athenian,* August 2, 1946.

33   *Knoxville Journal,* August 2, 1946; Bill White's account, International News Service, August 2, 1946.

34   *Chattanooga News-Free Press,* August 2, 1946; interviews with Charlotte Smith, widow of Cecil, and Ruly and Eddie Smith, brothers of Cecil.

35   *Chattanooga Daily Times,* August 2, 1946.

36   Written recollection of Bill White, in the possession of the White family; Bill White, audio tape.

37   Bill Grubb, written recollection, in the possession of the Grubb family; *Chattanooga Times,* August 2, 1946.

38   *Knoxville News-Sentinel,* August 2, 1946.

39   See, e.g., a photograph of seven spectators behind a car, *Chattanooga News–Free Press,* August 2, 1946.

40   *Oregonian,* August 2, 1946.

38. THE NIGHT WATCH

1   *Boston Globe,* March 15, 1974; United Press, April 19, 1954.

2   *Sweetwater Valley News,* reprinted in the *Tennessean,* August 11, 1946; interviews with Johnny McDaniel, son of Charles E. "Buck" McDaniel, with Helga McDaniel, his daughter-in-law, and with Lisa Lowe, his granddaughter; *Knoxville News-Sentinel,* August 2, 1946; *Maryville Alcoa Times,* August 2, 1946.

3   *Chattanooga News–Free Press,* August 2, 1946.

4   *Chattanooga Times,* August 2, 1946.

5   *Chattanooga News–Free Press,* August 2, 1946; *Washington Star* series on the Battle of Athens; *Knoxville News-Sentinel,* August 2 and August 4, 1946; Martin, "GI War," 396; *Daily Citizen* (Dalton, GA), September 21, 2008.

6   *Knoxville News-Sentinel,* August 2, 1946; *Chattanooga News–Free Press,* August 2, 1946; *Knoxville Journal,* August 2, 1946; four dynamite blasts of successive strength, the last shaking the jail, *Chicago Tribune,* August 3, 1946.

7   *Chattanooga Times,* August 2, 1946.

8   Bill White, audio tape.

9   *Chattanooga Times,* August 2, 1946; *Knoxville Journal,* August 3, 1946.

10 *Daily Post-Athenian,* August 2, 1946.

11 *Maryville Times,* August 2, 1946.

12 Interview with Jesse Ray Underdown, brother-in-law of Howard Thompson.

13 *Memphis Press-Scimitar,* August 2, 1946.

14 International News Service, interview with Billy White, August 2, 1946; *Newsweek,* "Veterans: Tennessee Siege," 1946.

15 *Daily Post-Athenian,* August 2, 1946; United Press, August 2, 1946.

16 *Chattanooga News–Free Press,* August 2, 1946; Martin, "GI War," 396.

17 United Press, August 2, 1946.

18 Interview with Chuck Redfern, McMinn County Living Heritage Museum; *Knoxville News-Sentinel,* August 2, 1946.

19 Martin, "GI War," 396.

20 Interview with Ray Wilburn and Tommy Buckner, nephews of Minus Wilburn, and Sandy Weeks, son of Paul Weeks; *Knoxville Journal,* August 2, 1946; *Home to War,* documentary, interview with J. B. Collins.

21 *Knoxville News-Sentinel,* August 2, 1946; *Chattanooga Times Free Press,* August 2, 1946; *Newsweek,* "Veterans: Tennessee Siege," 1946; the story of Ralph and Claudia comes from an interview with Steve Byrum.

22 *Chattanooga News–Free Press,* story dated August 2, 1946.

23 *Knoxville News-Sentinel,* August 12, 1946.

24 *Knoxville Journal,* August 2 and 5, 1946; International News Service, August 2, 1946.

25 Interview with Ralph Duggan, son of Ralph Duggan.

26 *Chattanooga News–Free Press,* August 2, 1946; *Knoxville Journal,* August 2, 1946.

27 Carmichael, *Two Memoirs,* 36–37.

28 Byrum, "Athens," 167.

29 *Knoxville News-Sentinel,* August 2, 1946; *Daily Post-Athenian,* August 2 and 7, 1946.

30 *Chattanooga Times* and *Chattanooga News–Free Press,* August 2, 1946.

31 *Daily Post-Athenian,* August 2, 1946; *Chattanooga News–Free Press,* August 2, 1946; Associated Press report published in the *Kingsport News,* August 3, 1946.

39. "GROPING BACK TO NORMALCY"

1   *Daily Post-Athenian,* August 2, 1946.

2   *Knoxville News-Sentinel,* August 4, 1946.

3   UP News Service, August 2, 1946, published in the *Knoxville Journal* of the same date; "M'Minn GI's Wait for Rumored Raid," August 3, 1946, loose clipping in the archives of the McMinn County Living History Museum; *Knoxville Journal,* August 2, 1946; *Tennessean,* August 6, 1946; *Chattanooga Times,* August 3, 1946.

4   International News Service, interview with Billy White, August 2, 1946; Biographical details on John Henry are from the *Columbus Dispatch,* June 1, 2015.

5   *Chattanooga News–Free Press,* August 2, 1946.

6   *Tennessean,* August 4, 1946.

7   *Chronicle* August 4, 1946.

8   *Knoxville Journal,* August 2, 1946.

9   Bill White, Oral History.

10 Thelma Wilson Memoirs, McMinn County Living History Museum; interview with Jean Wilson.

11 North American Newspaper wire service article, August 11, 1946, printed in the *Atlanta Constitution* of the same date.

12 *Chattanooga Times,* August 3, 1946.

13 *Tennessean,* August 4, 1946; Associated Press, August 2, 1946, reproduced in the *Philadelphia Record* of the same date; United Press, August 2, 1946.

14 *Knoxville Journal,* August 17, 1946.

15 *Philadelphia Record,* August 5, 1946.

16   *Washington Star* series on the Battle of Athens; *Chicago Tribune*, August 3, 1946.

17   *Chattanooga Times,* August 3, 1946.

18   Ibid., Associated Press, August 2, 1946.

19   *Chattanooga Times,* August 5, 1946.

20   *Knoxville Journal,* August 5, 1946.

21   Interview with Paul Willson, grandson of Paul Cantrell.

22   *Chattanooga News-Free Press,* August 2, 1946.

40. FORT ATHENS

1   *Daily Post-Athenian,* August 5, 1946.

2   *Knoxville Journal,* August 5, 1946; *Daily Post-Athenian,* August 5, 19, and 30, 1946; *Knoxville News-Sentinel,* August 4, 1946.

3   Interview with Chuck Redfern, McMinn County Living Heritage Museum.

4   *Knoxville News-Sentinel,* August 3, 1946; FBI file 52-771.

5   Associated Press, August 3, 1946; *Knoxville Journal,* August 5, 1946.

6   Photograph, *Chattanooga Times,* August 5, 1945.

7   *Knoxville Journal,* August 5, 1946.

8   *Washington Star* series on the Battle of Athens; *Knoxville News-Sentinel,* August 4, 1946; *New York Times,* August 12, 1946.

9   *Knoxville News-Sentinel,* August 4, 1946.

10   *The News* (New York), Monday, August 6, 1946.

11   *Knoxville Journal,* August 5, 1946; *The News* (New York), Monday, August 6, 1946.

12   Untitled newspaper clipping, August 1946, McMinn County Living Heritage Museum.

13   Felix Harrod, interview, McMinn County Living Heritage Museum.

14   *Knoxville Journal,* August 5, 1946.

15   *Chattanooga Times,* August 5, 1946.

16   *Knoxville Journal,* August 5, 1946.

17   *Chicago Tribune,* August 3, 1946.

18   *Daily Post-Athenian,* August 5, 1946; *Tennessean,* August 5, 1946.

19 *Chattanooga Times,* August 5, 1946.

20 United Press casualty list, August 2, 1946; *Daily Post-Athenian,* Focus '77 Edition.

21 Nashville *Tennessean,* undated article; Associated Press, August 2, 1946, Brasington, "McMinn," 35.

41. GLORIOUS VICTORY

1 Kennedy meeting Woods the night before is from Otto Kennedy's recorded talk to a classroom in the 1980s.

2 *Chattanooga Daily Times,* August 5, 1946.

3 *Knoxville Journal,* August 6, 1946.

4 *Daily Post-Athenian,* August 5, 1946.

5 *Chattanooga News–Free Press,* August 6, 1946; *Knoxville Journal,* August 6, 1946; *Daily Post-Athenian,* August 20, 1946; International News Service report, August 6, 1946.

6 *Daily Post-Athenian,* August 5, 1946.

7 *Tennessean,* August 3, 1946.

8 *Detroit Times,* August 2, 1946.

9 *Knoxville News-Sentinel,* August 6, 1946.

10 *Daily Post-Athenian,* August 6, 1946.

11 Eleanor Roosevelt, "My Day," August 6, 1946, retrieved online: https://www2.gwu.edu/~erpapers/myday/displaydoc.cfm?_y =1946&_f=md000410; *Daily Post-Athenian,* August 5, 1946.

12 Interview with Ray Wilburn, nephew of Minus Wilburn.

13 *Knoxville News-Sentinel,* January 19, 1947; *Daily Post-Athenian,* August 5, 1946; undated newspaper clipping, January 1947, in the files of Ralph Duggan.

14 *Knoxville News-Sentinel,* February 13 and 14, 1947; December 17, 1947.

15 *Chattanooga Times,* August 6, 1946.

16 *Washington Star* series on the Battle of Athens.

17 Brasington, "McMinn," 37; *Chattanooga Times,* August 13, 1946; *Daily Tribune* (Cartersville, GA), August 12, 1946; *Daily Post-Athenian,* August 8, 1946.

18 *Daily Post-Athenian,* August 8, 1946.

19 *Knoxville News-Sentinel,* August 17, 1946.

20 *Chattanooga Times,* August 21, 1946.

21 *New York Times,* August 13, 1946; Associated Press, August 13, 1946.

42. UNKNOWN SUBJECTS

1 See, e.g., *Daily Post-Athenian,* October 9, 1946.

2 *Tennessean,* August 27, 1946.

3 Bill White, audiotape, in the possession of the White family.

43. "LET US LIVE TOGETHER AND LOVE ONE ANOTHER"

1 Genevieve Wiggins, et al, *"Over Here" and After: McMinn County, Tennessee During WWI and the Twenties* (Athens, Tenn.: McMinn County Historical Society, 1986), 13.

2 Margaret Macmillan, *Paris 1919,* (New York: Random House, 2001) 183–84, 463–64, 467, 471, 478.

3 Interview with Billie Bea Kennedy Heltz.

4 Byrum, "Athens," 184.

5 *Knoxville News-Sentinel,* July 27, 1947; *Chattanooga Daily Times,* August 3, 1945.

6 Associated Press, August 6, 1948.

7 *Knoxville Journal,* August 24, 1952.

8 Ibid., July 29, 1956.

9 *Leaf-Chronicle* (Clarksville, TN), February 12, 1953; *Jackson* (TN) *Sun,* January 29, 1953.

10 *Daily Post-Athenian,* October 31, 1960.

11 Interview with Carroll Ross.

EPILOGUE

1 *Knoxville Journal,* June 29, 1953; *Chattanooga Daily Times,* September 9, 1951, January 22, June 29, and August 11, 1953.

2 *Knoxville News-Sentinel,* June 25, 1967; *Daily Post-Athenian,* April 27, 1965.

SOURCES

INTERVIEWS

Bill Akins (former county historian, McMinn)

Jim Buttram (son of Jim Buttram)

Steve Byrum (McMinn County native and historian)

Les Coomer (son-in-law of Millard Vincent)

Ann Davis (daughter of Charles "Shy" Scott)

Travis Davis (grandson of Bill White)

Bob Dooley (son of Tom Dooley)

Tom Dooley (son of Les Dooley)

Ralph Duggan (son of Ralph Duggan)

Joe Grubb (son of Bill Grubb)

Joy Guy (McMinn County sheriff and historian)

Mary Hendershot (niece of Otto Kennedy)

David Herrod (son of Felix Herrod)

Judy Howard (daughter of Cecil Kennedy)

Patty Hutsell (daughter of Ken Mashburn)

Ted Hutsell (son of Fred Hutsell)

Cindy Shamblin Jones (daughter of Thomas Shamblin)

Billie Bea Kennedy Heltz (daughter of Otto Kennedy)

Les Kennedy (son of Cecil Kennedy)

Randy Lockmiller (son of Jimmy Lockmiller)

Linda Rowland Loveday (daughter of George Rowland)

John Pirkle (son of Sweet Pirkle)

Carroll Ross (retired circuit court judge, McMinn County)

Charlotte Smith (widow of Cecil Smith)

Eddie Smith (brother of Cecil Smith)

Ruly Smith (brother of Cecil Smith)

Durant Tullock (Etowah historian)

Jesse Ray Underdown (brother of Charles Underdown)

Gabe Vestal (grandson of David Hutsell)

Tim Vestal (son-in-law of David Hutsell)

Larry Wallace (former sheriff of McMinn County)

Claude "Sandy" Weeks (son of Paul Weeks)

Jean White (widow of Bill White)

Ray Wilburn (nephew of Minus Wilburn)

Paul Willson (grandson of Paul Cantrell)

Jane Hutsell Yount (daughter of David Hutsell)

AUDIO RECORDINGS

Millard Vincent

Otto Kennedy

Chuck Redfern

Bill Seldon

Billie Bea Kennedy Heltz

Bill White tapes: description of Election Day 1946 and the Battle (34 minutes); early life through the Battle of Tarawa (1:28); interview with Paul Willson for the fiftieth anniversary of World War II, description of military service (52:10); description of military service, the events leading to the battle, and the battle itself (1:01); oral history for the University of Tennessee at Knoxville, focusing on World War II, but includes details of early life and a retelling of the Battle of Athens (3:03).

INDEX

Hannah DeRose

CHRIS DEROSE is the *New York Times* bestselling author of five books, including *Founding Rivals: Madison vs. Monroe, the Bill of Rights, and the Election That Saved a Nation* and *The Presidents' War: Six American Presidents and the Civil War That Divided Them.* He was formerly senior litigation counsel to the Arizona Attorney General, a professor of constitutional and international law, and clerk of the Superior Court, where he led a team of seven hundred in serving America's fourth-largest county.